THE CRISIS
OF THE AMERICAN
PRESIDENCY

SIMON AND SCHUSTER · NEW YORK

THE *Power*

TO *Lead*

JAMES MacGREGOR BURNS

For my students
in "Poli. Sci. 411–Leadership,"
who have taught me

Copyright © 1984 by James MacGregor Burns
All rights reserved
including the right of reproduction
in whole or in part in any form
Published by Simon and Schuster
A Division of Simon & Schuster, Inc.
Simon & Schuster Building
Rockefeller Center
1230 Avenue of the Americas
New York, New York 10020
SIMON AND SCHUSTER and colophon
are registered trademarks of Simon & Schuster, Inc.
Designed by Edith Fowler
Manufactured in the United States of America

10 9 8 7 6 5 4 3 2 1

Library of Congress Cataloging in Publication Data

Burns, James MacGregor.
  The power to lead.

  Includes bibliographical references and index.
  1. United States—Politics and government—
1945–2. Political parties—United States.   3. Po-
litical participation—United States.   I. Title.
JK1717.B87   1984   973.92   83–27105
ISBN 0–671–42731–8

Contents

I am not an advocate for frequent changes in laws and constitutions. But laws and institutions must go hand and hand with the progress of the human mind. As that becomes more developed, more enlightened, as new discoveries are made, new truths discovered and manners and opinions change, with the change of circumstances, institutions must advance able to keep pace with the times. . . .

—THOMAS JEFFERSON

Prologue:
The Desertion of the System

THE American political system faces a pervasive crisis of self-confidence that only the rarest kind of leadership can overcome. The roots of the crisis lie in structural problems that have been noted since the start of the system two hundred years ago. The symptoms of the crisis take the long-observed form of political disarray, institutionalized stalemate, and governmental ineptitude and impotence. But the situation today, I believe, has a different and ominous cast. Leaders at every level, whether in Washington or at the grass roots, are not merely attacking or defending the system. In various ways they are deserting it, and millions of the citizenry are abandoning it with them.

This desertion takes its most dramatic form in the massive failure of fifty million or so Americans to take part in even the most crucial elections. Once viewed as a moral failure, nonvoting was later seen as stemming largely from practical obstacles such as irksome registration requirements. We have made registration much easier— and still the voters flock away from the polls.

So we must stop deceiving ourselves. People stay home on election day not primarily because they had trouble registering, or because the voting hours are inconvenient, or because it is a working weekday. *People are staying home as a conscious act of withdrawal.* Hence reforms like Sunday voting or twenty-four-hour polling booths would make little difference, except to make voting easier for people who already do vote. After the two-year hullabaloo of presidential campaigning, half the audience fails to show up at the grand finale on election day, and two-thirds or three-fourths typically boycott state and local elections, the vaunted "foundation of democracy." They are not playing in our game of democracy, perhaps because they consider it only a game, a spectator sport.

Once we understand that people are deserting the system as a simple act of protest, or as a rational expression of indifference, we can stop berating them for "citizenship failure." We can start looking for the real causes. What lies behind this kind of withdrawal?

The most evident cause is a sharp decline in basic trust in government. Over a span of almost twenty years, a sample of 1,418 respondents has been asked, "How much of the time do you think you can trust the government in Washington to do what is right—just about always, most of the time, or only some of the time?" Those responding "just about always" or "most of the time" fell from almost 80 percent in 1964 to about 25 percent in 1980. During the same period, the proportion of people believing that government "is pretty much run by a few big interests looking out for themselves" as against "run for the benefit of all people" rose from less than 24 percent to almost 70 percent.

And how do people rate their leaders for honesty and ethical standards? In a 1983 poll in which clergymen were rated as "high" on this score by 64 percent of the respondents, and car salesmen were so rated by 6 percent, U.S. senators were given "high" ratings by 17 percent of the respondents, local officeholders by 16 percent, U.S. representatives by 14 percent, and state officeholders by 13 percent.

People, we are told, have alienated themselves from the system, but perhaps the system has alienated the people. They feel bored, repelled, excluded. Some recoil from the demands of democracy itself. In the face of intractable problems, pundits and others call for "consensus." People should stop arguing, suspend debate, look for some golden mean, appoint a commission, agree on a plan. I have made a small hobby of collecting issues over which some leader has called for consensus—a list that now includes defense policy, education, health, environment, economic recovery, labor, peace, and above all foreign policy ("party politics stops at the water's edge"). Obviously there are crisis situations requiring consensus (often a result of the failure of the system). But consensus as a way of life? In a democracy?

Or opinion leaders turn to gimmicks, such as the six-year nonrenewable term for Presidents. Amid the high-school-level debates on this question, the central point is lost—for hundreds of years men and women have fought for the sacred right to *fire* as well as to hire their leaders, yet this right would be given up without a quiver. To be govcrned by an endless, uninterrupted series of lame-duck Presidents—is this the culmination of the democratic dream in America?

A bizarre aspect of the present system is virtually a reversal of the democratic dream. This is a phenomenon called "voting through the looking glass." It has long been noted that voters by electing a right-wing candidate can sometimes produce left-wing outcomes, or by choosing a "peace" candidate can produce war. Thus the "militaristic" Nixon opens relations with China, and the Johnson who attacked Goldwater as the war candidate himself inflates the war in Vietnam. ("They told me if I voted for Goldwater we'd be at war in six months, and by golly I voted for Goldwater and we were," a Republican said wryly after the 1964 contest.) Such "reverse representation" has been noted in other democracies—thus it took the imperial Charles de Gaulle to withdraw French power from Algeria—but the phenomenon seems to be a markedly American one. Such a perverse tendency, while perhaps inevitable given our political disarray, hardly serves to strengthen citizen confidence in a system long touted as presenting voters with rational alternatives, majority decisions, and responsive policy.

Leaders themselves are turning against aspects of the political system, in part because it makes leadership so difficult. We have seen a steady drain from Congress of talented men and women who choose to return to private careers. A good many candidates detest aspects of the system—the desperate scrounging for money, catering to narrow group pressures, adapting one's personality and image to the demands of television and other media. Not only academic critics of the system but some of its most successful practitioners propose major constitutional alternatives permitting better leadership. Year after year leaders take part in task forces and commissions that urge major or minor changes in the system, few of which are adopted—while the symptoms continue. And is it significant, or only ironic, that when leaders announce that they will *not* run for President—Walter Mondale in 1976, Edward Kennedy in 1982, Morris Udall in 1983—the news brings a collective sigh not of regret but of relief?

When leadership fails in a democracy, we are told, the solution is simple—turn to the opposition party leadership. But Americans have little confidence in the parties and their programs. It has long been evident that both the public and its leadership were deserting the parties as institutions—the public by shunning party participation and even membership, the leaders by building their own personal organizations and operating outside the party structures. But now we find a new and even more alarming phenomenon—a strong public view that parties are not even fulfilling their central obligation of offering meaningful alternatives. Asked in mid-1982 whether the Democrats or the Republicans could do a better job in handling certain policies, or whether there was no real difference between the two parties, most respondents voted for "no difference." On such key issues as reducing the danger of nuclear war, handling inflation, dealing with the Russians, improving education, and "providing leadership," from 43 to 51 percent of the respondents gave *both* parties their vote of no confidence.

Voters distrust what the parties seem to stand for. The Republicans have strengthened their grip on conservatives at the expense of members of the old moderate Eisenhower-Rockefeller centrists. Democrats have been long on diatribes against Reaganomics and pitiably short on clear alternatives on which the Democracy could agree. The longtime student of parties David Broder described Democratic opposition to the Reagan budget of 1982 as an abject failure. One national poll found 20 percent of the respondents endorsing the Republicans' economic approach, 18 percent the Democrats'—and the rest neither. Inevitably people feel trapped in the system at the same time that they feel alienated from it.

The ultimate test of a political system is performance, and it is the failure of the American system to produce that has most alienated leaders and followers alike, whether the liberal left seeking social justice and economic equality or conservatives seeking a lean and parsimonious government. The failures are both old and new: the inability to resolve the problem of slavery without one of the bloodiest civil wars in history; the century-old incapacity of the American democracy to deal with undemocratic corporate power; the long delays in securing poor and vulnerable people—men, women, and children—the most elementary rights and protection, as reflected in a hundred-year failure to prevent child labor; a fiscal system beyond the control of the nation's elected leadership, as symbolized by an independent agency holding the critical power to set interest rates; a tax system that has become grossly unfair and inegalitarian; urban blight and sprawl; a deteriorating infrastructure of public facilities such as bridges and sewers; an inordinately expensive health system; enormous waste and profiteering in arms procurement; massive deficiencies in public education, especially in low-income areas; burning criticism of both our criminal- and civil-justice systems from practitioners within those systems.

This is an all-too-familiar list. We have a habit of fighting our policy wars over and over, for the very good reason that we fail to win them. Hardly a decade passes without a proclamation of a crisis in public education, followed by more pronunciamentos, media excitement, press conferences, appointments of "blue-ribbon" commissions, followed in turn by a quiet subsiding of concern as the crisis spotlight swings elsewhere while the real crisis continues. Presidents declare war on poverty—FDR in the 1930s, JFK and LBJ in the 1960s, even Ronald Reagan in the 1980s—and the poverty continues, with the number of poor children under eighteen, for example, rising to 13.5 million in 1982.

And what of the capacity of the political system to meet the transcending need for peacemaking and peace-keeping? Its capacity for war preparation and war making has not been in serious doubt for forty years. The White House today, and the Defense Department always, stand at the apex of a powerful structure of financial resources, arms procurement, manpower and womanpower recruitment, military and logistical deployment, and war planning that immensely dwarfs the feeble organization and efforts for peace. We have of course no Peace Department as such, and the State Department is too ambivalent and bureaucratic to serve as the cutting edge for strategic peacemaking. But the question of peace is even more a matter of will and commitment than of organization. It has become evident that only a long struggle of at least a decade or two could fashion and execute a comprehensive strategy of peace. Only collective, continuous, and committed leadership could conduct such a struggle. And this is precisely the kind of leadership we lack.

Such would be a liberal-left critique of the system, but conservatives have their own bill of complaints: a swollen federal government with seemingly built-in tendencies toward ever more fat and bloat; a federal debt that a conservative Administration inflates rather than controls; continuing government intrusion into private and business affairs; spiraling taxes; bureaucratic waste, corruption, ineptitude. Right and left differ heatedly over the ends of government; they agree on the inability of popular majorities, whether liberal left or conservative right, to control the government, and of government to control itself. For both sides a meandering, centrist government is a great muddle, responding to expediency rather than to the interests of the majority, whether left or right.

It is the loss of governmental direction and authority, of social coherence and control, that disturbs many social scientists. The distinguished sociologist Morris Janowitz, summing up half a century of social change in America, sees "weak or stalemated regimes," unable to "produce effective or authoritative policies to manage economic and social tensions and political conflict," as a key indication of that loss of coherence and control. "In Janowitz's institutional analysis," another sociologist reports, "leaders play a unique role in defining a vision of collective justice and rationality. It cannot emerge automatically from all the shifting about of individual maximizers looking for a score. Only leaders can formulate solutions for the strains of the system."

"Only leaders" . . . this is the eternal appeal of a people who have lost their way, of a political system in disarray, of a government out of control. I believe it to be a rational and valid appeal, depending on what we mean by leadership. I mean by leadership not only the top cadre of Presidents and nationally known politicians, but the second cadre of political leaders of group interests and professions and states and regions, and the vital third cadre of grass-roots political activists. And I mean by leadership not only the transactional leaders who thrive on bargaining, accommodating, manipulating, and compromising within a given system, but the transforming leaders who respond to fundamental human needs and wants, hopes and expectations, and who may transcend and even seek to reconstruct the political system, rather than simply to operate within it.

The central question in this book is the capacity of today's political leadership in America to respond to fundamental human needs and American values of security, peace, liberty, equality, and justice. I pose the key issue: Is leadership failure in the United States caused primarily by institutional, constitutional, and other structural failings deeply rooted in the American political system? Or does that failure lie mainly in the leaders themselves, in deficiencies of skill, intellect, integrity, policy commitment, moral purpose? If the latter, why have we had such magnificent leadership in the past, as in the constitutional founding period, and such a paucity today? As Janowitz sees it, the "new breed of politicians forswears the hearty task of leading; they will not brave the dicey search for rational policies. Like binge-eaters, they crave the short-term pleasure of re-election. Hand in glove with public relations specialists, they turn the art of politics into show business." Is this true?

Or, if the leadership failures are rooted in structural forces, why did the Framers of the Constitution, perhaps the most brilliant single group of intellectual and political leaders in the history of the West, bequeath us such an anti-leadership system? Why have we had a host of excellent leaders in the past, despite the system, and so few today? Has the "mass media" in fact changed things that much? Does the system encourage—indeed require—a King-of-the-Rock brand of politics—highly personal contests among feuding politicos, a Hobbesian struggle of each against all, reflecting our individualistic culture and ethics and leading to policy discontinuity and impotence? What structural changes would be necessary to create a foundation for creative, principled, and moral leadership—for transforming leadership—in the America of the 1980s and 1990s? And what are the prospects for such change?

Even as I spell out these questions, the radio brings new reports of American interventions and adventures abroad, of tens of thousands of Europeans and Latin Americans massing in the streets and at military centers and shouting against our government, of feeble and futile efforts to curb the nuclear arms race. I wonder again, where is the principled government action that speaks for the true needs of the people? Where is the principled opposition party? Why is there such a leadership gap in this large and abundant nation, with its diverse and talented people? The answer, I think, lies not in our stars but in ourselves and our institutions.

PART ONE

Three Presidents

ONE

Carter:
The Verdict of November

I T was, the press rejoiced, a Camelot Jubilee setting: a shining new castle rising by the ocean, a meeting of kings and courtiers amid resplendent heraldic banners fluttering in the sea breezes, on a day that had turned fair and hazy after the morning fog had cleared, with rain banned until sundown. It was, some felt, one of those rare occasions when past and present, poetry and politics, humor and hope, the old politics and the new, mingled for a few brief shining moments. It was the dedication of the John F. Kennedy Library, October 20, 1979, in Boston.

It was a day that conjured up the past but portended more of the future than those present could have been aware.

Three political generations converged by the new library building. Eighty-seven-year-old John McCormack, the venerable former Speaker, was there, and Averell Harriman, and aged clerics and politicos. Hardly any of the aging JFK generation was not there; former Cabinet members and envoys extraordinary genteelly maneuvered for standing space below the long stage, like lords and ladies-in-waiting. The third generation of Kennedys, headed by each brother's oldest son—John, Joe, and Teddy, Jr.—trooped onto the stage in their blazers and sweaters. Media stars were even more recognizable than many of the old Kennedyites: John Chancellor, Theodore White, Roger Mudd, along with a huge press corps, were present. One Boston pol, seeking media attention, took pictures of every reporter in sight, muttering under his breath, "Ah, what a rogues' gallery, what a bunch of turkeys!"

It was, indeed, the kind of event you see through media eyes even as the events unfold before your direct gaze. Watching the soft clouds scudding in from the ocean, I could not help thinking of Teddy White's starting a chapter with the soft clouds scudding in from the ocean. Later that day, when I told him this, he drew back in mock indignation and cried out, "You have stolen my lead!"

The crowd, called naturally the "greatest concentration of America's political elite in history," still responded to White House vibrations like a fire bell in the night. There was a great stir as President Carter and Rosalynn Carter strode onto the stage. The crowd, some of whom had been shut out from the Carter Administration or ejected from it, had long anticipated this moment, which had been hailed in the press as the real start of the Democratic presidential sweepstakes. Edward Kennedy had not yet announced his candidacy, but all knew he would do so within a few weeks. "I will whip his ass," Carter had boasted earlier in the year.

By now Carter's political stock was low, in the polls, in the press, and in the view of the vast majority of the nation's leaders attending the dedication. It seemed an act of audacity, almost of desperation, for the President to come into "Kennedy country" and compete with one of the party's foremost orators. When the President went down the long line of the Kennedy family kissing the women, including Jacqueline Kennedy, who responded with a glacial frown, the court attendants reflected that this symbolized Carter's situation—this far but no farther.

The Boston Pops Esplanade Orchestra offered Beethoven and Bernstein. Humberto Cardinal Medeiros gave the invocation. Caroline Kennedy introduced her brother, John, who recited a poem of Stephen Spender's:

> *I think continually of those* . . .
> *Who wore at their hearts the fire's center.* . . .

Then came the first surprise of the day. Young Joe Kennedy had been asked to speak as part of a family plan for his father, Robert Kennedy, to share in the commemoration. Joe plunged into a fiery account of his father's dying while he was "waging a struggle" for miners toiling in unsafe mines and ravaged by disease, for tenant farmers laboring long and hard with little to show for it, for Indians "hurt, manipulated, betrayed," for black people, Eskimos, Appalachians, "ordinary working families" sweating it out at work and too often getting a raw deal. Young Kennedy was not content with generalities. While many of his elders squirmed in their chairs, while his Uncle Ted held his forehead in his hand, he demanded to know who was protecting the poor from the ravages of inflation, who was stopping the big coal companies from "squeezing us so hard all the time," who was standing up to the "agri-businesses that rake in the dough and give precious little" to migrants. And as he spoke thus Joe cast admonishing glances at the President of the United States, who sat stonily gazing at the audience.

Now it was Carter's turn. Conspiracy theorists in the crowd were sure that Joe Kennedy's speech was a put-up job, an old Massachusetts "bag operation," but Carter was unruffled. Joe's indictment, indeed, made it possible for him to begin with a humorous riposte he had not been sure would be appropriate. He recalled John Kennedy's press conference of March 1962, when the "ravages of being President were beginning to show on his face," and a reporter had reminded President Kennedy that his brother Ted, after seeing the cares of office on the President, had doubted that he himself would ever be interested in the job; the reporter had then asked President Kennedy "if you could tell us whether, first, if you had to do it over again, if you would work for the presidency, and second, whether you could recommend this job to others." And Kennedy had replied, "Well, the answer to the first question is yes, and the second is no. I would not recommend it to others—at least for a while."

As laughter and applause swelled among Carter's listeners, he turned toward Senator Kennedy to drive the point home: "As you can well see, President Kennedy's wit and also his wisdom is certainly as relevant today as it was then." The Senator appeared to join in the general mirth.

As Carter moved into the substance of his talk, it slowly dawned on listeners that he was giving a superb media performance. He struck just the right note of recognition of the late President's accomplishments. He deftly evoked a common remembrance of the news of Kennedy's death: "I remember that I had climbed down from the seat of a tractor, unhooked a farm trailer and walked into my warehouse to weigh a load of grain," when farmers there had told him the news, and then he had "wept openly," for the first time since his own father had died barely ten years before.

But the President was not content with uttering condolences. He smoothly turned to the new challenges and problems that, he insisted, were quite different from those of twenty years before. "President Kennedy was right: change is the law of life. The world of 1980 is as different from what it was in 1960 as the world of 1960 was from that of 1940. . . . We have a keener appreciation of limits now; the limits of government, limits on the use of military power abroad; the limits on manipulating without harm to ourselves a delicate and a balanced natural environment. We are struggling with a profound transition from a time of abundance to a time of growing scarcity. . . . But in this age of hard choices and scarce resources, the essence of President Kennedy's message—the appeal for unselfish dedication to the common good—is more urgent than it ever was. . . ."

By the time he finished, Carter had managed to distance himself from his young challenger and yet virtually lay claim to being John Kennedy's legatee. Edward Kennedy's own touching tribute to his brother evoked many phrases from the past—of the man who "could make lightning strike on the things he cared about," whose life was a voyage of discovery, a President who called upon all governments to be as "a city upon a hill." And it foretold perorations of the future: "The spark still glows. The journey never ends. The dream shall never die." Yet there was an impression that Kennedy had been upstaged.

As people drifted away after the last musical performance, they seemed to agree that this had been marvelous theater, just right for a dedication. In retrospect it also seemed to have some of the apartness, the separatedness, the unreality of the stage. If the troubles of the nation and the world seemed remote at the moment, those of Boston were close at hand. Its schools were filled with racial violence; its finances were shaky; its transportation system was approaching crisis. Only half a mile from the library sat Columbia Point, one of the most ravaged, crime-ridden, demoralized housing projects in the nation. It stood as a mocking reminder, in the Kennedys' back yard, of the failures of the great dreams. A black resident told a reporter that, after being robbed nine times in the past years, he was packing a gun.

"Next time someone tries to rob me I'm going to shoot 'em," he said. "No calling the police on 911 or the Housing Authority!! I'd like to get out of here. . . . But where the hell can I go? I'm stuck."

Thus when people returned from the performance to the reality of America, Joe Kennedy's speech in cold print had a strangely old-fashioned, populistic ring. Some wanted to ask if the country was still in the condition that Joe described, why had his uncle the President and his father the attorney general not been more successful? If Boston's leadership had been asked to be as the "city upon a hill" two decades before, why was the city still in such dire straits? President Carter's remarks also seemed divorced from reality. If John Kennedy had not produced more lasting results in his two years and ten months in office, why had Jimmy Carter produced so little in his two years and nine? Was it, as he contended in his address, because presidential power was so limited?

The crowd at the dedication had hardly seemed aware of the people in the slum nearby. But the people in Columbia Point were quite aware of the ceremony. They felt that as next-door neighbors they should have been invited, but they were not. A few accosted the police barrier, made a fuss, and were tossed into jail. Mrs. Dorothy Baskin and her grandchildren did get a glimpse of President Carter's limousine as it sped away.

"They went by fast and the people inside were small, they seemed so far away," she said, "but I think the President waved at us."

THE HOPES OF JANUARY

It is hard today, though only seven years or so have passed, to recapture the positive mood of the nation when Jimmy Carter entered the White House. After years of witnessing government in the hands often of well-intentioned mediocrities or outright scoundrels, here was a man of fine ethical standards, with a kind of sunny morality. After years of drift and deadlock and delay in government, here was a man of proved competence, tough, demanding, clearheaded. He seemed a man of parts—Annapolis graduate, Navy officer, successful businessman, effective governor, and above all a brilliant campaigner who had come from "nowhere" to win the Democratic presidential nomination and then knock off an incumbent President.

He was, he said, an "idealist without illusions," and many liked that. He was a man who read Reinhold Niebuhr and appreciated the great theologian's hardheaded view of political morality, his ironic conception of American history, and his "Christian realism" that recognized the evil—the greed, selfishness, injustice—as well as the good in humankind. The new President seemed to be religious but not pious, compassionate but not sentimental, moral but not moralizing or moralistic. He seemed able to deal with the famed power brokers of Washington on his terms, not theirs. He seemed both "above politics" and "with it."

His sheer air of competence attracted people—competence at running a business and a state, a submarine and a tractor, and several tough political campaigns. At a time when the nation seemed weary of the big, ideological issues, many welcomed a no-nonsense type who seemed more concerned with getting the job done. They liked his emphasis on the *process* of government, on prosaic but crucial matters like budgeting and administrative reorganization. With more and more Americans protesting and clamoring about ever-increasing taxes and government spending and bureaucratic incompetence, it was good to have an economizer at the head of the Administration.

If his southern Baptist ways occasionally put people off—his joyful hymn singing and hand holding with fellow parishioners, his rhetorical exaggerations and appeals for more "love" among humankind, his southern accent that seemed to grow thicker the nearer he was to Plains—many were happy too that he was from the Deep South, that he was the first President to come out of that region for well over a century, that he would bring fresh regional and cultural perspectives to bear on the governmental behemoth in Washington. Above all people honored him for transcending the old racial conflicts that had so badly hurt the nation, the South, and the Democratic Party. He seemed the perfect spokesman for the New South.

The political environment also seemed right for a successful Administration. Carter had won a close but clear victory over Gerald Ford. Democrats still held majorities in both houses of Congress, and the kind of men with whom Carter could work—Robert Byrd in the Senate and Tip O'Neill in the House—headed the Democratic majorities there. Even more, the President had "momentum" going for him. A vast number of Americans wished him well. Many Republicans wanted him to succeed, if only because they perceived him as an efficiency expert who would cut the federal budget and save money.

Hopes only increased during the "first hundred days," which the press has made into the testing period for new Presidents. He got off to a media-perfect start, within minutes after the inaugural ceremony, when he bounded out of his limousine and walked hand in hand with the new First Lady and daughter Amy down Pennsylvania Avenue. He gave a fireside chat, reminiscent of Rooseveltian days, pardoned Vietnam draft violators, announced that he would reduce federal regulations and cut down on presidential staff perquisites, such as free use of White House limousines. Then, when he fulfilled a campaign promise that he would keep close to the people by conducting a presidential "town meeting" in the small community of Clinton, Massachusetts—and then handled himself with skill and aplomb—we concluded that he rivaled John Kennedy and even FDR in his mastery of the symbolic potential of the presidency.

There were some doubting Thomases, of course. To some it seemed that the President was far more interested in the mechanics of policy making, and especially in the symbolic potential of policy, than in the substance of it. They wondered how long he could sustain his imagery and popularity when hard choices had to be made. He had run against the Establishment—the rich, the big interests, the city elites, the Washington officialdom—yet he seemed curiously dependent on the expertise of some of the old hangers-on. Soon journalists and scholars were digging more deeply into Carter's record as governor of Georgia and coming up with mixed evaluations.

In campaigning for governor, reported Professor Betty Glad, who conducted the most penetrating inquiry, Carter had run as a relative unknown against "Atlanta" and the Establishment, emphasizing his own qualities as an outsider, as one of the people, just as six years later he would do in his campaign for the White House. "But having won office as governor, he then became an insider. . . ." He was already mainly interested in administration, making the reorganization of the Georgia state government his top priority. "In the programs he embraced," Glad summed up, "Carter had shown himself to be a conventional good-government man, pushing mainstream reforms favored by good-government people in his and other states. The net result of his reorganization program, which he had made the hallmark of his administration, however, was less impressive than his later claims were to suggest. His other accomplishments were in the areas of natural resource development and protection of the environment, judicial reform, improvement in the treatment of the retarded and mentally ill, and certain modest changes in the prison system. In the promotion of sexual and racial equality he had a mixed record. When judged on a scale other than his own, Carter had proved to be a good, but not extraordinary, governor."

Carter had displayed a tendency in Georgia to go it alone, sometimes getting too far ahead of other state officials and politicians and having to back down, showing almost too much flexibility when he may have "switched friendships and positions a little too fast, been a bit too facile in accepting the support of persons he would quickly forget."

Anyone intimately familiar with Carter's gubernatorial ways could hardly have been surprised by reporter Robert Shogan's findings that after ten weeks in the White House, "as during the transition, Carter's image as a methodical and sensitive political planner had been overshadowed by other aspects of his personality. Restless and aggressive, he plunged ahead, sometimes heedless of the timetables established by his advisers, and even of his own political interests. . . ."

Most of these deeper analyses of the earlier Carter were published in book form and hence appeared months or even years after the "honeymoon period."

For every doubt expressed about Carter during this period, however, there seemed to be a convincing answer. Had he shown himself essentially a master of the media arts rather than of policy substance? Talent in public relations was crucial to exercising leadership in the presidency. Did he lack extensive national political experience? The White House was a marvelous teacher—and besides, some of those "politicians of great experience" had been mediocrities or worse in the White House. Had he practiced all the wiles of politics while pretending to be "above politics"? All effective politicians had done the same. Had he avoided taking stands on major issues? That was the oldest political game in town. Had he used in Georgia all the weapons of traditional politics—patronage, use of discretionary funds, putting supporters into key legislative and executive posts—to maximize his influence? What else was new?

It was, above all, Carter's absolute self-assurance that had impressed many of us. "Even in a trade where egos are unbounded," Jack Germond wrote during the campaign, "Carter's self-confidence is dazzling"—it would shame Muhammad Ali. Carter aspired to combine all the virtues of the previous great Presidents. "I've studied the finer aspects of previous Administrations," he said shortly after his nomination, "the humility and courage and tenacity of Mr. Truman's Administration, the inspiration of Kennedy, the elimination of discrimination and inequity by the Johnson Administration. I would like to exemplify the finest aspects of each one of those great Presidents of the past. Whether that would be possible it is too early to say, but that is my goal."

Four years later Jimmy Carter left office amid almost universal judgment that his Administration had been largely a failure. Was it? The answer typically turns on diverse standards and mixed perspectives.

By and large the Washington journalists had given their own negative answer by election time, but many of them understood the fragility of such early judgments and were willing to appeal to the "bar of history." But the verdict of that bar would not be in for a long time, and it was certain to change over the years as new historians achieved more comprehensive views of the era, and as revisionists and counterrevisionists fought their battles in the scholarly journals. Still, those who conducted intensive studies of Carter and his Administration—notably Betty Glad (*Jimmy Carter: In Search of the Great White House*, 1980) and Clark Mollenhoff (*The President Who Failed: Carter Out of Control*, 1980)—were highly critical of his presidency.

The bluntest verdict on the President's performance came from the people themselves. By August 1980, when the Democratic National Convention met in Madison Square Garden, presidential popular support in the polls had dropped to one of the lowest levels in the entire history of the Gallup poll. Then came the voter's eight-million-plurality verdict for Ronald Reagan in the fall election. No President is as "failed" as a defeated President. But Americans had become rather sophisticated about polls and the polled. Popular judgments would change in time; moreover, being out of favor, at least temporarily, could ultimately be seen as the badge of courage, commitment, and indeed success. So the popular verdict was not all that convincing.

Perhaps the most illuminating verdict on Carter's Administration was that of Carter himself. And in his own disarmingly honest way, he awarded himself mediocre grades at best. Indeed he *literally* gave himself grades, telling Dan Rather on CBS's *60 Minutes* a week before his defeat that he thought his presidency merited a B or a C plus on foreign policy, C on overall domestic policy, A on energy, C on the economy, and "maybe a B" on leadership. For a President, grades of B and C are failing grades. According to Joseph Califano, as early as April 1978, at a specially convened Cabinet meeting the President stated that "my government is not leading the country. The people have lost confidence in me, in the Congress, in themselves, and in this nation." He would change his "life-style," he said, and he would change his Cabinet; later he sacked four of his Cabinet secretaries. It was reported two months after Carter left office that at a meeting with Princeton upperclassmen he admitted that he had not been "as effective as a President as he could have been."

Perhaps the most damning indictment of the Carter Administration lay not in critiques but in the enormous gap between what Carter had promised as a candidate and what he achieved in the White House. Perhaps no candidate had made so many pledges, had raised expectations so high, and hence had set so formidable a standard for himself, as did Jimmy Carter. And he had made a special pledge about his pledges. "I don't intend to break a single promise," he had told a New Hampshire audience during his 1976 campaign, "I'm giving you

my word of honor." After his election Carter was even more auda-
cious—he had his transition team compile all his promises (they to-
taled 660) and then hand out the list to the press. Later two *New
York Times* writers went through the list and concluded that the
President had "broken" at least two hundred of these, and especially
the more important ones. Thus he had promised that by 1980 both
employment and inflation would be 4 percent or less, the economy
would be expanding at a 4 to 6 percent rate, the 1,900 federal agencies would be reduced to 200 or less, the defense budget would be cut
$5 to $7 billion.

Presidents who fail to live up to expectations—their own and the
public's—are granted a standard defense: the problems were intractable; events were beyond anyone's control; Congress was too negative
and fragmented to help the Administration program; lobbies and special-interest groups were too strong, etc. These excuses are usually
quite justified. But they beg the central issue—the gap between what
the candidate promised and the President produced. Most of the obstacles are predictable: the problem of Congress has existed for almost two centuries; lobbies and special interests are not new; the political system has long been fragmented. Candidates and Presidents
have been far more persuasive as to *what* they wanted to do than *how*
they proposed to do it. But the "how" has become as important as the
"what." For all Carter's interest in process, he never came up with a
political strategy to deal with governmental deadlock, or with specific
suggestions except for administrative reorganization, which hardly
touched the fundamental problem.

This matter of candidates' excessive raising of expectations and
underfulfillment of promises by Presidents brings us to the essence of
the question of why leaders fail in America. Do these failures stem
mainly from the leaders themselves—from their personal failings or
political inexperience or intellectual incapacity and the like—or from
the political, institutional, or psychological environment in which they
operate? Every presidency is a testing out of this question. Hence we
have a series of (typically) four-year laboratory experiments in the
behavior of leaders in interaction with the political structure around
them. Carter was an especially illuminating test in this series of experiments, because of his own impressive personal qualities and because of many favorable elements in the political environment. In
short, is it *Presidents* who fail us, or is it the presidential-congressional-
judicial system? Or both? Or neither?

THE LONELINESS
OF THE LONG-DISTANCE JOGGER

Jimmy Carter had a choice of several strategic alternatives, when he entered the White House, as to what kind of President he would be. He could choose to stress one or more of the old textbook functions of the President—chief executive, party chief, chief legislator, bipartisan chief of state, and others. He could choose among various real-life presidential models, including Franklin Roosevelt's loose, open, competitive administrative arrangements, Eisenhower's command-and-staff system, and John Kennedy's way of combining charisma and symbolism with traditional methods of building reputation, guarding power, and bargaining in a hard-nosed way with friends and adversaries at home and abroad. In the most fundamental sense, Carter could choose whether to be mainly a transactional, transcending, or transforming leader.

As it turned out, Jimmy Carter did not make a choice. His Administration attested not so much to political or administrative incompetence as to a collapse of political strategy stemming largely from a failure of intellectual leadership.

The usual explanation of Carter's failures is political ineffectiveness owing to political inexperience. This strikes me as oversimplified. A man who won campaigns for state senator and governor, who suffered the educational sting of defeat in another gubernatorial race, who later swept through the 1976 Democratic primaries to sew up the nomination long before the convention, and then defeated a President—such a man is hardly inexperienced. Still, electoral politics calls for different qualities of leadership than administrative or legislative politics, and Jimmy Carter before his inauguration had spent far more time running for office than serving *in* office. But this was not the heart of the matter.

Carter was not good at a *certain kind* of politics. "He's not a political animal," his campaign manager, Robert Strauss, told me during the last days of the Carter Administration, by which Strauss meant that the President would not conduct the kind of bargaining with senators and congressmen that got bills through. Strauss said that he would have sent Carter's congressional liaison man to the Hill with this admonition, "Here's two dams and three grants—you go up there and spend them. You bring me back thirteen goddamned votes in the

Senate and forty-two from the House." But Carter would not give his liaison people the dams and grants and jobs to spend. Carter, Meg Greenfield noted astutely, "has no appetite for and certainly takes no joy in that combination of management, manipulation, inspiration, deceit, psychiatry and arm-wrestling that it takes to get things to happen when you are President, and so, often as not, they don't."

In dealing with key congressmen and senators Carter was bent on his own kind of politics—explaining, analyzing, detailing, urging, perhaps moralizing a bit. He saw no need to "cut deals" because he felt that the legislators, if sufficiently informed, would see things his way. Strauss may have been right in believing that Carter talked with more congressmen and senators and indeed had more of them to the White House than any other President had done. But something was lacking. Carter could not indulge in the "blarney, bludgeon and boodle" that the Kennedyites boasted of employing in their (not always successful) efforts to push bills through Congress. It was not that the President was inept or crude in these contacts; no one could be more gracious or reasonable in talking over the phone or face-to-face with legislators. But he was not seen as "one of them," not seen as a good trader and accommodator.

The President much preferred to rise above this bargaining level, to transcend the kind of politics he associated with the Georgia Senate and House. He wanted to be a teaching President, as Wilson and FDR had been, a preaching President who set the tone of moral uplift so clearly that it would guide his Administration and impress his adversaries, perhaps even Congress. He wanted to be something of a charismatic leader, American-style. He wanted, in short, to be a transcending leader. Even so, he shunned the notion of taking on the symbolic trappings of that kind of elevated leadership. He carried his own bags, worked in his shirt sleeves, and banned the playing of "Hail to the Chief." Beyond platitudes about honesty and morality, however, and specific policies the President was interested in at the moment, it was not clear what this transcending leadership was *for*.

Tragically for Carter's presidency, the one vehicle that might have helped shape and support a coherent program—the Democratic Party—was the one he most neglected. Carter had never been a strong party man. He had moved to the top outside the national Democracy; he had looked on the presidential primaries as rungs on the ladder of his own ambition rather than the mechanisms of a great political organization. The Democratic Party was in a parlous state when he took office, but he did virtually nothing to arrest its further decline; he largely ignored it. The people around him who were as party-minded as Walter Mondale made little effort to rejuvenate the Democracy as an organization. As the President prepared to leave office, partisan Democrats on his staff were eyeing the Republican Party organization enviously and talking about the need of the Democrats to revitalize themselves and surpass the GOP. But they had no explanation of why the Carter White House had not tried to revitalize the party when it had the chance—and the clout.

The absence of a strong party was especially damaging to Carter, for he needed not only the party's constituency but even more a broad political organization and program that would have bound him together, politically and organizationally and programmatically, with Democratic leaders in Congress, state legislatures, county courthouses, and local party committees. Even the weakened national Democracy of the 1970s could have served this role to some degree. Party-minded people in the White House tended to attribute Carter's abdication as party leader to the President's nonparty background in Georgia politics, but the staff too had muddled priorities, perhaps because it came from the same background. They prated about building up the party from the grass roots, for example, while opposing a 1982 midterm conference that would provide a role and recognition for hundreds of grass-roots party activists, as well as momentum and a strengthened image in national affairs.

Looking back on his presidency Carter believed that he had failed as party leader. He should have taken a more active personal role in shaping the character of the national Democratic Party, he told me in an interview in Atlanta about fifteen months after he left office. "If we could have kept the image of compassion and competence and fiscal responsibility that I wanted the Democratic Party to have, if I had played a leading role, for example, in the replacement of some of the delegations of the party, if I had attended the National Committee meetings, if I were to shape the platform, if I had played a larger role in the mini-convention, it would have changed things to some extent." But this was never on his list of top priorities, he added. "I never did try to mold the character of the party in my own image or to the image of what Democrats in the country represented."

The former President, I believe, still did not understand the nature of his failure as party leader. His great regret was that he had not made "sufficient use of the Democratic Party." His idea of party leadership was not to engage with the collective leadership and followership of the party as partners on a reciprocal basis, but to use the party, shape it, restrain it, moderate it, for his own political purposes. The fact was that Carter feared the party too much to work with it. "Almost any candidate who wants to be elected as a Democratic President could only look on the party's national convention with trepidation," he told me. "We saw it as a spectacle that would alienate a substantial portion of the American people from the party." He remembered the delegates as essentially proponents of causes—"worthy causes in their eyes—abortion, gun control, homosexual rights, equality of women. They are so highly motivated that they are willing to sacrifice the election of a candidate. . . . They have little interest in who the Democratic nominee might be—apart from how he is involved with their cause." It would be good, he added, to have more "Democratic Party functionaries" represented at the convention who would concentrate on getting a Democratic President elected. Carter still showed little understanding of a party as a vast partnership of leaders and followers collectively interested in electing not merely a President but hundreds of national, state, and local candidates, in pursuit of a national program stated in a democratically endorsed party platform.

Behind this and other missed opportunities lay an intellectual failure by the President. Critics kept saying he lacked vision or broad purpose or a theme, yet he spelled out high moral goals in speech after speech. He also, with his clear engineering mind, was on top of a multitude of policy details. What was lacking was the linkage between the two—a clear ordering of priorities, a well-formulated set of goals, an explicit marshaling of ends and means. That explained why, in Greenfield's words, there was so little collective sense that Carter "represents an identifiable program—certain values and choices and priorities— that an identifiable group of voters thinks is right." It also explained why Carter himself may have felt a lack of *policy* mandate.

One result of this strategic myopia was instability of policy—and of public and congressional perception of policy. Lacking a firm and coherent set of policies of his own, lacking commitment to a party platform that dealt with a wide range of issues, Carter zigzagged on policy. He proposed at least four anti-inflation plans. Even in the first year, according to an analysis by Howard J. Silver, "Carter reversed himself on issues. For example, the retreat from the $50 rebate caused credibility problems. In addition, Carter repeatedly overpromised and then backed off from his policies. A loudly publicized human rights program faded when an arms control agreement with the Soviet Union took precedence. An energy crisis that was the 'moral equivalent of war,' a crisis which would require great sacrifices from the American public, two days later became a program that would bring benefits to the people." Policy zigzagging continued throughout the Carter years and increased in some policy areas.

The wavering on program that afflicted the Carter Administration in domestic policy at times could be a positive advantage in foreign affairs. In dealing with a hundred or so sovereign nations in an essentially anarchical world polity, a President may benefit from loose guidelines and limited program constraints. Opportunism as well as vision may be the key strategy in this area. Perhaps it was not surprising that Carter's main successes—the Panama Canal treaty and the Camp David agreements—occurred in a relatively open policy and political environment. But even as the aura of Camp David fell away, Califano observed, the Administration fell back into the "inept and confused vacillation" that even Carter had deplored.

Policy zigzagging more than anything else explained the Administration's difficulties in working with Congress and department heads. Legislative and bureaucratic leaders are involved in a continuing process of deciding among competing policy demands and among budgetary pressures. These day-to-day decisions are almost insuperable unless there is some sense of priority, timetable, substance. I remember standing in the office of a United States senator while a legislative aide talked at length to a White House policy aide. The senator's man was not urging a position on the Administration but simply trying to *divine* its position. Long moments went by punctuated by such remarks as "That's very interesting *but just where does the Administration stand?*"

All Administrations run into difficulties after the honeymoon; a test of leadership is how the President and his lieutenants react to them. FDR was assailed by forces on both the right and the left during the early New Deal, castigated for poor staff work, loose administrative practices, even vacillating policy. Soon he proceeded to broaden his Administration, forging closer ties with labor and farm groups, reaching out to the millions who were responding to the appeals of Huey Long, Father Coughlin, the Townsend movement, and the like. John Kennedy, in his third, abbreviated year, took a bolder position on civil rights and in effect brought much of the black leadership into political and program coalition with him. Roosevelt of course had a relatively strong set of national and state Democratic parties to fall back on, as did Kennedy to a lesser extent.

Jimmy Carter's main response to vacillation and turmoil in his

Administration was to fall back on his personal resources—on his personal staff, his wife, and himself. He had risen to power through an individualistic, personalistic political effort, and this is all he had still working for him in the face of frustration. In the strife that erupted between his staff and the Cabinet—conflict absolutely predictable in any Administration—he sided with his staff and let some of his ablest department heads go. He made Hamilton Jordan "chief of staff," called (not very originally and perhaps unfairly) one of the most inappropriate appointments since Caligula made his horse a proconsul. Fortunately Jordan, having even less interest in an executive role than aptitude for it, concentrated more on political and personal chores, so the damage was minimal.

Politically the President fell back on his personal organization, painstakingly built up in his long campaign of 1974–1976 and broadened during his presidency. The White House development of this organization, headed by one of Carter's ablest political operatives, Anne Wexler, was a quite remarkable operation. Day after day, week after week, she invited to the White House persons who were somehow involved in presidential policies, appointments, or interests, and who might swing some weight with their senator or congressman. The visitors received a royal welcome—meetings with relevant government officials, a pep talk in the White House, a brief address and perhaps a quick handshake from the President himself. Anne Wexler ran follow-ups on these visitors and kept in touch until election day.

It was a fine idea, bringing grass-roots activists and good citizens into the glow and hospitality of the White House, but there was a price to pay. Anne Wexler cultivated Republicans as well as Democrats, since she was primarily interested in roll-call votes—including those of Republican legislators—in Congress, and in votes from any and all live bodies for her boss on election day. Inevitably she caused flaps in the precincts when local Democratic Party chieftains heard that she was entertaining local Republicans. She would long remember how furious Democratic Senator Patrick Leahy became with her when she brought a group of Vermont Republicans—including the state GOP chairman himself—into the White House for a "briefing" that would help win support on the Hill from the Republican congressman from Vermont. White House mobilization of short-run bipartisan support for Carter clearly hurt the Democracy's morale, legitimacy, and self-esteem. One wonders how much the Democratic Party would have been strengthened if Anne Wexler's efforts had been concentrated on party building rather than nourishing her boss's personal organization. But of course the benefit to the party would mainly have been long-run, whereas the President wanted to win the next legislative victory in Congress and the next election.

Carter's falling back on *personalismo* and personal organization had an even broader effect—a swing to the center and even right of center in policy and program. Here again there was an interesting contrast with FDR's and John Kennedy's shift to the left during the pressures of their first two or three years in office. It is still difficult to gauge how much this shift in Carter was inherent in his attitudes from the start; within five months of his inaugural he said he was making a balanced budget by 1981 his top priority, despite the glaring inconsistency of this undertaking with his commitment to reduce unemployment, aid the needy, and fulfill several hundred other campaign promises. By his third year in office his position on many issues was hardly distinguishable from those of liberal Republicans and in some instances from true-blue conservatives—a shift that Edward Kennedy and other potential rivals eyed with a wild surmise.

In the end the President was reduced not only to defeat but to a kind of ignominy. Harshly opposed in his own party, battered by his Republican rivals, defeated in Congress on bill after bill, he was reduced to making telephone calls to local citizens during his self-imposed campaign inactivity as a result of the hostage crisis. As in all matters of detail, he was thorough and well organized. It is said that he made twenty thousand telephone calls. It was a delightful surprise for these twenty thousand, who would remember the call from the White House for the rest of their lives (save for a woman in Iowa who was watching Kennedy on television when the President telephoned and who refused to take the call). But this ploy had very little evident effect on the election outcome. It had nothing to do with the serious business of politics. And it left the spectacle of an earnest and intensely well-meaning leader bereft of party and popular support, forced back into ultimate political loneliness and self-dependence, stacks of three-by-five cards at his elbow, making calls to anonymous persons, far out into the night.

SO—WHY NOT THE BEST?

"Is it in our institutions or in ourselves?" We return to our central question: Did the failures of the Carter presidency stem mainly from the personal failings of the President and the White House staff or more largely from the institutional and ideological environment in which they operated? Verdicts came in quickly after Carter's re-election defeat. "It's hard to be successful and popular in this town," Hamilton Jordan complained a month later; "there are a lot of forces at play today that make the art of governing very difficult. It is not only true of this President but for all recent Presidents, and it'll be even more difficult for President-elect Reagan."

Jordan listed the things that made life hard for all Presidents: the fragmentation of political power, the new generation of complex problems, an "active and aggressive" press that had gone from being properly skeptical to negatively cynical, congressional resistance, special-interest groups, and limited presidential resources to deal with all these forces. "I suspected that issues would be tough," he added, but things were tougher than they had dreamed.

Certain President watchers jumped on the "impossible situation" theory. That defense, said political scientist Erwin C. Hargrove, left "no place for skill by a president at winning political support for his policies. . . . The argument will not work. Carter's failure was that he did not address himself to the problems which were worrying most people. Few people care about government reorganization or even the Panama Canal. But inflation and the power of the U.S. in the world are of concern to people. Carter lacked a firm strategic grip and thereby the majority of citizens came to believe that he was not in control of the events which most concerned them." Hargrove's view is typical of the "personal failure" theory held by many journalists and some scholars.

This dispute far transcends the issue of Carter's presidency. If Jordan and the other Carter apologists are right, *no* President can succeed under the circumstances of the 1980s. If they are wrong, we should simply do a better job of choosing Presidents, and Presidents should do a better job of running the railroad.

The "personal failure" theory tends to be skewed by the notion, widely shared in Washington, that Presidents and their staffs must be privy to a set of special skills and arcane arts in political persuasion, manipulation, communication, pressure, management—and that the possession or nonpossession of these skills and arts makes all the difference in a President's political leadership. This is the "skill mystique." Because Carter's White House was poor at returning phone calls, because his legislative liaison office was unusually incompetent, because manipulation was often applied clumsily, because Washington abounded with rumors about the latest blunder in the White

House, Carter slowly lost the reputation for political brilliance he had won in his primary and election victories. I doubt though that these day-to-day slips and stumbles made a profound difference amid the literally thousands of exchanges that took place weekly between the White House and the departments and between the White House and Congress. Far more fundamental forces were at work.

We have no calipers to measure where personal failures leave off and situational forces take command—and even if we did, it would be hard to measure the interplay between the two—but I would lean far more toward the "impossible situation" theory in measuring the Carter presidency than toward the "personal failure" interpretation. To begin with, the fact that governmental fragmentation faces every President does not make its impact seem any lighter to a particular President. The dispersion of legislative power among committees and subcommittees, among personal staffs and committee staffs, between Senate and House, faced the Carter White House every day of its existence. The "iron triangles" of interlocked congressional faction, bureaucratic power group, and single-interest group were no less consequential for having been well analyzed by scholars and well publicized by the media.

The state of the Democratic Party also supports the "impossible situation" theory; Carter inherited a Democracy that was more a problem than a prop. As usual the party in Congress ranged ideologically across the spectrum from left to extreme right, so that it was not easy for the Administration to organize majority support behind major bills. The Democratic "Boll Weevils" who emerged so dramatically during the early Reagan days as fiscal conservatives had long been at work, albeit more quietly, nibbling away at Democratic Party fiscal undertakings. Not only was party discipline in Congress woefully spongy; the party foundations in the country were eroded, cracked, and splintered, for reasons we will be exploring. The Democracy has long been divided between liberals and conservatives, but now it was further divided among what Scammon and Wattenberg called New Politics Liberals, Old Fashioned Liberals, and Conservatives; and it further subdivided into numberless factions within each of these groupings. It would be easier to eat hot consommé with a fork than pack these factions into any kind of political base.

Behind much of this division was a liberal ideology in disarray. As long as old-fashioned—New Deal or Fair Deal—liberalism dealt mainly with redistributionist economic issues, it sustained a credo around which a vast number of Democrats could unite. The failure of some of the old New Deal-Fair Deal programs, the cost of most of them, and the very *success* of many of them have helped produce a new era of "tired liberalism" and the exhaustion of many of the earlier hopes and dreams. Even more, the decline of the relative salience of economic issues in a time of greater middle-class affluence has helped burning social issues such as abortion and crime to come to the fore. American liberal thought has lacked leadership innovative and creative enough to cope with these divisive issues, which, for example, have split sections of organized labor's constituency away from middle-class liberals. Thus the ideological foundations for a united Carter Administration were as pasty as the political.

One could hardly expect the Carter White House, in the two or three years it was given for governing, to overcome such deep-seated political and intellectual obstacles. But Carter's presidency must be seriously faulted for making the problems *worse* rather than better. Rather than seeking to overcome the fundamental conditions that made its governance so difficult, it made those conditions even more intractable.

Thus, instead of taking leadership in the modernizing and reshaping of a cogent liberal doctrine, perhaps with a strong Niebuhrian component, Carter tended to rely, rhetorically at least, on conventional liberal and Democratic Party wisdom. Instead of renovating old party doctrine, he stood on the Democratic Party platform of 1976, with all its inherent contradictions between the costs of programs and their financing. Indeed, his people at the 1976 Democratic convention had agreed that the party platform must be presented as a "contract" with the American people. That is a pretty strong term, considering especially that so many of the previous Democratic Presidents had left so much of the contract unfulfilled. Carter, to repeat, shared one of the oldest weaknesses of American liberal thought—a tendency toward sermonizing and uplifting at one level, and toward a vast range of specifics at a lower level, but lacking linkage between the two, lacking, that is, an orderly relating of high aims and specific policy, of financial outlays and incomes, of explicit ends and concrete means. Thus the President alternated between born-again moralizing and engineering specifics, without connecting the two.

Surely, the Carter White House cannot be faulted for not renewing and vitalizing the Democratic Party; that would require committing political brains and resources at least for a decade. But here again Carter and his people made the situation worse by letting the Democratic National Committee wither on the vine, under the direction of amiable mediocrities; by largely ignoring other Democratic Party candidates; by refusing to divert funds from his personal re-election campaign coffers to the good of the party as a whole.

Not only did the Carterites fail seriously to confront the institutional malaise that was frustrating them; in the end they seemed to yield to it and be diminished by it. In analyzing Carter, Betty Glad quoted Karen Horney on the introvert: "He lives . . . by his private religion . . . abides by his own laws . . . within the barbed-wire fence of his own pride and with his own guards to protect him against dangers from within and without. As a result he not only becomes more isolated emotionally but it also becomes more difficult for him to see other people as individuals in their own right, different from himself. They are subordinate to his prime concern: himself." According to Barbara Kellerman, the "president who is an introvert will experience some of the following politically relevant outcomes: 1) vulnerability to isolation, 2) excessive dependency on a few key staff people, 3) limited contacts and successes with politically important others in the realm of both domestic and foreign policy, 4) restricted input into the decision-making process, 5) restricted ability to dramatize and sell his concerns and to make his presence felt, 6) limited number of political allies who will lend national and international support, and 7) a tendency to extreme sensitivity that will hinder him in his ability to take the rough and tumble of hardball politics and encourage him still further to retreat from the world of people." With one or two exceptions Carter could hardly be better described.

All told, Carter was one of the few Presidents in our history diminished by the office rather than enlarged by it. Just as he fell back on his wife and personal staff, so he and the staff fell back on a kind of phantom realism to justify their failures. I was not surprised by this. I have spent many hours talking with members of the Truman, Kennedy, and Johnson staffs while they explained to me, kindly and patiently, why all the things they promised could not be done—in short, advancing the "impossible situation" defense. But they had a special argument: the need to win elections. "Professor," they would explain to me, "you can only do so much. If we hadn't compromised on this piece of controversial legislation or that, we would have lost in 19—."

The Carter people explained all this to me in identical terms— the need to compromise, to pull back from the party platform and the early promises, to retrench financially, to move toward the center, to try to hold on to the party moderates and conservatives. They were still saying all that in the last week of the Carter Administration, even as they were surrounded by packing boxes. You had to be in the White House, they were saying, to get a realistic grip on things. They had made all the compromises and retrenchment, I reflected, and still had not won. And that was realism?

The puzzlement remains: Why did the Carterites make the "impossible situation" worse? Why did such talented presidential-primary winners let themselves be defeated by the institutions through which they had to operate, rather than at least seeking to outwit, transcend, or transform them? Why could they not at least exercise better transactional leadership—that is, serve as more effective accommodators, brokers, persuaders, and manipulators within the system?

The answer lies in the presidential recruitment process. Presidential primaries call for qualities almost precisely the opposite to those necessary for presidential governance and leadership. Those primaries require a kind of dexterity, opportunism, volatility, expediency, and short-run manipulation that have little to do with the steady, persistent, year-long efforts of Presidents to develop programs, form broad policy coalitions, mobilize continuing support, control policy, and ultimately to produce outcomes that are quite different from the quick pulling of levers or scratching of X's in polling booths on a certain day in a certain state.

Of all his triumphs, Carter's primary victories of 1980 were the most convincing demonstration of his genius for King-of-the-Rock electioneering. Granted that he commanded the political resources of the White House, but he also had the formidable opposition of Edward Kennedy; and the President could hardly forget that the last President had almost succumbed four years before to a formidable adversary in *his* party. Carter rose to the occasion. He readily shifted from the role of pugnacious campaigner ("I will whip his ass") to the "nonpolitical" President in the Rose Garden. He agreed to debate Kennedy, then refused to, without any apparent political damage. He was good at little ploys; thus he leaked to the press a memo that had the President's advisers urging him to go through with the planned debate in Iowa, and he responding nobly that he could not "break away from my duties here" no matter what the "adverse political consequences." The President's campaigning without appearing to campaign was an interesting twist on his often appearing to govern without actually governing.

Above all, Carter's presidential-primary campaigning tactics called for two related qualities that were counterproductive in the presidency—emphasis on personality and on going it alone. His media experts in 1980 planned campaign ads emphasizing personal qualities rather than accomplishments: "Husband, father, President—he's done these three jobs with distinction"—an interesting equation of those three tasks. Who a man is, the ad continued, "is frequently more important than what he's done." This was not only an invidious reference to Kennedy and a rationalization of lack of presidential accomplishment; it was a genuine expression of the strategy, so useful in the primaries, of emphasizing *personalismo* rather than issues, policies, and governance.

Carter's go-it-alone tactics worked well in the presidential primaries. The primaries were, after all, essentially battles of all against all, or in his case, one against all. Negative campaigning—that is, cutting down opponents—was more crucial than creating coalitions. In 1980 Carter seemed far more effective in undermining support for Kennedy than in building support for himself; he made the challenger rather than the incumbent the issue. No wonder Cyrus Vance concluded that the "present primary system isolates the candidate from party and Congressional leaders. . . . Parties tended to produce candidates accustomed to working with diverse groups and to forging a consensus among the competing factions within the party. . . . [Primaries do] not insure that the successful candidate will have the . . . political skills needed for leadership. Nor do [they] insure that a candidate will have the support of political leaders whose alliance may be essential in enacting legislation." The final and most remarkable demonstration of Carter's go-it-alone campaign tendency was his early concession of defeat by Reagan, with costly impacts on Democratic turnout and voting for other Democratic candidates on the West Coast.

So, why not the best? Because we possess, judged by the Carter example and others before him, one of the worst top-leadership recruitment systems in the democratic societies of the world. One does not need to glorify the old convention system, with its own forms of manipulation, corruption, destructive competition, malrepresentation of rank and file. But at least that system was able to produce effective leaders when needed—or at least nominees who would prove to be effective leaders—and it did so largely because experienced leaders at all levels of the party were able to measure candidates by their potential for doing the one thing that is crucial in a divided political system—develop coalitions for governing.

Jimmy Carter's rise and fall stands as the most striking case to date of the presidential game of King of the Rock. Stripping the story to its essentials, Carter emerged from the grass roots, gathered a band of followers, shouldered his rivals out of the 1976 Democratic nomination, pushed a President off the top, climbed to the pinnacle of the rock, fought off his rivals for a time, and finally was toppled by a new challenger with a bigger following. All this made for wonderful media coverage; it did not make for responsible politics or effective government. Still, it will be far more typical of future presidencies under the present political system, I expect, than the presidency that immediately followed. Ronald Reagan would try a quite different experiment in presidential leadership.

TWO

Reagan and
the New Republican Party

AT first many in the media viewed Ronald Reagan as another Jimmy Carter—another outsider who had come in from the political cold to defy the Washington Establishment. And they predicted that he would undergo the same metamorphosis as had previous Republican candidates: He would enter the arena breathing fire, preach good old conservative Republican doctrine strongly enough to win the GOP nomination, then move to the center in order to win the presidency. "A remodeled conservative," *Newsweek* summed him up on the eve of the 1980 election.

Then if Reagan did win office, it had been predicted, the education of this political outlander would really begin, as he discovered the "realities" of American government. He would become more moderate, more conciliatory, more pragmatic. Had not Eisenhower departed from his 1952 rhetoric to embrace most of the New Deal program? Had not both Richard Nixon and Jerry Ford moved from the right or moderate right wing of the GOP to its center? Democrats had done the same, we were reminded, only in the opposite direction. Both John Kennedy and Jimmy Carter had entered office as "rhetorical radicals" and soon turned into fiscal moderates. Preempt the center—that was the great rule of practical politics.

When Reagan refused to follow this script, President watchers groped for other explanations. He was simply an old performer looking for a new stage, little concerned with hard-core policy, confident he could talk his way to success. Or he was a candidate of nostalgia, with no real vision of the future. Or perhaps there were really two Ronald Reagans—the dogmatist who stuck to his principles no matter how hard the going, and the politician who adjusted his views to the latest polling returns. How the two Reagans lived together was never made clear; perhaps the President himself did not know.

The media had a hard time understanding Reagan because they had never quite encountered his type before—an ideologue with charm. In the American stereotype, ideologues are wild-eyed extremists, abrasive, rigid, unyielding. Indeed, American politicians must not even be allowed to be ideological, at least in the press. Typically a newsmagazine or Sunday feature covering a politician of strong and explicit doctrine will admit that he is a dogmatist but—all is well!— he is also a practical man; he does carpentry down in the basement or coaches a local Little League team. He is—the highest encomium—a *pragmatist*.

But here was Ronald Reagan, who could say the most terrible things with a disarming quip or smile. Even after he had governed three years we had only begun to take the measure of the man. Yet the facts were so breathtakingly simple as to be perplexing in an age used to the complexities and nuances of politics.

In his middle years Ronald Reagan came to embrace a set of conservative beliefs. He proceeded to publicize these beliefs, to gain a following, to enter politics, to speak for other conservative candidates like Barry Goldwater. Then he proceeded to build a majority following within the Republican Party, to capture its presidential nomination, then to build a majority following within the American electorate, and to win the presidency. Then, most surprising of all, he proceeded to govern on the basis of his beliefs. What he did *not* do was also important. He did not in his inaugural address paraphrase Jefferson and say that "we are all Democrats—we are all Republicans"; he knew that would be nonsense. He did not appoint a batch of Democrats or liberals to his Administration or start "rising above party politics" or talk about a national consensus. He simply acted for the slim electoral majority that had voted for him on the basis of the promises that he and his party had made to them. People found this hard to understand.

People found this hard to understand because Reagan combined his firm strategy with a certain tactical flexibility as well as a flair for public relations. Thus he had to win thirty or forty Democratic votes in the House for his budget and his tax proposals, so he talked a little bipartisanship. He had to win support from congressmen facing pressure from special interests, so his envoys to the Hill indulged in a good deal of bartering, ego massaging, and favor dealing. But there is a vast difference between a leader who has a general strategy and tempers it here and there to shifting winds, and a leader who has no strategy. Reagan has a strategy, and his strategy emerges from his doctrine, his ideology.

This makes Reagan far more dependent on ideology than is the case with typical "pragmatic" politicians who can adapt their views to meet the demands of opportunism and expediency. And it makes it necessary for the student of his kind of leadership to understand the peculiar nature of the ideology that sustains and guides him, and which he in turn has revivified.

THE TWO REPUBLICAN PARTIES: CONSERVATIVE ROOTS

Ronald Reagan's early electoral and legislative feats were all the more impressive if you looked at them in the context of conservative thought in America. A major, though little publicized, question when the new President took office was whether our conservative tradition would provide his Administration with reasonably clear guidelines for day-to-day policy decisions. Some working politicians, proud of their practicality and "pragmatism," disputed the need for such a credo. Better to proceed "by guess and by God," they felt, adjusting to new problems and conditions as they arose, rather than following some blueprint. But Reagan conservatives came into office prepared to follow not a blueprint but a peculiarly American form of ideology, well defined by James Reichley as a "distinct and broadly coherent structure of values, beliefs, and attitudes with implications for social policy."

American politicians, despite their public skepticism about party platforms and their frequent departure from them in practice, have found platforms indispensable as part of their broad political and governmental strategy. As embodied in convention resolutions, platforms serve as rallying points for party leaders, activists, and supporters. As elaborated in campaign speeches, they serve as policy commitments to the voters. As enunciated by a President and his associates, they serve as guidelines for officials, means of setting priorities, devices for settling disputes. They reassure the public that the nation's leaders have a sense of purpose, a settled direction, a foundation for teamwork.

Judged by these standards, the Reaganites inherited a potent but curiously truncated conservative credo.

The living body of conservative thought forms a rich and creative part of the Western intellectual heritage. With its sensitivity to the communal and organic needs of society, its grasp of the role of authority and hierarchy, its recognition of the place of family and church and community in the great organism that we call a nation, its nourishing of stability and continuity amid the torrents of change, its awareness of human limitations—narrowness, selfishness, blindness, fallibility—as well as human potential, its hope above all of *preserving* authentic qualities of civility, reason, order, and decency among humankind, Western conservatism has served as a powerful antidote and balance to the liberal, radical, revolutionary, and reactionary forces that swept through the eighteenth and nineteenth centuries. For Anglo-Saxons, at least, the great exemplar of conservative thought and action was Edmund Burke, who doubted the wisdom and perfectibility of men and the need and possibilities of reform, while he defended the institutions and values that preserved the best qualities of rational and civilized humankind.

For a time this kind of conservatism seemed to be taking root in America and bearing fruit in the words and deeds of the remarkable cadre of leaders who fought a "conservative" revolution and then built a nation. The Framers of the Constitution inherited the liberal traditions of Locke and Hume and Montesquieu, but in their faith in the orderly processes of government, their fine balance between optimism and skepticism, their belief in orderly change, their fear of volatile and radical majorities, their recognition of the role of authority and even of elites, their capacity to combine traditionalism and inventiveness, their respect for property rights as bulwarks of liberty, the men of 1787 acted out of a powerful conservative tradition. Political leaders as diverse in outlook as Alexander Hamilton, John Adams, and Fisher Ames took on the visage of die-hard conservatism, or were assigned this role at the time by Jeffersonian critics and later by liberal historians. But the first party to be established under the Constitution—the Federalist—not only embodied central assumptions and values of conservatism, such as the belief in social order and restricted suffrage; it offered a creative and dynamic national policy, especially in the economic domain.

As the decades of the new century passed, however, irresistible economic and political forces leached away the foundations of the broader, more positive and variegated conservatism, leaving thin soil in their wake. Notions of stability, continuity, orderly and organic change disappeared in a welter of competitive economic development, heedless social alterations, and ceaseless innovation, usually at the hands of self-styled conservatives. Old conservative doctrines of authority, hierarchy, and religious duty or at least affiliation wilted in the heat of democratic, egalitarian, and secular energies. Family and community structures were imperiled by capitalists' needs for migrants, immigrants, child labor, labor mobility, while public authority was diminished or flouted by men who made the crucial economic decisions. Decentralization, local autonomy, and "states' rights" dwindled in the face of railroads that knit the nation together, creating new communities and bypassing others, strengthening national authority over interstate commerce, establishing great national markets and market cities that left many a small town withering on the vine.

What was left in place of a rich and spacious conservatism was the ideology of the marketplace, an ideology that for many years was as much a liberal as a conservative credo.

That ideology extolled the virtues of personal acquisitiveness, capital accumulation, private enterprise, economic competition, corporate property rights, individual freedom from governmental restraints. Like any other full-blown ideology, it pervaded politics, religion, education, the professions, and the arts almost as much as it dominated the economic world. Some of the financial leaders of the marketplace were also the intellectual leaders of marketplace doctrine. Andrew Carnegie was a notable example. A practitioner of the harshest economic competition, an accumulator of enormous riches, an apostle of the Horatio Alger, Jr., credo of rags to riches, he preached that capitalistic competition served broader goals of human progress, social welfare, and moral values through the practical philanthropy and moral conscience of those who had money.

At the heart of the ideology of the marketplace lay a theory of individualism—the theory that the individual, as a free economic entrepreneur, could act out of personal self-interest to work, accumulate, innovate, invest, build, accumulate more, and spend. Entrepreneurs hence carried the hopes of the broader society on their shoulders. The ideologists of the marketplace had one message for friend and foe: Individualism works—leave it alone. A nosy, interfering government was the main threat; it should be taught to keep hands off while the economic contestants ran their race. All runners had to be given their opportunity to get ahead, without favoritism for the rich or wellborn.

No one expressed this philosophy in the 1920s more cogently than a young mining engineer and government executive named Herbert Hoover, in a book called *American Individualism*. We must,

Hoover said, through free and universal education and other means, create the conditions for full equality of opportunity for all individuals, so that all could be at the starting line of personal advancement. America must "provide the training of the runners; we give to them an equal start; we provide in the government the umpire of fairness in the race. . . ."

Powerful ideas do not float somewhere in the clouds; they engage leaders (who in turn engage with them), mobilize some voters and repel others, find their way into party platforms, candidates' speeches, congressional oratory, presidential inaugural addresses. In the nineteenth century the linkage between political ideas and party credo was especially strong. Parties were a form of "instant ideology," an institutional expression pulling together ideas, interests, institutions, and individuals into a somewhat coherent pattern. Parties established the political boundaries and the articulate major assumptions within which politicians played out their games of coalition and conflict.

Throughout the nineteenth century the growth of marketplace conservatism, of economic individualism, both prompted and mirrored the ideas of party leaders. Consider the old Whigs of the 1830s and 1840s. Born in opposition to Jacksonian "autocracy," the Whigs had inherited some of the old Federalist notions of elitist rule, aristocracy and hierarchy, noblesse oblige. We tend to think of the Whigs in the age of Harrison "as stealing the egalitarian thunder of the Democrats," Louis Hartz wrote, "but actually they did more than that. They transformed it. For if they gave up Hamilton's hatred of the people, they retained his grandiose capitalistic dream, and this they combined with the Jeffersonian concept of equal opportunity. The result was to electrify the democratic individual with a passion for great achievement and to produce a personality type that was neither Hamiltonian nor Jeffersonian but a strange mixture of them both: the hero of Horatio Alger."

The Republican Party underwent a similar transformation following the Civil War. Born largely as a reform party bent on blocking the spread of slavery, but appealing also to businessmen concerned over tariffs, trade, and transportation, the party played a vital role in carrying through emancipation and partial reconstruction, but then moved sharply toward doctrines of marketplace conservatism and economic individualism. The party had so closely engaged with corporate interests by the end of the century that Republican chieftain Mark Hanna was able to raise a war chest of $16 million mainly from a militant "money power." If "Conscience" Whigs had finally yielded to "Cotton" Whigs before the Civil War, so later did "Radical" Republicans yield to "Railroad" Republicans.

So powerful was the credo of marketplace individualism that it penetrated all major political parties and virtually all major social movements. Thus many late-nineteenth-century liberals came to be as devoted to propertied capitalism as had Whig and Republican conservatives. The philosophical core of this liberalism was individualism; its intellectual method, rationalism; its economics, free enterprise and competition; its politics, moderation and constitutionalism; its theology, the idea of progress. Under brilliant editors like Edwin L. Godkin of *The Nation,* American liberalism had positive and reformist impulses, as in its support of intellectual freedom, free trade, and civil service reform, but its economics was hardly distinguishable from that of conservative Republicanism. The credo of individualism penetrated organized labor as well. After flirting with the radical collectivist ideas of Knights of Labor and Industrial Workers of the World ("Wobblies"), most American unionists by century's end seemed content with Samuel Gompers' craft elitism and business unionism—that is, with the idea of competing for a larger slice of the capitalistic pie.

So widely embracing had the creed of conservative, Horatio Alger individualism become by the early twentieth century that it tended to divide among itself, just as it divided many who embraced it. It tended to divide party factions too, as Cleveland and Bryan Democrats battled with each other over currency and other economic issues, and Republican Stalwarts and Mugwumps fought over moral issues like honest government and protection of the poor. As American business and industry expanded and consolidated, conservatives differed among themselves as to whether giant trusts represented a natural culmination of the doctrine of competitive individualism, or a contradiction of it. This struggle assumed dramatic form in Theodore Roosevelt's loud battle against the "trusts" and in Woodrow Wilson's effort to police trade and finance. Trustbusters were two-minded, Hofstadter noted, for they feared bigness but respected property. Should consolidation be accepted and regulated, or should competition be restored and regulated?

Politically this struggle expressed itself not merely between Democrats and Republicans but within the two parties. As liberal Democrats turned militantly under FDR against big business or corporate capitalism, the Republicans were left as the biggest and best defenders of the old individualism. But the fight over the nature and defense of true individualism continued in even sharper form within the party. As party lines re-formed after the partial bipartisanship and consensus of World War II, a congressional Republican Party and a presidential Republican Party stood uneasily side by side under the broad umbrella of the GOP. Each of these parties had its own distinctive leadership, credo, institutional support, electoral roots, and set of constituencies.

The congressional Republicans, under the leadership of Senator Robert Taft and later of Senator Barry Goldwater, was preeminently the party of small businessmen and northern farmers, especially Midwestern farmers. Goldwater spoke for most members of the party when in the early 1960s he called for spending cuts in the federal government, a balanced budget, taxation of all incomes at the same rate, turning welfare programs over to the states, going easy on civil rights laws, ending aid to education and housing subsidy programs and the farm subsidy program and the like. He had a tough foreign policy: Encourage captive peoples to revolt against their Communist rulers; in the event of a major revolt, such as Hungary, send Russia an ultimatum forbidding intervention; if Moscow rejected it, move American forces into the area. At the same time drastically cut foreign economic aid, limiting assistance to military and technical help.

The institutional roots of the congressional Republicans lay in their minority leadership in the major fiscal committees of House and Senate, and in the seniority rule for choosing chairmen—a rule that favored those who had served continuously in their chamber for many years. Their electoral roots lay in the rural, one-party districts that tended to provide such longevity. The party drew ideological inspiration from—and in turn provided "constituents" for—columnists like David Lawrence and Westbrook Pegler, radio commentators like Fulton Lewis, Jr., magazines like the *Reader's Digest,* newspapers like the Indianapolis *Star* and the Chicago *Tribune.*

The presidential Republicans represented a quite different political thrust. For leaders they could claim some of the most illustrious political names of the twentieth century: TR, Charles Evans Hughes, Elihu Root, Henry Stimson, Wendell Willkie, Thomas E. Dewey, Dwight Eisenhower, Earl Warren, Nelson Rockefeller. Their institutional roots lay in the presidency, in the electoral-college system that tended to favor liberal Republicans from populous states for President, in the nation's Republican governorships; their electoral foundations lay in the large urban states that held a balance of power in national elections, and in the corporate and middle-class constituencies in eastern and western cities and suburbs.

The two Republican parties at times fought each other, as in the battles between Taft and Eisenhower and between Goldwater and Rockefeller for the presidential nomination; and at times cooperated with each other, as in trying to elect the man who *was* nominated; and most of the time bargained and dickered with each other, as in passing or blocking bills in Congress. Both parties believed in economic individualism and private enterprise, but they would reach these goals in somewhat different fashion—"presidentials" through executive initiatives and authority, better management of big government (as reflected in the outlook and goals of the first Hoover Commission), variously promoting, subsidizing, and regulating big business, extending their influence abroad ideologically and economically; the "congressionals" through protecting the "little man" in business, reducing governmental regulation of business, curbing executive power in government and enhancing legislative power, raising tariffs. In foreign policy the presidential party was oriented more toward Europe, toward financial aid, toward presidential authority, the congressional party more toward Asia, toward military intervention, toward legislative delay and veto.

All this made for a shaky foundation for leadership and policy when the Republicans controlled the federal government. Such indeed proved to be the case with the Nixon and Ford presidencies. Appealing to the major Republican Party factions—especially to both the Goldwater and Rockefeller groups—had been Nixon's winning grand strategy for gaining presidential nominations in 1960 and 1968; he seemed to feel as President that he could make policy in this fashion too. But instead of following some kind of firm Nixon line between the various factions, he flip-flopped on economic, welfare, and foreign policy. Not only did he denounce Lyndon Johnson's Great Society and then continue most of LBJ's programs; he deserted his own preachments. After years of condemning governmental intervention in the marketplace, he decided to go for price and wage controls; after years of denouncing big federal spending, he turned to deficit financing, even confiding to ABC correspondent Howard K. Smith, "I am now a Keynesian in economics."

This turn produced budget deficits of $45 billion in fiscal year 1975 and $66 billion in fiscal 1976. "The administration that was against expanding the budget expanded it greatly," Nixon economic

adviser Herbert Stein commented; "the administration that was determined to fight inflation ended up by having a large amount of
inflation."

Nixon also shifted on welfare policy, as he moved toward a fam-
ily-assistance program that called for the kind of close federal super-
vision that he had long attacked. At the same time he favored federal
revenue sharing with the states—a move toward delegating policy and
administration to states and localities. One of the more humorous moments in the Nixon White House occurred when the President's speech
writers—especially William Safire—were asked to produce an articu-
lation of Nixon's "political philosophy, of his vision of America," as
H. R. Haldeman instructed. Safire valiantly went to work, cooking up
a "New Federalist Paper No. 1," signed "Publius," that proclaimed the
need "for *both* national unity and local diversity," a need to protect
both "individual uniqueness" and attain national goals, etc., etc. Conservatives' efforts to write more New Federalist papers broke off in
disagreement. Safire later let the cat out of the bag when he admitted,
"Strange, fitting a philosophy to the set of deeds, but sometimes that is
what must be done."

By far the most dramatic shifts in Nixon policy lay in foreign relations. The man who had symbolized militant Republican anti-Communism, even to the point of calling for American atomic intervention
in Vietnam during the French debacle in Dien Bien Phu, the man who
had practically built a political career on anti-Sovietism, the man who
had flatly opposed recognition of "red China"—this same man conducted a long effort at détente with Moscow, concluding with a series
of accords; took a conciliatory posture toward Mao's China after a
diplomatic pilgrimage there; and even contended that his policies were
no longer mainly intended to contain the two big Communist nations,
thus admitting a turnabout in his foreign policy as sharp as his embracing of Keynesianism in his domestic.

If Gerald Ford had been granted more years in the White House,
perhaps he would have shown more doctrinal consistency than Nixon
demonstrated in his term and a half—or perhaps less. As it was, Ford
was running for a full presidential term before he had much chance
to develop his own program. The former congressman and Vice-
President did exhibit his own brand of inconsistency, or flexibility,
however, in shifting away from the neo-isolationism and economic conservatism that had made him a luminary of the congressional Republicans, to the traditional posture of presidential Republican leaders. The
relative ease with which both Nixon and Ford moved out of their

congressional parties to leadership of presidential Republicans was a tribute both to their doctrinal suppleness and to the absence in American conservatism and Republicanism of any core idea aside from competitive individualism and marketplace capitalism.

THREE RIGHT WINGS: REAGAN'S DILEMMA

Ronald Reagan was an FDR Democrat in the 1930s and 1940s, a Truman Democrat and ADA liberal in the late 1940s, an Eisenhower Democrat in 1952, a Nixon Democrat in 1960, and a registered Republican not until 1962. After galloping across the political spectrum, he plunged into the ranks of conservative Republicanism at the time that the congressional and presidential Republican parties were locked in deadly combat over the nature and strategy of the GOP. From the rich and diverse heritage of American conservatism, from the wide alternatives within the Republican Party, he made clear choices. He chose to be a right-wing Republican, embracing the old creed of marketplace individualism.

Why he made this choice is not wholly clear. Certainly it was not expediency, because neither the old individualism as a creed, nor the conservative Republicans as a party, was prospering politically at the time he enlisted. Some day psychobiographers may find the roots of Reagan's conservatism in the conditions of his early life—a poor, constantly moving family, genteel poverty, an ineffective, alcoholic father, a devoutly Protestant mother, a feeling of boyish vulnerability owing to his frail physique and his nearsightedness, but the connections will not easily be made. A Democrat and something of a liberal in the 1930s, Reagan seems to have taken on his political coloration during his early mid-life years, a period in people's lives that has been winning more attention from students of personality. Some contend that Reagan moved rightward during the many years he served as leader of the Screen Actors Guild and had to deal with "Communists and radicals" in the film industry. But in fact he was actively anti-Communist in this respect since immediately after the war. Then for a decade he moved steadily farther to the right on domestic and foreign policy.

That he made a full ideological commitment to economic individualism during this period cannot be doubted. The test came in the mid-1950s, when he left his flagging movie career to become the host of a drama series sponsored by General Electric. The job also called for Reagan to tour GE plants talking up the company's products and helping the company with its labor and community relations efforts. Soon he was talking more and more politics, less and less products. "My speeches underwent a kind of evolution," Reagan recalled, "reflecting not only my changing philosophy, but also the swiftly rising tide of collectivism that threatens to inundate what remains of our free economy." For some years General Electric tolerated—doubtless even welcomed—Reagan's politicizing of his role, but it feared pressure from its unions and customers too, and the show was canceled after Reagan declined to stick to products. That Reagan was willing to give up an annual salary of about $150,000 was testament to his commitment to conservatism, and an answer to those who called him just a performer who would dance to whatever tune the piper called.

A commitment to conservatism—but of what kind? Dealing with GE executives and selling GE products had brought Reagan into a network of capitalistic thought and action bound to strengthen his credo of economic individualism. When he moved into Republican politics after he left GE, however, he entered a world of competing doctrines and factions—the world of Nelson Rockefeller and liberal Republicans as well as that of Goldwater and the right wing. How narrowly he defined his conservatism became evident in the "speech of his life" for Goldwater in the 1964 campaign. Reagan had such a reputation as a rightist by then that even Goldwater had to go over Reagan's draft, by phone, finally barking out, "What the hell is wrong with that? Go ahead."

For a speech that brought in a flood of congratulatory messages and half a million dollars in contributions, a speech alleged to have made Reagan's political reputation, his "A Time for Choosing" campaign oration reads disappointingly today. It was a talk that had been given a thousand times not only by Reagan but by Herbert Hoover, Alf Landon, Wendell Willkie, Robert A. Taft, and Barry Goldwater— a long denunciation of big government, creeping socialism, the threat to private property, government planning, federal spending, the "schemes of the do-gooders," planned inflation, and the kind of moral, economic, and military weakness that would provoke Communist aggression, war, and defeat. Why was the talk so well received? Evidently because Reagan delivered it with uncommon style, smoothness, and good humor.

Both Reagan and Goldwater said things that would outrage people, but the ebullient Californian could get away with things that the caustic Arizonan could not. He demonstrated the kind of ironic, self-deprecating wit that John Kennedy had used so deftly. And his professionalism stood him in good stead: how to move, talk, shrug, smile, stand. "Very few of us," he wrote in *Where's the Rest of Me?*, "ever see ourselves except as we look directly at ourselves in a mirror. Thus we don't know how we look from behind, from the sides, talking, standing, moving normally through a room." Reagan knew these things. A photographer who took thousands of pictures of Reagan could not find one showing him with a frown, or in an awkward posture.

Reagan's likability, his persona, his way of presenting himself were also deceptive, however, because many in the media concluded that he was a political lightweight, a performer, a crowd pleaser, just as men as insightful as Walter Lippmann had taken a long time to perceive the steel behind Franklin Roosevelt's genial façade. Through the 1960s and 1970s Reagan demonstrated a consistency of credo and a persistency of combat quite unusual in American politics. Beaten out by Ford for the 1976 presidential nomination, he rallied his forces the next day by quoting from an old Scottish ballad: "I'm hurt but I'm not slain, I'll lie me down and rest a bit and then I'll fight again." Like the Horatio Alger hero, with a lot of pluck and a little luck he would overcome adversity and rise to the top.

But he did not jettison his doctrine in doing so. "Perhaps no politician on the national scene has enunciated his philosophy so often, over so many years, with such consistency," wrote Robert Lindsey in *The New York Times*. "I see less change in him than in any political figure I have ever known," said one of his strategists. "He has a set of values, and everything stems from those values." He was one of the few American politicians openly to deride pragmatism and "pragmatists." The true leader, he felt, was the opposite of the typical American trimmer and opportunist.

Reagan's 1980 campaign strategy was based on the belief that Americans saw in him great leadership qualities and viewed Carter as an "ineffective and error-prone leader." A television advertisement had Reagan looking straight into the camera and saying, "We have the talent, we have the drive, we have the imagination. Now all we need is the leadership." A poll of voters leaving the polls indicated that Reagan was seen above all as a "strong leader." Though he had never held presidential office, he had established this image of himself through years of taking consistent stands on issues.

Developments in the Republican Party, moreover, made it increasingly rewarding for Reagan to take a consistently conservative position. By the late 1970s the GOP had made up its mind to do the same. Partly because of the death of leaders like Nelson Rockefeller and the defeat of others, partly because of the growth of Reagan-type conservatism within the party, the old right-wing elements were clearly coming to dominate the GOP by the end of the decade. The old presidential party faded away, as some moderate and liberal Republicans switched to the Democratic Party, while a few conservative southern Democrats moved over to the Goldwater-Reagan phalanx.

At the same time—and partly because the Republicans had found themselves ideologically—the GOP had become immensely stronger as an organization. Fundamental efforts at party renewal, begun after the 1964 Goldwater debacle by national chairman Ray Bliss of Ohio, extended under successors like George Bush, and immensely expanded under the leadership of William Brock, began to pay off in a series of state and local victories. While the Democrats were fighting among themselves over procedural reform, the Republicans were working on *organizational* improvements calling for regional political directors, an organizational director program spurring state parties to improve local parties, modern political technology such as data-processing and computer services, greater national financial contributions to local—especially state legislative—contests, and a general unifying of the whole party structure.

A powerful new party credo allied to a revitalized party organization—no wonder the Republicans were winning major elections by the end of the 1970s.

Early in December 1980, about a month after Reagan's stunning election victory, the *National Review* staged an elegant twenty-fifth birthday celebration with a black-tie dinner at the Plaza Hotel in New York. Editor William F. Buckley, Jr., founder of the journal, presided with his usual aplomb. Appropriately for an enterprise that had spawned and nourished a multitude of conservative causes with the solicitude of a mother hen, conservative ideologists of a variety of hues were gathered at their separate tables, eyeing one another a bit warily. Conspicuously present were notables from the intellectual New Right—Norman Podhoretz, editor of *Commentary;* Irving Kristol, editor of *Public Interest;* and others.

Conspicuously absent was the promised guest of honor, Ronald Reagan, promised both by Buckley and by Reagan. Although the event had been publicized in advance, the White House had telephoned Buckley to explain that the President's "schedulers" had, alas, tied him up that night. Buckley made only a tart comment or two about the President-elect, and the incident passed with far less mention in the media than would have been the case if, say, a liberal President had promised to keynote a conference of Americans for Democratic Action and failed to show.

It was at least of symbolic interest, however, that Ronald Reagan did not appear. It was not because he disagreed with the views of the *National Review* or of the conservative leaders present. After all, he had been the main speaker at the journal's twentieth birthday celebration. It was in part, I suspect, because he so agreed with the old conservatives and new conservatives present that he had little to say to them, or they to him. And therein lay the poignance of this gay evening—the neo-conservatives, rather than serving as a source of creative criticism and innovation to Reagan, had become just another voting constituency, to be wooed in 1975, when Reagan was seeking support, and waved away after victory was won.

The tip-off to this state of affairs came that same evening when columnist George Will, the substitute speaker, proclaimed that "it took approximately sixteen years to count the vote in the '64 election, and Goldwater won." With the election, he said, "American conservatism came of age." For a leading neo-conservative to reach back to the Goldwater campaign and platform, filled with stale ideas and hoary clichés even in 1964, and proclaim it as the truth for the 1980s, was a measure either of the intellectual sterility of the neo-conservative mind, or of Will's willingness to adapt himself to the polemical demands of the occasion.

For two decades and more, neo-conservatives had conducted a brilliant attack on liberal and radical assumptions, shibboleths, and practices. They had derided "liberal guilt," radical chic, the tendency of the left to devour its leaders, leftist sentimentalism and utopianism in foreign affairs, overdependence on the rational potential in humankind, the willingness of liberals to overload government while failing to recognize the importance of authority and efficiency. In particular they had castigated liberal "isolationism" and "pacifism" in the face of Communist aggression abroad and subversion at home.

But when it came to the question of what the neo-conservatives proposed in place of these "failed doctrines," one could discern little beyond the old call for a marketplace free of government regulation, an economic individualism free of external restraints. Neo-conservatives—or the Market Right, as I shall call them—proposed lower taxes, less government spending (save for defense), smaller government, balanced budgets, respect for private property, fewer bureaucratic controls. The great rallying cry of Jack Kemp et al. was still "Get government off our backs." This was a natural reaction to the expansion of federal and state government, increased taxes, and bureaucracy, but it was also narrow, self-interested dogma, routine to the point of boredom.

One wondered what had happened to the intellectual promise of an earlier generation of conservatives—to the vigorous effort to transform conservatism from a shallow creed of petty negativism and self-interest to a transcending and positive philosophy embracing the public and community interest, social and national responsibility, of the sense of social duty combined with individual excellence that one identified in men so diverse as Theodore Roosevelt, Oliver Wendell Holmes, Henry Stimson, and Wendell Willkie. What had happened to Edmund Burke's respect for reverence and humility, Russell Kirk's concern with prescription, authority, and ordered freedom, Stephen J. Tonsor's search for identity, Stanley Parry's call for the restoration of worthy tradition, Walter Lippmann's evocation of a public philosophy? Market Rightists dealt with many of these topics, of course, since they were as prolific as their liberal counterparts, but they did not follow through on their implications, perhaps because many of these conservative ideas contained an implicit attack on cherished notions about the marketplace, commercialism, private profit.

"Will we," Russell Kirk had asked twenty years earlier, "like George Bowling in Orwell's *Coming up for Air,* revisit the scenes of our youth only to find the country which 'progress' has touched an abomination of shoddy new bungalows, juke joints, concrete, billboards, and jaded faces? Too many of us already have experienced that abysmally dreary survey. Some generations of indiscriminate getting and spending are certain to develop a remarkable type of man. The automobile will be his deity, and to it he will sacrifice sometimes nearly half his annual income, his domestic comfort, his family life, and his church. The television set will be his preacher, and inanity will compete with inanity for his attention, applying Gresham's Law to amusement. . . ." Throughout his manifesto, *A Program for Conservatives,* Kirk denounced competitive individualism as severely as he did the centralized state.

Market Rightists advance their doctrine of individualism with as much zest as their warnings of the doctrine of egalitarianism. They argue for equality of opportunity as against equality of condition. This is the most serious example of their unwillingness to follow through on their own premises. With Herbert Hoover they would grant that all must have an equal place at the starting line, and then prosper or fail depending on individual effort, merit, luck, and pluck. But where should the starting line start? After a certain amount of schooling, most neo-conservatives would answer. But this response begs the central issue. If we *really* mean equality of opportunity, we would try to grant life chances to persons at a point before circumstances—poverty, poor nourishment, ill health, neglectful parents, shrunken or distorted motivation, community hatreds, ravages of war, lack of education, damaged self-esteem—begin to close off myriad opportunities and crush the potentials for individual development and self-fulfillment. Neo-conservatives are cool to such analysis because it would imply the need not only for family and community and educational intervention in the life of a child but also governmental as well, for only government would have the capacity to compensate for most of the massive closures and deprivations in the structure of poverty.

Because neo-conservatives have shrunk from the radical implications of some of their own premises, they have hardly done more than rationalize and prettify and intellectualize the biases that a man like Reagan already holds. Hence the Market Right can be of lesser use to him. A hundred years ago the capitalists of the nation gathered at Delmonico's to honor Herbert Spencer, articulator of the doctrine of social Darwinism that underlies the central thinking of Ronald Reagan today. In this age, Market Right intellectuals gather at the Plaza to honor the top politician, even though he may not come.

It is this ultimate subserviency to power that marks the near-bankruptcy of neo-conservatism. But the loss is ultimately Reagan's, for the men of power ultimately need the men of thought far more than the intellectuals need the politicians. Thus a man like Reagan needs a conservative like Kirk or Clinton Rossiter to remind him that a tax bill radically favoring the rich has serious moral and human as well as economic and political implications. But a President will hardly receive such advice from intellectuals obsessed with marketplace concerns over taxes, budgets, and profits.

Two months after taking office President Reagan addressed a conservative audience even more divided than those at the *National Review* dinner. This was the Conservative Political Action Conference, comprising the nation's key right-wing organizations. The main division lay between Market Rightists essentially satisfied by the President's 1981 economic program—cutting federal spending and regulation, balancing the budget, lowering taxes (especially on the rich)—and those who wanted all this but wanted even more for Reagan to get on to his "social agenda." Addressing the crowd as "fellow truth seekers," the President treated them as one big family. "Our victory," he said, was less a "victory of politics" than "a victory of ideas. . . . We do not have a separate social agenda, a separate economic agenda and a separate foreign agenda. We have one agenda. Just as surely as we seek to put our financial house in order and rebuild our nation's defense, so too we seek to protect the unborn, to end the manipulation of school children by utopian planners and permit the acknowledgment of a Supreme Being in our classrooms."

These words fell pleasurably on the ears even of listeners unhappy about Reagan's postponement of the "social" or "moral" budget. These listeners represented groups coalesced in what had become known as the "New Right," or the "Moral Majority." The first title was confusing, for the neo-conservatives constituted a New Right, and the second was misleading, because the Moral Majority, in its preaching and sermonizing and evangelizing, was moralistic rather than moral, and it did not yet, at least, constitute a majority. A better term, which I will use, is the Moralistic Right, covering a wide range of groups united by four basic "moral" principles, described by a conservative leader as *"pro-life,* which holds that human life is sacred from conception; *pro-traditional family,* which revolves around husband and wife; *pro-moral,* which centers on the spread of pornography, mind and spirit pollution and the drug epidemic; and *pro-America,* focusing on support for a strong national defense."

Pleased by Reagan's reassuring words, the Moralistic Right was still rather skeptical toward the Administration as a result of Reagan's selection of George Bush as his running mate, some of the President's moderate appointments, and his total immediate emphasis on economic policy. Still, leaders as conservative as Representative Mickey Edwards of the American Conservative Union, Cal Thomas of Moral Majority, and John T. Dolan of the National Conservative Political Action Committee (NCPAC) expressed fealty to the President. But the Moralistic Right leaders had less good will toward leaders of the Old Right, which seemed remote and anachronistic as a cause, and they showed even less benevolence for neo-conservative spokesmen, many of whom they considered elitist, Ivy Leagueish, eastern-oriented "pointy-heads." For their part, these two groups were even more con-temptuous of the Moralistic Right. Old conservatives saw its credo as a caricature of the ancient virtues of family, community, organized society, harmony, and stability. Neo-conservatives feared above all the Moralistic Right's desire not to "get government off our backs" but to intrude government into family, school, and private life by passing restrictive laws on divorce, homosexuality, abortion, crime, secular education, drugs, and "living together," as Senator Jesse Helms had put it. The differences over intervention in citizens' lives between traditionalists, as William Safire called them, and "libertarians" were to Safire a matter not just of degree but of kind.

How could Ronald Reagan hold these disparate groups together, along with regular Republicans and old-fashioned Russell Kirk con-servatives? Perhaps by following the same strategy that helped him to win office and to govern during his first year in the White House— keeping together his core majority of Old Right, Market Right, con-servative Democrats, and moderates, and making only the necessary tactical concessions to the Moralistic Right necessary to win votes in Congress and in elections. He could always rally them with a "godless communism" speech. Such concessions for a time would be relatively easy for Reagan to make, since to some degree he shared the Moral-istic Right's views on social issues.

Eventually, however, he would probably see cracks opening up in his coalition because of the nonnegotiability of many social issues of the Moralistic Right as compared with the brokerage possibilities of dealing with the Market Right over economic policy, which usu-ally *is* a matter of degree rather than kind.

If his coalition did begin to disintegrate, Ronald Reagan had quickly available a supremely dangerous recourse—reuniting his fol-lowers over a provocative policy toward Moscow. The Old Right, the New, and the moralists shared an abiding hostility toward Bolshevism, and while they might disagree over specific foreign policies and tactics, such as the Panama treaty or lifting the grain embargo, they would doubtless fly the flag together if the President faced a showdown with the Russians. Barring such an extreme situation, one may predict that the most likely fissure in the Reagan coalition would rise over the role of government on social issues in general and its invasion of privacy in particular. In that "Good Right Fight" over order versus privacy, Safire said, "count one wiretap-remembering pundit among the lib-ertarian hawks."

FOREIGN POLICY—STRATEGY OR STANCE?

Rhetorically, at least, Ronald Reagan entered the White House as the most bellicose President since Theodore Roosevelt. While TR had tended to strike out in all directions, however, Reagan had eyed his Communist foes with the steely concentration of a frontiersman targeting a band of Indians. His anti-Soviet rhetoric had long been unbridled. "We are faced with the most evil enemy mankind has known in his long climb from the swamp to the stars," he wrote in a 1968 volume. The North Vietnamese, seen as controlled by Moscow, were "hard-core, hard-nosed, vicious Communists who had a goal and who still have that goal and who are going to fudge, cheat and steal every chance they get," he said in a 1973 press conference. "When it suits the Communists to have a confrontation with the United States, . . . they will have it, whether we do any provoking or not. It won't depend on anything we may choose to do," he said in a 1972 press conference.

A showdown seemed inevitable, according to Reagan's rhetoric. In the event of a compromise in the Middle East, Reagan warned in 1972, "I think West Berlin would disappear in a minute and a half. You could choose the spots around the earth that would disappear. And then you've got to go back to Lenin's strategic plan in which he said: 'We will take Eastern Europe, we will organize the hordes of Asia, then we will move on Latin America.' And, he said, 'Eventually the United States, the last bastion of capitalism, will be surrounded. We won't have to take it; it will fall into our outstretched hand like overripe fruit.' " Americans should be equally tough, Reagan advised. Korea, our first "no-win" war, would have been won if MacArthur's advice had been followed. Once in Vietnam, we should have stayed in, gone all out, and won. Over and over he repeated his theme: accommodation was appeasement.

When this fire breather entered the White House, with the nuclear trigger at his elbow, veteran observers professed not to be worried. Reagan, they said, would be tamed by the burden of power. It was one thing to rant outside the White House, trying to get in. It was something else to handle the awful day-to-day responsibilities of foreign and war policy; no rhetorician, however drunk on his own words, could fail to be sobered up by cold blasts of reality. Wait until he had to consult with a vast range of foreign envoys, with heads of state in summit conferences; wait until he had to confront cables bristling with the endless complexities and nuances of real-life international relations; wait until his own advisers, many of them professionals and holdovers from previous Administrations, monitored his speeches and toned down his rhetoric. After all, hadn't Teddy Roosevelt in the White House become a conciliator, mediating the Russo-Japanese War and even winning the Nobel Peace Prize?

Sure enough, Reagan for a time did tone down his rhetoric some-what after entering the White House. He preached peace sermons, called the nuclear threat "a terrible beast," told the British Parliament that nuclear weapons threatened "if not the extinction of mankind, then surely the end of civilization as we know it," described negotia-tions on intermediate-range nuclear forces in Europe and the START talks as "critical to mankind." Within a year or so of the inaugural, journalists were talking about a new, consensual Ronald Reagan. Hedrick Smith found a "substantial shift from the sharply ideological, anti-détente rhetoric of the 1980 Reagan campaign to a more mod-erate, mainstream foreign policy."

But after three years in office one crucial attitude had not changed—Reagan's cold and implacable antagonism to Soviet Com-munism. The President might have softened his language, a close aide said, but not his attitude. "He hasn't changed one bit in how he thinks about the Russians." In March 1983 Reagan warned Christian evan-gelists in Florida that America's struggle with the Soviet Union was a struggle between right and wrong, good and evil. Labeling Soviet Russia an "evil empire," he called totalitarian states "the focus of evil in the modern world." "Adopting a perspective very similar to John Foster Dulles in the fifties," Betty Glad wrote, "Reagan has not changed—as technology and political development in the world made the assumption of a kind of a Pax Americana an even less appropriate guide to policy in the late 1970s and early 1980s than it had been in the 1950s."

How is it possible that this charming, sophisticated, personally benign septuagenarian could denounce the creed of a large portion of humankind as diabolical, much like the Ayatollah Khomeini castigat-ing his enemies as "the great Satan." Perhaps because he is right, per-haps because the Russians really are the primary if not the exclusive source of evil in this world. Certainly this is explanation enough for true believers. But even for the far right the implications were hor-rendous: If any kind of Communism is Satanic, nothing—not even the most barbaric African or Latin-American despot, or even Nazism itself—is worse than Communism, and hence that barbarism or despotism must be preferred when the chips are down.

Others, finding grays and shadows within the Communist societies, even aside from the indigenous Communisms of Yugoslavia, China, and North Vietnam, have looked for less primitive explanations of Reagan's rigidity. One of these is "social-cultural." Ronald Reagan, we are reminded, grew up in a rural Illinois town in which the old values of independence, initiative, private property, hard work, thrift, individual liberty—in short, the credo of individualism—were imprinted in the minds and souls of the young. Reagan's simple anti-Communism is a direct product of that small-town culture. Reagan's own career, however, challenges this theory. During the 1930s and 1940s—and thus during Reagan's own twenties and thirties—the movie star embraced Franklin D. Roosevelt, the New Deal, organized labor, Americans for Democratic Action, Hubert Humphrey, Helen Gahagan Douglas, all of whom had little connection with the small-town conservatism of rural Illinois. Reagan's father, Jack, indeed, was the head of the WPA in that little town of Dixon.

Another explanation of Reagan's obsessive anti-Communism is psychological. His unhappy, insecure childhood, his embarrassment over his alcoholic father who in turn mistreated him, produced a displacement of Reagan's anger, hostility, and loss of self-esteem onto a treacherous outside world in general, it is said, and especially onto the Communists who challenged the small-town virtues. "The quality of Reagan's reaction to communism in Hollywood, the protesters at Berkeley, or the Russians and the Cubans and the Koreans," according to Glad, "suggests that a kind of displacement is going on. His purple prose suggests that he is discharging an anger that carries emotional weight from the past."

Surely cultural and psychological forces helped sustain Reagan's antagonism, but the main explanation may lie in the sustaining power of ideas. Throughout his life Reagan embraced a narrow but powerful doctrine of liberty in his devotion to individualism. Brushing aside the rich, humane, and variegated elements of individualism, he seized on those most protective of private property, profit, and business enterprise. For years Reagan felt that this kind of individualism was safe in the hands of FDR and the New Deal, and in Roosevelt's day-to-day policies, but as the onetime movie star worked for General Electric, powerful reinforcing influences came into play. He married an outspoken young woman from a conservative family. His GE asso-

ciates and bosses—especially Lemuel Boulware, the apostle of tough-
ness toward unions—hardened his own attitudes. And his reading—
mainly *Reader's Digest* and conservative journals like *Human Events,*
perused on the run—further reinforced Reagan's growing conservatism.

In his California governorship and in the White House, Reagan
fortified himself—and his ideas—by surrounding himself with men of
similar libertarian ideas. He might still pay tribute to Franklin Roosevelt, but he had no use for FDR's penchant for exposing himself to
a variety of political and social views. In choosing men like David
Stockman in budget and finance, Alexander Haig and later George
Shultz at State, James G. Watt in Interior, and scores like them in his
administrative posts, Reagan not only set the course and "stayed the
course" but guaranteed that the needle would be fixed far to the right
on his political compass. He long had adjusted his specific ideas to the
overriding one of hatred of Bolshevism. "Anti-communism had not
driven him into the right wing," Ronnie Dugger noted of Reagan's
early "liberal" stage; "he had simply made anti-communism part of
his liberalism."

To describe Reagan's ideas as narrow and rigid, however, is not
to argue that they were superficial and ahistorical. On the contrary,
they represented a concept far older than the nation itself, rooted in
the intellectual heritage of the American people, pervasive of the political climate. Unhappily, his individualism and Algerism immensely
exaggerated the narrowly self-serving components of liberty, and utterly ignored the doctrines of equality and justice, of fellowship and
sharing, that made up a rich part of the American intellectual heritage.

Reagan, in short, pitted against the powerful appeals of Communism a free-enterprise individualism, a truncated libertarianism,
and cold-war fundamentalism. This kind of response, wrote Stanley
Hoffmann, tried "to find remedies in old verities: not in the spirit that
led to past successes, but in the mythified recipes that worked before,
in the rituals of national celebration, in the rationalizations that attribute troubles or temporary decline to internal dissolvent forces or
evil men and ascribe recovery to a rediscovery of traditional ways."
The result was not a strategy, nor even a policy, but a stance, an attitude, a knee-jerk reaction of the sort that conservatives used to attribute to liberals.

Could a stance beat a strategy? Soviet behavior might be mystify-
ing and Soviet intentions might be opaque, but the rough dimensions
of Moscow's strategy had emerged from sixty-five years of history.

The Soviets had (1) persistently opposed any intervention in a country on its borders by a hostile power; (2) consistently, in later decades, subordinated its drive for "Communizing the world" to the requirements of national security, sometimes to the point of simply abandoning a foreign Communist party or leadership; (3) moved opportunistically to seize advantages on the chessboard of international relations, advancing here and sidestepping there, fishing in troubled waters where it seemed worth the gamble, but usually willing to pull out, as from Egypt, or to pull weapons out, as in Cuba.

Reagan had no counterstrategy worthy of the name. He had a stance—an unbridled rhetoric, a propaganda campaign, a moral posture. But he did have something else—he had a *party*. Just as the President had obliterated the old presidential Republican Party of Willkie and Dewey in domestic policy, so he had submerged the "internationalist" Republican Party of Eisenhower, Rockefeller & Company. He had made the Grand Old Party into the Big Stick Party of the 1980s. Could the Democrats respond with a peace party? The party was still trying to make up its mind as the 1984 election neared.

REAGANISM WITHOUT REAGAN

As Ronald Reagan headed into the fourth year of his presidency, he was still king of his particular rock. He continued to command the right-center of American politics. Democrats might still laugh at his historical malapropisms, his vagueness about policy details, his cowboy image. They had to acknowledge his strategic control of the right half of the political continuum. Warned in advance that as President he would face a fragmented governmental system and a declining party system, but that "you *can* govern" through strong leadership, Reagan had combined tactical skill and media appeal with ideological commitment and, over all, policy consistency. "The simple truth is," he said as he neared the midpoint of his term, "I haven't changed one bit in what I intend to do, what I want to do, and I think some of them"—his critics—"are beginning to realize that."

The President happened to address these words not to Democrats but to members of the Moralistic Right who were complaining about his compromises and concessions. Could the President maintain his coalition of old and new conservatives, of Market and Moralistic Rightists? Longtime party prophet Kevin Phillips warned that Reagan's economic policy alone might split his following, but the Reaganites showed enough tactical flexibility to keep the diverse economic conservatives within the presidential tent. As for the Moralistic Rightists, Reagan fended them off with the one thing they wanted as second best to policy—uplifting sermons of the kind Reagan had become so expert at.

Moreover, he consoled his right-wing critics, he would always come back and ask for more. "It is one thing to stand for something— and I do, and I know they do, also—but it's another thing to have to make a choice if you can't get all you want at once, when you are faced with hostility in at least one house of the legislature. Do you jump off the cliff with the flag flying and never get any of it, or do you say, 'O.K., I'll work as hard and get as much of a chunk as I can, and come back later and go for the rest of it'?"

But would Reagan be around to go back for the rest of it? Even if he won re-election, he would have only a year or so to carry through his program. Automatically a lame duck, he would see many of his followers depart for other political camps, and old forces of fragmentation would close in on him. Unless he was able to weld his three right-wing followings into a coherent and continuing support for *governing,* he would find them drifting away as Carter's followers had done, and he could no more deliver them to Bush or some other Reaganite than Carter had been able to turn over his personal supporters to Walter Mondale, if he had wished to.

The crucial test for a continuing Reaganism was whether the President could complete the conversion of the Republican Party into a solid right-wing vehicle able to coalesce and represent the diverse conservative groups, and here he was making considerable progress. This would be the supreme test of Reagan as political strategist, as a man who could rise above transactional politics, indeed as a transforming leader. The tests would be practical ones—whether he shared his popularity with other Republican candidates, whether he shared White House political money with the Republican Party, whether he made the further strengthening of the party organization a top priority for his Administration.

If Reagan did all this, he would have "dished the Democrats" with a strategy reminiscent of some of the great British party turnabouts in the past. By one of the ironies of history, Reagan was following a party strategy that had been often recommended to the Democrats and as often spurned—a strategy of program making, of program commitment, of collective party leadership, of moving away from the center to a posture that would represent the interests of *po-*

tential as well as present Democratic activists and followers. By an even sharper irony, he was mobilizing Republicans behind one of the most narrow, negative, and backward doctrines—market conservatism—any major party had embraced in modern American history, and behind a most dangerous foreign-policy doctrine of indiscriminate, belligerent, hard-nosed anti-Communism.

As campaign year 1984 dawned, President watchers were still seeking to take the full measure of Ronald Reagan and his Administration. They continued to be surprised by the intensity of his anti-Communist attitudes and by his adventurous and aggressive policies in Latin America, Europe, and the Middle East. It was difficult for some to realize that his actions were governed by a set, implacable hostility toward Soviet Communism, that he would stick to his anti-Communist posture through thick and thin, that his occasional compromises in speech and action were temporary tactical concessions that a "principled" man can afford to make, and that a "pragmatist" makes at his peril. It was hard to realize that Americans had as President an ideologue who, despite his occasional collisions with reality, would not heed Herbert Spencer's famous warning about "the murder of a beautiful theory by a brutal gang of facts."

"The fox knows many things," wrote the poet Archilochus, "but the hedgehog knows one big thing." Isaiah Berlin sees a "great chasm between those, on one side, who relate everything to a single central vision, one system less or more coherent or articulate, in terms of which they understand, think and feel—a single, universal, organizing principle in terms of which alone all that they are and say has significance—and, on the other side, those who pursue many ends, often unrelated and even contradictory, connected, if at all, only in some *de facto* way, for some psychological or physiological cause, related by no moral or aesthetic principle; these last lead lives, perform acts, and entertain ideas that are centrifugal rather than centripetal, their thought is scattered or diffused, moving on many levels, seizing upon the essence of a vast variety of experiences and objects for what they are in themselves, without, consciously or unconsciously, seeking to fit them into, or exclude them from, any one unchanging, all-embracing, sometimes self-contradictory and incomplete, at times fanatical, unitary inner vision." The first kind, said Berlin, is the hedgehog, the second the fox. Surely Ronald Reagan is a political hedgehog.

Some hedgehogs wander forever in an ideological wilderness; they are "not for real," practical people say. Some hedgehogs are the transforming leaders of history. Which will Reagan be? Certainly he has transformed the Republican Party, remaking it in his own image. Having officiated at the marriage of the Market Right and the Moralistic Right within the Republican church, he has so far kept the skittish couple together. Now he must bring them more firmly into the church itself—he must bring these powerful movements into the structure of the GOP. In no other way can he ensure that the party will possess a galvanizing set of ideas, and that right-wing leaders will make a solid commitment to the Republican Party as their vehicle of political action.

Will he succeed? As I write this, I am reminded of his persistent effort to unite party and ideology. In the mail I find a "personal" letter from the White House. "The Honorable Ronald Wilson Reagan, President of the United States," it reads, "requests the honor of your support and participation in the congressional elections as a Sponsor of the GOP Victory Fund." Just a campaign ploy? No, because the Conservative-in-Chief is making an effort for his *party* and its candidates. The money will go not into President Reagan's coffers but toward recruiting "outstanding candidates," sponsoring training schools, and giving "direct cash" to congressional aspirants. Reagan is extending his coattails to the whole national party. He is continuing to pose the question for the Democratic Party leadership: Can the opposition party make an equally principled commitment to the liberal-labor left?

THREE

Kennedy:
Governing Without Camelot

E ARLY in November 1979, two and a half weeks after the dedication of the John F. Kennedy Library, Edward Kennedy announced his candidacy for the Democratic nomination for President. Once again a Kennedy occasion generated media images of politics and glamour, poetry and history. Outside Faneuil Hall in Boston stood a large crowd enlivened by signs evoking Chappaquiddick and obscure conspiracies. Inside were gathered old Boston pols who might as well have stepped out of the pages of *The Last Hurrah,* along with the whole Kennedy clan, headed by Rose Kennedy looking exquisitely fragile in a royal-blue bonnet and matching suit.

As the Senator read his announcement speech, which focused on the need for leadership, with appropriate literary allusions, bursts of applause broke out from the younger members of the family, to which the Senator responded with an almost self-mocking smile and genial shaking of his fist. The press promptly questioned him not about his leadership theme, but about the hostage crisis in Iran, an interview with Roger Mudd that had gone badly, and whether Joan would campaign with him, in light of the couple's physical separation. As Kennedy tried to hush scattered hisses and boos evoked by this last question, Joan Kennedy suddenly rose to say that she would campaign—and that she looked forward to her husband's victory. Jacqueline Onassis was there too, and screams of "Jackie! Jackie!" broke out as the former First Lady left the hall.

In Faneuil Hall more than two centuries before, Samuel Adams had aroused revolutionary colonists in behalf of men's rights and liberties; in Faneuil Hall leaders such as William Lloyd Garrison and

Wendell Phillips had thundered against slavery. Edward Kennedy proposed to demonstrate the same kind of idealism and commitment. To Elizabeth Drew two days earlier he had defined leadership as setting out a "vision and purpose and goal" for the nation and then developing "a team" that would work with the institutions that could release "the enormous forces in this society who want to be productive and to be involved in the solution of the problems." The energies of the people had to be mobilized in order to galvanize the government. "The leader," he said, "wants to be able to release those energies and play a critical role in setting out the agenda. I think those forces out there—the elderly, youth, church groups—have a synergistic effect on each other, and that moves this nation. . . ."

Kennedy announced at a time when Americans were calling almost desperately for presidential leadership. Fear of the imperial presidency seemed almost to have disappeared as a popular impulse. Asked in 1976 whether the country needed "some really strong leadership" or whether such leadership would be too "dangerous," respondents divided about equally, but three years later chose strong leadership, however dangerous, by more than two to one. Of all the necessary qualities of the President, respondents rated leadership as the most important. A telephone opinion survey found two-thirds of a nationwide sample rating Carter as a weak or very weak leader. By 1979 Edward Kennedy's leadership rating had soared; in 1973 one-third to one-half the respondents were saying that he had the "personality and leadership qualities a President should have" and he would "take courageous stands on basic issues facing the country," while in 1979 approximately two-thirds of them affirmed these views. "Kennedy by the fall of 1979," Thomas E. Cronin said, "had the largest lead over any incumbent in polling history, the largest lead over the rivals in another party. . . . Americans seemed to be calling him."

In making his decision to run, Edward Kennedy could hardly have forgotten the heady days of 1959–1960 when John Kennedy, then barely forty-two, had launched his seemingly quixotic campaign for the presidency. While JFK had not taken on a sitting President in his own party, he had defied the well-established party leadership of Adlai Stevenson, Eleanor Roosevelt, and Lyndon Johnson, along with that of a host of state and city bosses. Memories of his brothers' victories and defeats had become part of Ted Kennedy's political lifeblood. JFK's presidential campaign, and indeed his presidency, would serve as something of a model. There might indeed be a Kennedy-style government.

It is doubtful, though, that Edward Kennedy or his associates comprehended the full implications of his brother's campaign strategy for JFK's strategy of presidential government. John Kennedy's quest for the office was an example of pure King of the Rock—a mobilizing of his family, personal following, clan money, political credits, and above all of his own resources of media appeal, glamour-magazine coverage, and celebrity familiarity to wrest the presidential prize from the Democratic Party "Establishment." This was by no means the first such occasion in American history. In 1912 Theodore Roosevelt had mobilized his personal constituency in a failed effort against President William Howard Taft and the other GOP regulars. In 1952 Dwight Eisenhower had exploited his immense personal popularity and military prestige to seize the presidential nomination from Taft's son Robert.

King-of-the-Rock politics provoked the danger that a candidacy based on such personal factors would make it more difficult for a President to work with, or overcome, the Establishment and the institutional leadership entrenched in the political system. John Kennedy's presidency had sharply posed this problem. Jimmy Carter's had confirmed the seriousness of the problem. How to *lead* collectively and *govern* effectively after winning as an independent "free lancer"— this is the question that haunts Presidents who want to carry out their party promises but who have come in from the political cold.

JFK: MEMORIES OF THE FUTURE?

For the rest of their lives a whole generation of Democrats and liberals as well as his young brother will remember John F. Kennedy's campaign for the presidency and his three years in office. Cherished images will crowd in on one another: the dramatic convention roll call in Los Angeles; the young face turned to the sky in the fall campaign; the taut finger jabbing the air; the staccato calls for a new generation to "get the country moving again"; the great crowds baking in the western sun or waiting long after midnight in the eastern cities; the cool and composed television figure besting Nixon at his own trade. And then the White House, with its further summons to greatness, the bitter-sweet portraits of family life in the White House, the triumphs and tragedies of Cuba, Big Steel, Berlin, Vietnam, black rights, Dallas . . .

John Kennedy's career as a campaigner had been a sensational success. He had never been defeated in five House and Senate races, and in a host of presidential primaries. He had won the presidency during the era of Eisenhower popularity. And he would have been re-elected by an enormous majority in 1964—Democrats were sure—bringing in a huge congressional majority with him.

Guardians of the Kennedy flame will venerate JFK as a political leader with major accomplishments in the White House and with the promise of even greater achievements ahead, only to be cut down by an assassin. Many younger Americans who came into political consciousness in the late 1960s and 1970s still consider him a Cold Warrior abroad and a trimmer at home. In the longer and broader judgment of history, I think, he will be seen as a politician of extraordinary personal qualities who rhetorically summoned the American people to a moment of activism and greatness, who fell back on a conventional politics of brokerage, manipulation, and consensus once he attained office, who found the institutional constraints on action—especially in Congress—far more formidable than he had expected, who was intellectually too much committed to existing institutions to attempt to unfreeze them but lacked the passionate moral commitment necessary to try to transcend the restraints—and then, in his third year in the presidency and his last year on earth, he began to find his true direction and make a moral and political commitment to it.

"I have premised my campaign for the Presidency," John Kennedy told the autumn crowds in 1960, "on the single assumption that the American people are uneasy at the present drift in our national course, that they are disturbed by the relative decline in our vitality and prestige, and that they have the will and the strength to start the United States moving again." If he did not make explicit in what broad direction he would lead the country, he did make clear that he would fight on a number of fronts, including old New Deal-Fair Deal bread-and-butter liberalism. And a "new generation" would be required by "science and technology and the change in world forces" to face "entirely new problems which will require new solutions." Again and again the words rang out—until they became the leitmotif of the campaign—"to get America moving again."

Would America "move"? The new President achieved some of his immediate, short-term goals by exploiting the oldest political techniques in America—personal influence, patronage, bestowing of presidential recognition and other forms of "stroking," rational persuasion, emotional pressuring, brokerage, swapping pork-barrel tidbits for votes—all summed up in the Administration's favorite term, "blarney, boodle, and bludgeon." All this was enough to protect New Deal and Fair Deal programs and to extend them in significant respects. But it was sadly inadequate compared to the sweeping promises offered in the Democratic Party platform of 1960 and in Kennedy's own campaign.

The President turned toward some minor institutional reform, but only reluctantly, for he had a Burkean conviction that tampering with long-accepted institutions and processes was risky and unrewarding. "When it is not necessary to change," he liked to quote, "it is necessary not to change"—an elegant precursor to Bert Lance's later dictum, "If it ain't broke, don't fix it." But standing in the way of even Kennedy's moderate reforms was the lean and cadaverous figure of Howard Worth Smith, chairman of the House Rules Committee, which could delay, block, destroy, or amend liberal measures and for decades had been doing just that. Liberals in both parties had long wanted to destroy the power of the committee as an anachronistic weapon of the conservative coalition entrenched in the power structure of Congress. But Kennedy had to settle for a plan to enlarge and slightly liberalize the committee, and he was lucky even to gain this. As for the other flagrant expression and symbol of conservative rule on the Hill, the power of filibuster, the Administration had to accept it, with its obvious implications for delaying and destroying civil rights bills.

As the conservative coalition that dominated congressional leadership blocked or vitiated or sidetracked some of Kennedy's key proposals during 1961 and 1962, why did not this vibrant young Administration challenge the institutions of delay and deadlock in which they were enmeshed? Partly because the Kennedy tacticians feared that to defy these power structures would be to precipitate a tremendous struggle with the forces of conservatism entrenched in them, that even winning this struggle would be a diversion from their day-to-day efforts for incremental changes, and that they might lose both the struggle for institutional change *and* their immediate program. I believe that the main reason, however, was intellectual—the considered view of the President and his immediate circle that they ultimately could make the system work by the input of sheer energy, pressure, legislative skill, public persuasion.

This is the point, in my view, where the Kennedy people made a sensible decision for their immediate, limited, and short-run goals but a crippling one for their broader goals and those of subsequent lib-

eral-left presidencies. The dilemma was a severe one. To seek to mod-
ify the filibuster and break the power of the oligarchy of committee
chairmen was to challenge the power system on Capitol Hill that in
turn was entrenched in a wider structure of power based in the politics of congressional constituencies, the financial power of affluent organized interests, electoral arrangements, political party weakness and
fragmentation, and a diffused public support for the existing constitutional distribution of political power. This would be a daunting enterprise for any leader. But not to attack the entire power system all
along the front meant accepting the likelihood that the main thrusts
of the New Frontier would be blunted and contained. Kennedy's refusal to tilt against these real windmills can be understood. But it is
important to note that his choice of the other strategy—a vigorous effort to democratize and reinvigorate the system—was precluded from
the start—that, in short, a fair consideration of strategic alternatives
was never possible.

The reason for this lies in the intellectual tendencies at the heart
of Kennedy's first two years in the White House. The Kennedy circle
prided itself on being practical, realistic, hard-nosed, "pragmatic." It
prided itself on not being emotional, sentimental, dreamy, mystical,
or passionate. Kennedy's mind, wrote Arthur Schlesinger, "was not
prophetic, impassioned, mystical, ontological, utopian or ideological.
It was less exuberant than Theodore Roosevelt's, less scholarly than
Wilson's, less adventurous than Franklin Roosevelt's. But it had its
own salient qualities—it was objective, practical, ironic, skeptical,
unfettered and insatiable." Kennedy attracted to his side men and
women of similar minds.

Realism and practicality are so prized in the American political
culture that few criticized the Kennedy circle for displaying such qualities. But a price was paid. Political practicality and skepticism in
American government easily shift into minor, ad hoc activism, loss of
a sense of purpose, a derangement of priorities, expediency, cynicism,
the elevation of means over ends—and hence ultimately into extreme
impracticality. "The pragmatic realist," wrote Henry Fairlie, "acting
within a consensus he fosters, frees himself from political values, only
to find he has bound himself to react to events pragmatically as they
occur, judging their urgency rather than their importance." The result, in Fairlie's words, tends to be "action without direction, purpose
without belief, energy without thoroughness, activity without result."
It is seldom clear by what standards practicality, realism, and "results"
are to be judged.

In domestic policy Kennedy operated so largely in the New Deal-Fair Deal tradition, and as legatee of his own and his party's promises, as to give his social and economic program considerable coherence, even if limited acceptance in Congress. But in foreign policy his tough-mindedness and practicality were employed in an intellectual and political context so divided as to encourage and legitimate a range of varied and even inconsistent policies and postures. He entered office breathing fire against Communism and at the same time holding out the dove of peace. His first two years in the White House brought the Peace Corps and the Alliance for Progress, the Bay of Pigs invasion, the Berlin and missile crises, the flexible-response doctrine for NATO (as an alternative to the "trip wire" possibly triggering a nuclear response), and deeper involvement in Vietnam.

John Kennedy's third year in the presidency, however, seemed to bring the start of a sea change leading to a fresh and more coherent global policy, save probably for Vietnam. Most notable was the Administration's leading role in negotiating the limited nuclear test ban treaty with Moscow and other signatories. In the last weeks of his life, moreover, Kennedy was having deep misgivings over Vietnam. He criticized the Saigon government and insisted that the United States could play only a supportive role. Perhaps the President was responding to rising peace sentiment that had been spurred by his own earlier speeches for détente. On the other hand, the Administration tacitly approved Diem's assassination, and Kennedy continued to feel, in Theodore Sorensen's view, that "we had to stay in Vietnam," for better or for worse, "until we left on terms other than a retreat or abandonment of our commitment." And in his remarks planned for Dallas on the afternoon of November 22, 1963, was an admission that assistance to Southeast Asian and other nations could be risky and costly, but "we dare not weary of the test."

It was the civil rights struggle at home, however, that brought the most marked change in Kennedy's moral posture in 1963 and illuminated most sharply both the problems and the promise of his leadership. Kennedy's fiery speeches and flowery promises of 1960 had helped mobilize the civil rights community as they had other constituencies. Kennedy's almost adventitious but comforting telephone call to Coretta King when her husband was taken off to a rural prison farm in Georgia in itself had a galvanizing impact on black voters. After his election Kennedy had adopted a posture of energetic executive action for black rights, of limited moral leadership, and of very few legislative demands or pressure. He tried to cool the passions of both sides, north and south, while his brother the attorney general urged a big registration and voting effort. But Kennedy's effort to calm feelings and "maintain a consensus" collapsed in the face of dramatic civil rights confrontations in the South, rising black unrest and protest, and militant black leadership. Urged repeatedly to "wait," black leaders told the Kennedy brothers that they had waited for 150 years, they were tired of waiting, waiting meant "never."

For a time the Administration kept on trying to "cool it," but a new and powerful tide of protest swept the South early in 1963, and now the President himself could wait no longer. On June 11, 1963, he gave a television speech that in Carl Brauer's words represented a momentous "turning point." Now Kennedy was decrying delay. Who among us suffering the plight of the American Negro, he demanded, "would then be content with the counsels of patience and delay." The nation faced a "moral crisis as a country and as a people." The heart of the question was whether all Americans were going to be granted equal rights and equal opportunities. "A great change is at hand, and our task, our obligation, is to make that revolution, that change, peaceful and constructive for all."

At last John Kennedy had not only placed himself at the head of the political movement for civil rights but he had taken moral leadership. In his speech he had put himself and all white Americans in the position of the blacks, and thus had assumed the high ethical posture of empathy with suffering humans through an effort to take on their black skins and all the hate that followed. And at last he called on Congress for a sweeping civil rights bill that would protect the right of all Americans to be served in public hotels, restaurants, theaters, retail stores, and the like, and shortly the President endorsed the concept of banning discrimination in employment. He was now, Herbert Parmet concluded, more interested in sending up legislation that could be enacted than in "political ploys."

But moral leadership exacts its own price. Eleven weeks later, when 250,000 black and white Americans gathered in front of the Lincoln Memorial, the President felt it wise to remain in the White House, receiving black leaders after the meeting. Twelve weeks after that the President flew to Texas in order to raise campaign money for 1964, repair political fences, and conciliate a South seething over his civil rights and other radical postures. One of his stops was Dallas.

1980: THE DEATH OF CAMELOT

At the time Edward Kennedy plunged into the race in November 1979, he had been campaigning for weeks as an unannounced candidate, hauling around a large press contingent and sundry observers. When late in November he invited me to join his campaign tour of California, I accepted. As a longtime student of leadership I was especially curious as to how he would define and exhibit leadership qualities in a presidential nomination effort. While I did not yet know of his remarks to Elizabeth Drew, I did know that he was flailing Carter for lack of confidence in the people—specifically for the President's "malaise speech" of the previous summer—and that Kennedy was making leadership a central issue of the campaign.

I was also eager to see a presidential nomination campaign from the candidate's perch, in contrast to the two perspectives I had held. As a political scientist I had long been critical of the presidential primary system as unrepresentative, cumbersome, overly personalistic, dominated by the mass media, and divorced from the political party in whose name the winning candidate ultimately would campaign for election. As a local Democratic Party activist, however, I had exploited the system in order to become a convention delegate myself both in earlier days when most delegates were chosen from within the leadership network and later when delegate selection had been somewhat "democratized," or at least made less elitist. In 1956 I had spent a hot Midwestern summer trying to round up delegates for Averell Harriman in Iowa, Nebraska, and Kansas. We hadn't bothered with motorcades, mass meetings, street-corner rallies. I simply worked through the existing party leadership network. In succeeding election years, as I saw the system "democratized," I felt no happier about it. To become a delegate in the 1950s and early 1960s, I mobilized what influence I could within the leadership of the Massachusetts Democracy. I was put on the primary ballot, with no opposition. Later the delegate-choosing system was "opened up" to allow more voters to participate, but the process seemed to me to have become complex, chaotic, and divisive, if more open.

Now Edward Kennedy, and a dozen other candidates, Democratic and Republican, were testing themselves in this kind of system, through a six-month ordeal. They were also testing the system itself. I wondered how candidates would operate through a vast array of state presidential primaries and caucuses, and how the system would influence leaders. Kennedy talked about mobilizing the people. Could he do so through such a complex system, campaigning against a President of his own party, enlisting support in thirty or forty states with their diverse political cultures? Could he *engage* with a fragmented electorate increasingly bored or alienated by the posture and policies of liberals and Democrats? That is, would he reach out to them and respond to them, would he mobilize them and would his finer impulses and more creative instincts be mobilized *by* them?

I caught up with the Kennedy entourage at the Bonaventure Hotel in Los Angeles, where the senator was addressing a large luncheon gathering of public defenders and other lawyers. He spoke forcefully, without much variation in style, and then handled rather skillfully a barrage of questions, some of which enabled him to display considerable knowledge of Hispanic concerns, especially over Mexican immigration. He was then rushed to the conference room of the Los Angeles *Times,* where he and the editorial board confronted each other rather warily. Little was said of interest to the reporters waiting expectantly outside. A meeting with Jewish leaders followed, back at the Bonaventure. Everything went cordially until it was clear that Kennedy would not favor the recognition of Jerusalem as Israel's capital. The candidate was then whisked to a fund raiser in a private residence, and then back to the hotel, where he sat through a long dinner and awards program of the Mexican American Legal Defense and Educational Fund, gave the main address, and later—around 11 P.M.—gathered with a group of contributors to the Fund.

During the next two days, as Kennedy met with black leaders and with union heads in Los Angeles, then spoke at another huge dinner, then flew on to San Francisco to go through a similar schedule, I decided that one view of Kennedy could be put to rest—the view that his heart was not really in the campaign, that he did not actually want to run for President or even be President, that he was merely responding to some old call of family duty or Camelot noblesse oblige. Nor, on the other hand, was he doing all this for the fun of it. He did not especially enjoy campaigning, he told me as he was driven out to the Los Angeles airport; he could not think of any part of it he liked, except for the learning process in visiting farms and factories. But he expected this would be his life for eleven months, and he would stay with it.

Kennedy told me, with a kind of wry, detached humor, of an incident the previous day that must hardly have tempered his taste for campaigning. The morning had been reserved for "R & R"—rest and recreation—by his campaign planners, and he and members of his family had stayed at the home of former Senator John Tunney. Had he relaxed a bit? Not much, it seemed. His fund raisers had instructed him that he must see Barbra Streisand that morning, for she was a queen bee; other celebrities would fall in line with financial help if she gave the word. But Barbra, he was told, insisted that he drive several miles to her house to make his pitch. And he had done so. A political superstar paying court, hat in hand, to a *real* superstar. Nothing, it seemed to me, better symbolized the crazy, upside-down world of presidential nomination politics.

The trip out to the airport was a pointed reminder of another aspect of the campaign. Kennedy's limousine, preceded and followed by security people, was elaborately detoured around an overpass. On the freeway, I realized with astonishment that even in the rush hour we could see no cars ahead of or behind us—only a long, empty ribbon of concrete, save for the motorcycle police passing us every few seconds as they moved ahead to block off access roads to the freeway and fell behind to reopen them. Clearly the Los Angeles police were not going to allow another Kennedy to be shot on their turf. All this reminded the senator of a piece I had written for *The New York Times* urging candidates to avoid "political macho" and shun sidewalk hawking and handshaking on street corners, in stores, at subway exits, and other conspicuous and pre-announced places. He agreed with me in principle, he said, but in practice it was hard to be fully protected. I had seen little protection for him, indeed, as he moved in and out of Los Angeles buildings.

Watching Kennedy during these California days I had a growing impression that something was dampening his campaign, even aside from the boredom of barnstorming and the constant danger. He was saying the right things to the right groups, but something was lacking—a sense of excitement or novelty. He was taking conventional liberal Democratic positions, but he was also hewing to a more centrist line—his staff preferred to call it "pragmatic"—than he had been taking in recent years in the Senate. The newspeople "on the bus"— the fifteen or twenty national correspondents and local reporters who drove and flew with him—were clearly bored by his campaign talks. Instead of reporting his policy stands, however, or analyzing why he was taking such standard liberal ones, they were seizing on every small slip or blunder, minor campaign crisis, and trivial "human" angle that they could put on wire or film.

Kennedy's occasional slips and gaffes and erratic performance had overshadowed the campaign from the start as a result of a CBS network interview with Roger Mudd in which Kennedy had been remarkably vague and halting as to why he wanted to run for President. It turned out that the interview had been filmed weeks before the Senator's Faneuil Hall announcement, at a time when Kennedy had not finally made up his mind and in any event was not going to announce his candidacy on Roger Mudd's program, but it was not aired until the eve of his candidacy, when it would have the sharpest effect on his candidacy.

Still, it was a poor performance on the part of a man who, after exploiting the mass media for his own purposes, should have been aware of the tricks of the trade. It seemed like an even poorer performance to millions of Americans, however, because they thought that this apostle of leadership would come across their television screens looking more like a leader. The media, in the course of many years of exploiting the Camelot mythology (with help from the Kennedys themselves), had built up such an image of invariably magnificent Kennedy oratory, fantastic campaign organization and management, compelling, clear-cut positions on policy, that the public could hardly recognize this man who from time to time stumbled in his speeches, made campaign errors, and took standard liberal positions on new and emerging problems.

I was disappointed by the unoriginal and uncompelling positions Kennedy was taking on issues, especially in light of the efforts some of us had made to develop a channel into the campaign for fresh ideas. During the summer I had talked with Arthur Schlesinger, Jr., John Kenneth Galbraith, Doris Kearns, and Richard Goodwin—all of them old friends and allies of the Senator—about developing a "bank" of intellectual input along these lines. The Kennedy staff was appreciative but basically not interested. One night, while we were sitting through an interminable campaign dinner, a Kennedy aide explained why. The whole effort, he said, had to be directed toward the media, especially television, which wanted only sharp, vivid, controversial or otherwise juicy tidbits that could be aired in one minute or less.

What would happen when the media had a really solid piece of news? On the evening of the last toilsome day of his California tour Kennedy responded to a television interviewer's probings with an emotional attack on the deposed Shah of Iran, who, he said, "had the reins of power and ran one of the most violent regimes in the history of mankind—in the form of terrorism and the basic and fundamental violations of human rights, in the most cruel circumstances, to his own people." Kennedy was angry also about a report that the Carter Administration had decided to admit the Shah to the United States. How could we justify, Kennedy stormed, "on the one hand accepting that individual because he would like to come here and stay here with his umpteen billions of dollars that he's stolen from Iran and, at the same time, say to Hispanics who are here legally that they have to wait nine years to bring their wives and children to this country?"

The incident produced a media fire storm. Pouncing on Kennedy's outburst with alacrity, the Carter campaign people issued a torrent of criticism, ranging from the indignant to the suave; campaign chairman Robert S. Strauss tut-tutted that Kennedy did not understand the "full impact of those statements." This response was to be expected, but the more serious question was whether the media could help convert Kennedy's statements into the opening gun of a national debate over the treatment of the Shah and indeed the whole issue of the hostages, how such crises came about, how they could be averted or resolved. On the contrary, press and television treated the affair as a *campaign* incident, with endless speculation about its impact on candidates' standings, rather than as a vital *policy* issue.

Kennedy's remarks about the Shah had stemmed in part from his frustration over the startling surge in Carter's popularity. The Iranian seizure of the American Embassy in Teheran, which happened just three days before Kennedy's declaration of candidacy, had produced a powerful rally-around-the-President sentiment, which seemed to intensify every day that the hostages were held. Like Boss Plunkitt of old, the President "seen his opportunities and he took 'em." Carter proclaimed: "I, as President, have got to maintain the accurate image that we do have a crisis, which I will not ignore until those hostages are released. I want the American people to know it. I want the Iranians to know it. I want the hostages' families and the hostages to know it. I want the world to know that I am not going to resume business-as-usual as a partisan campaigner out on the campaign trail until our hostages are back here—free and at home." So he suspended campaigning—including the debate that he had promised to have with Kennedy.

The senator accused the President of hiding in the Rose Garden, but few were listening. The Soviet invasion of Afghanistan some weeks later enabled the President to cling to his posture of being above the battle. One could not fault Carter; previous Presidents—notably FDR—had exploited foreign crisis to enhance "bipartisan" and party support. But one could fault the media. After the Bay of Pigs, Vietnam, the Tonkin Gulf crisis, and other recent episodes, one might have expected the press to be wary of the rally-around-the-flag tendency, to scrutinize the case for "consensus," to stimulate rather than discourage criticism, to call for stepped-up national debate. But once again the media discussed Carter's exploitation of the Iranian "crisis" without challenging basic assumptions; once again it emphasized the impact of the issue on the campaign rather than its significance for war and peace. Clearly, flag-waving still worked in American elections.

In January I flew out to Iowa with students taking a Williams College winter study course that allowed them to campaign for the candidate of their choice. Iowa was a different kind of battleground from California. Instead of voting in a presidential primary, Iowa Democrats would meet in Democratic neighborhood caucuses to choose pro-Carter or pro-Kennedy delegates to congressional-district conventions. Hence the campaign, instead of trying to mobilize a mass electorate in a climactic primary, had to dissolve into numberless local efforts to activate third-cadre activists throughout the state. Even Kennedy's large family and entourage seemed to be swallowed up in the great farm areas and numerous small towns of Iowa. The campaign plane was of little use here. Once again, though, I was impressed by a phenomenon almost unique to Kennedy campaigns: the arrival on the campaign field of a small host of true volunteers—students, business and professional people, housewives, workers—who had only to hear that a Kennedy was campaigning to quit assembly line, desk or kitchen and hurry to the scene of battle. There they would live off the land.

My students and I ran a one-car mini-campaign, following mainly the university and college circuit, and keeping as far away from the Kennedy effort as possible. Even in the dead of winter the countryside looked lovely, with its undulating snow-covered fields, huge barns, and modest, comfortable-looking homes. It was hard to reach those homes, though, or even the students on their campuses. Apathy seemed thick enough to cut with a knife. This seemed rather surprising in the case of students, for draft registration was an issue of the moment, and the students had the same right as any other voter to attend the local party caucuses, in either their college town or their hometown. My own students became so desperate at the lack of turnout in a rural part of Iowa that they spent a whole day in one small college visiting every dormitory room and urging the occupants to turn out for the rally. Two showed up.

My own morale must have reached a low point when, about a week before the caucus meetings, I picked up a newly arrived copy of the *Reader's Digest* in a college library and noted its featured article, a thirty-page "exposé" of what really happened at Chappaquiddick. It was a rehash of old allegations, and since the five or six other current "exposés" of Chappaquiddick differed as much with one another over the "true" explanation as they did with Kennedy's version, this article had to be dismissed as a carefully timed thrust at a liberal Democrat by the nation's leading conservative magazine. Obviously Chappaquiddick was still a grievous question, but my heart sank when I reflected that for some days I had been drawing at best audiences of fifty or one hundred or perhaps two hundred students in give-and-take sessions, while this one piece of propaganda would sit on desks and coffee tables in ten thousand or more Iowa homes.

The Kennedy people were prepared for a knife-edge win or loss in Iowa, but not for the two-to-one shellacking that President Carter gave his rival in the caucus outcomes. The first severe electoral defeat a Kennedy brother had ever suffered, it sent shock waves through the whole campaign organization. Since the senator had rashly made Iowa a crucial test of his electoral hopes, the media at once speculated that he would drop out of this now "hopeless" race. The political prospects at this point looked very bleak, Kennedy said in an interview a year later. It seemed impossible to "focus attention on the campaign"; the outlook for three contests coming up in Maine, New Hampshire, and Vermont—usually considered part of Kennedy turf—was not promising; and "there was even the possibility of a very close race in Massachusetts," an outcome that would hurt his "ability to be an effective leader in the Senate in the future" and might "even have some very serious adverse implications in regard to the 1982 race." Some in the Kennedy camp wanted him to pull out, but the Senator decided to stay in, as much on policy grounds as political grounds.

His "decision to continue," Kennedy remembered later, "came at a rather interesting confluence of events." One, of course, was the final announcement of the figures on the economy for the end of the year [1979] which indicated that we were going to be at a 13 percent rate of inflation, and that the interest rates were moving up in a rather dramatic fashion, and it was very clear at the time that there was going to be no corresponding action at all by the Administration and that a more dramatic alternative was going to have to be taken. Clearly, Carter wasn't going to move.

"And that really triggered my decision to make the announcement in regard to wage-price controls as being the really last resort to get a handle on the escalating rates of inflation and interest rates. . . ." He hoped, Kennedy recalled, that such measures would foster increased productivity in a competitive market. But he had been as concerned about Carter's foreign policy as his domestic, for the President had just delivered a fire-eating speech, confronting what Carter called "the most serious threat since World War II," asking Congress for more arms, offering an American guarantee of protection over "the Persian Gulf region . . . even to include military force," and in general playing his "Afghanistan card."

Carter's speech, Kennedy recalled, "set in motion a lot of very deep concerns in my own mind. It was really an announcement of a nonpolicy. It was not a policy that had been worked out with the countries in the area, . . . but an open-ended policy that was never really supported by our European friends and allies. . . . It was really going to be a dangerous policy with regard to a unilateral American involvement."

His mind made up to continue, and suffering no anguish or second thoughts, Kennedy called his advisers together at his McLean home to consider *how* to continue. His brother-in-law and campaign manager Steve Smith was there, along with regular staff members Paul Kirk, Carey Parker, Bob Shrum, Carl Wagner, and others. The senator summoned Arthur Schlesinger, Jr., down from New York; Richard Goodwin took part, and Allard Lowenstein came by. A debate broke out as to whether Kennedy should take a softer or harder line than Carter on the Near East. The senator reasserted his own pro-détente feelings late in the evening, when he asked Schlesinger to rewrite a draft prepared by the staff. Debate continued until around midnight; then Schlesinger, quoting Samuel Rosenman's line, "There comes a time in the life of every speech when it has to be written," went to work, finishing around three in the morning. Another group labored over a strong economic policy statement.

The result was the Georgetown speech, a powerful statement powerfully delivered in favor of a firmer policy of détente and cooperation with allies abroad, and "an immediate six-month freeze on inflation—followed by mandatory controls, as long as necessary, across the board—not only on prices and wages, but also on profits, divi-

dends, interest rates and rent." At last Kennedy was presenting a focused, deeply felt, and boldly stated policy that sharply differentiated
him from the President and from the Republican aspirants. His immediate reward was a morale boost among his staff, a sudden jump in
campaign contributions, and some unwonted praise in the media.

Well received though it was, the Georgetown speech brought no
change in Kennedy's electoral fortunes. He lost in New Hampshire
and Vermont, won easily in Massachusetts, took a shattering defeat in
Illinois, and kept in the race with victories in New York and Connecticut. But Kennedy had won a big victory over himself and for
himself—a clear sense of self-identity and of political direction. One
reason for Kennedy's floundering in the early part of the campaign,
Schlesinger said later, "was that he was saying things which didn't
come from his heart and trying to take a line which really was not
consonant with his line as a senator or what he really felt. . . . He
was betrayed in his stumbling, stammering, and so on. Once he began
talking what he really believed, all the complaints about his inarticu-
lateness disappeared. . . . People in politics should never get out of
character; when they do, they betray themselves. And Ted Kennedy
started his campaign out of character—and got back and recaptured
his identity in Georgetown."

Kennedy's early defeats, his resurgence, and his ultimate failure
to capture the nomination marked the death of the Camelot legend.
Part of that legend was Kennedy's invincibility at the polls—that myth
had dissolved. Kennedy to some degree had been captive to the legend,
perhaps unconsciously. Just as royalty expects to have the fealty of
the lords without asking for it, so Kennedy found it difficult to solicit
commitments—even from those who had begged him to run. Some of
these supplicants had earlier feared being weighed down by Carter's
drooping political coattails; when Carter's star soared later, some of
these "Kennedy friends" soared away with the President. Next time
Kennedy would extract political commitments.

Kennedy had not swallowed the idea of royal privilege; he knew
that the nomination would not be handed him on a gold platter. But
there seemed to be an assumption in the Kennedy camp that if you
did work for it, if you revved up the old troops and machinery, victory
was all but certain. Then, too, Kennedy's move to the center earlier
in the campaign had smacked a bit of the hoary political technique of
rising above parties and issues and conflict in order to maximize one's
votes. It was a political technique for kings, not Presidents or prime
ministers, as was Kennedy's heavy reliance on his family, exemplified

by his almost automatic choice of Steve Smith for campaign manager, despite Smith's severe and often-stated reservations about his brother-in-law running in 1980. At its worst, Camelot in politics had meant, in Ronnie Dugger's words, "the personalization of our politics, its conversion into a star system, the debasement of the nutritious politics of issues, ideals, programs and values into the junk politics of personal tragedies, myths, themes and slogans."

One other myth may have died in 1980—the myth that Kennedy's personal failure under stress after the Chappaquiddick accident demonstrated that he would fail under public stress in the White House. Crushed and even humiliated by the Iowa defeat, bone-tired and media-battered, Kennedy had shown remarkable resiliency in confronting and resolving the crisis in his own campaign. Watching Kennedy go over the drafts of the Georgetown speech, which was now the last desperate throw of the campaign dice, Schlesinger had been impressed and reassured by his performance. "He asked the kind of hard, critical questions which his brothers would have asked. He wanted to know exactly what he was being committed to by these various words. . . . He wasn't satisfied with facile verbal formulations."

As he went through the final primary battles, his campaign more forlorn, underfinanced, and disorganized than ever, Kennedy impressed friend and foe alike with his humor, stamina, gusto, and refusal to scapegoat. During the brief span of this campaign, at least, Kennedy proved himself worthy of membership less of Camelot than of that small aristocracy described by E. M. Forster—sensitive but not weak, considerate but not fussy, plucky in his power to endure. In the midst of the campaign turbulence, as his final thin hope of nomination was shattered, he proved himself to be a hardy if not happy warrior.

DIVIDED DEMOCRATS:
TWO LEFTS AND A RIGHT

Not least of the benefits of the fall of Camelot will be the better opportunity it gives us to focus more on Democratic Party and liberal-left ideas and less on *personalismo*. For Kennedy or any other Democrat who takes a clearly liberal-left position in domestic policy and a consistently pro-détente posture in foreign and defense policy, some disturbing questions must be posed. Is there an authentic and coherent body of liberal or radical ideas on which left-of-center Democrats can draw, to serve them as guidelines for political strategy and policy innovation? Is there an organized Democratic Party today that could serve as a political home for such Democrats and a vehicle for such ideas? And if the entrance into the presidential sweepstakes is still largely through King-of-the-Rock politics, how does a candidate shift from personalistic strategies to policy and program politics?

Historically the Democrats have almost always been divided, as they have responded to an enormous diversity of popular impulses. As Jeffersonian Republicans, democrats of the early years of the nineteenth century shared the early liberal ethos of agrarian individualism, states' rights, private property, the separation of powers and checks and balances, as against the alleged Federalist belief in elitism, industrialization, centralized finance, a consolidated national government. The liberal and democratic credo centered in the idea of an easy, independent, self-regulating rural society that would cultivate the virtues of the honest yeoman. These early American democrats had a passionate faith in liberty—but liberty was defined negatively, as liberty *from*. The aim was to get governments, armies, churches, and all other establishments off the people's backs.

As the nation inexorably urbanized, industrialized, and centralized, the potential cleavage within liberalism between notions of negative and positive liberty intensified. Jacksonian Democracy inherited the individualistic ethos of the Jeffersonians, with the old bias against centralized finance and government, but powerful egalitarian as well as libertarian impulses quickened within American liberalism, impulses that were expressed also in the widening of the suffrage, the decline of the gentry and of deference, and the rise of the political professional, massive patronage, and a party politics of caucuses, conventions, election rallies, parades, and vote huckstering. But though the Democracy dubbed itself the party of the Common Man and attracted labor, agrarian, and reform support, the national Democrats were centrally compromised over the southern embrace of slavery and broke into pieces on the coming of the Civil War.

As marketplace individualism—negative liberty, free enterprise, "equality of opportunity"—became the dominant American ideology in the post-Civil War years, the national Democratic Party split between laissez-faire economic libertarians and urban and farm populists demanding help from government. A party that over a seventy-year period nominated for President Horace Greeley, William Jennings Bryan, Woodrow Wilson, Alfred E. Smith, and Franklin D.

Roosevelt on the one hand, and Samuel J. Tilden, Grover Cleveland, Alton B. Parker, and John W. Davis on the other, was clearly a party that hardly knew its head. One portion of the party did know its head, however—the southern Democracy, which developed a whole political strategy of its own based on the continued repression of the black and protection of "southern interests" against northern interference.

The Depression and Roosevelt's New Deal brought profound alterations both in the Democratic Party and in the shape of American liberalism. FDR took on the conservative southern wing of the party—successfully in his gaining repeal of the two-thirds Democratic convention vote requirement for nominating a President, unsuccessfully in his effort to purge Senator Walter George of Georgia and other conservative officeholders from the national Democracy. Far more significant was Roosevelt's influence on liberal thought and action, especially on the need for positive liberty. Evoking words and memories of Wilson and Al Smith, and the more egalitarian aspects of Jeffersonian and Jacksonian doctrine, he preached year after year that government—including most particularly the federal government—could be the common man's friend and not his enemy, that government was simply the means through which Americans could make collective efforts to help themselves and other Americans, that "necessitous men are not free men." Early in the struggle against Nazism he proclaimed the Four Freedoms, including the positive liberties of security against want and fear as well as the classic liberties of speech and religion. At the height of World War II he announced that "we have accepted, so to speak, a second Bill of Rights under which a new basis of security and prosperity can be established for all—regardless of station, race, or creed. . . ."

Americans emerged from the Roosevelt and Truman years with a permanently altered Democratic Party and a more coherent, more broadly supported credo of liberalism. The Democracy was now a committedly New Deal-Fair Deal party, aside from bastions of conservative thought and practice, mainly in the South. The Democratic Party's concept of liberalism had broken away for good, it seemed, from the classic free-enterprise market individualism of the last century, and now embodied the crucial idea that government had both a constitutional right and a moral duty to intervene in behalf of the deprived, the poor, blacks suffering discrimination, women, children, the elderly. These developments had key spin-off effects too on the Republican Party, which had to accept most Democratic ideas of social-welfare liberalism and positive liberty while promising that it could do things "better, quicker, and cheaper."

The Roosevelt-Truman years left Americans with a four-party system, arrayed from moderate left to right: the *presidential Democrats,* headed by such as Adlai Stevenson, John Kennedy, Lyndon Johnson, and Hubert Humphrey, inheritor of New Deal-Fair Deal policy and philosophy, centered in the presidency, the Electoral College, and the big urban states with their labor, urban, and ethnic populations; the *presidential Republicans,* led by Dwight Eisenhower, Henry Cabot Lodge, Nelson Rockefeller, John Foster Dulles, and the like, founded and funded in the growing suburban areas of the East and West Coasts and in top corporate networks, also centered in the presidency; the *congressional Democrats* led by Sam Rayburn, Lyndon B. Johnson (initially), and a relatively obscure group of Democratic committee chairmen, centered in the congressional committee structure of House and Senate, the seniority system, and rural, conservative, mainly one-party districts operating through that system; and the *congressional Republicans,* led above all by Senators Robert A. Taft and Barry Goldwater, as well as by former House Speaker Joe Martin, rooted in much the same congressional system and rural, one-party constituencies as the congressional Democrats, but more in the Midwest than in the South.

Today, some thirty years later, Reagan-type congressional Republicans have swallowed the presidential wing of the GOP. What has happened to the two Democratic parties?

The congressional Democratic Party has survived as a shrunken but still significant grouping. Deserted by a number of old-time leaders who have gravitated into the Republican Party, shorn of much of their power as a result of a now-truncated seniority system and a diffused committee and subcommittee structure, overshadowed by the self-proclaimed conservatism of the Reagan Republicans, the old-time oligarchical committee heads still exercise considerable, though mainly negative, influence. The conservative congressional party survives at the grass roots because of the strong traditionalist and right-wing attitudes that persist in the Sun Belt and continue to produce heavily Democratic state political structures there. The old congressional party manifests itself nationally most dramatically in the forty or so House "Boll Weevils," who deserted Tip O'Neill's ranks again and again in 1981 to support Reagan's tax and budget proposals. O'Neill and moderates like Jim Wright are compelled to mediate between the conservatives and the liberal rank and file. This party split, combined with the divisive impact of single-interest groups, has produced a divided Democratic leadership in Congress.

The presidential Democrats have prospered until recent times. Their nominees—Stevenson, Kennedy, Humphrey, McGovern—invariably won presidential nominations in contests with conservative Democrats such as Richard Russell and Lyndon Johnson. Only when LBJ firmly set himself in the Roosevelt-Stevenson-Kennedy tradition after succeeding to the presidency did he establish himself in 1964 as the undisputed leader of the presidential Democrats. For most of three decades this party leadership, operating through the presidency and majorities in Congress, was a powerhouse of social-welfare programs at home and political and economic intervention abroad. Presidential Democrats often collaborated on both domestic and foreign policy with their close ideological neighbors on the political spectrum, the presidential Republicans, while congressional Republicans like Taft and Goldwater and Reagan castigated the unholy combination of "liberal," eastern, Ivy League, corporate interests in both parties.

By the mid-1970s, public-opinion analysts could report that social-welfare liberalism, as nourished by the presidential Democrats with a lot of help from presidential Republicans, had won a wide consensus among Americans. Analyst Everett Ladd could speak of the "almost universal acceptance among Americans of the general policy approach of the New Deal." Sometimes, however, nothing fails like success. Not only did the presidential Democrats overextend themselves and their country in military and political commitments in Southeast Asia and elsewhere. Not only did they clash with a "quality of life" radicalism less concerned with economic issues than with "social" ones like the environment, criminals' rights, women's liberation, legalization of marijuana, rights of homosexuals, abortion. Even more important, a fundamental weakness and ambivalence lay at the heart of social-welfare liberalism in the United States.

If New Frontier-Great Society liberals had rejected the old hard-nosed, competitive, marketplace Horatio Alger liberalism of the nineteenth century, they have embraced a twentieth-century extension of it—a credo of pluralistic liberalism and a polity of interest-group representation. While the liberal movements and programs of this century have unquestionably benefited the nation as a whole—the poor as well as the rich—they have been peculiarly responsive to the needs and demands of organized interest groups and in turn have stimulated and strengthened these groups. Thus the Wagner Act of

1935 responded to labor's demand for the right to organize, but in turn, and as part of its very success, that Act helped build the foundations of the powerful labor organizations that arose after World War II. Farm, business, transportation, and other policies had similar mobilizing impacts on client groups, which in turn helped spawn—or vastly expand—a host of single-interest groups that operate through the whole political system today.

The result, as presciently described by Theodore Lowi in the late 1960s, "was not the strong, positive government of which the pluralists spoke but impotent government, no less impotent because it was getting bigger. Government that is unlimited in scope but formless in action is government that cannot plan. Government that is formless in action and amoral in intention (i.e., *ad hoc*) is government that can neither plan nor achieve justice. . . ." Lowi pictured contemporary liberal government "as a gigantic prehistoric beast, all power and no efficacy . . . power without definition, finesse, discrimination, ending in disappointment. . . ."

Among the disappointed were members of both the disillusioned Old Left and the New Left. Old liberals or radicals—now "neo-conservatives" or the New Right—such as Norman Podhoretz, Irving Kristol, Aaron Wildavsky, and Nathan Glazer, through such journals as *The Public Interest* and *Commentary,* lamented that organized interests, following a doctrine of maximizing freedom for private and group appetites, were reducing government itself—its legislators, executives, judges, bureaucrats—to a jumble of naked interests; that governmental regulation, originally proposed as a means of protecting the public interest, actually frustrated the public interest; that the huge social-welfare economy was leaching money and vigor away from the creative private sector; that New Deal liberalism, for all its great achievements, had run down to the point of exhaustion.

The New Left had its own indictment of pluralistic, interest-group liberalism. As organized interests extracted more money, protection, and recognition from government, their upper-level beneficiaries tended to earn more, to live better, to move out of the world of poverty both physically and psychologically, and to take on middle-class attitudes toward the poor, and toward government helping the poor. Even more, the whole pluralistic, interest-group polity tended toward equilibrium, conservatism, stasis. Both these developments thwarted what was really needed—a popular, grass-roots, liberal-radical New Left coalition of labor, women, blacks and other minorities, and the poor and deprived generally, a coalition that would transcend the age-old divisions among lower-income people, fashion a strong and cohesive popular majority, and win control of the government.

The New Right and the New Left grappled over these philosophical and political differences, but this of course is not what they chiefly argued about. The most heated disputes raged over social policy at home and military-political policy abroad. "Old liberals" derided the permissiveness, self-indulgence, sentimentalism, and irresponsibility they discerned in the New Left's positions on crime, pornography, homosexuality, abortion, drugs, and the rest; this was individualism gone wild. Defending its "humane" positions on these issues, the New Left attacked the neo-conservatives for their alleged willingness to use repressive measures against persons seeking to control their own minds and bodies; this was statism gone wild. On foreign policy the New Right, some of whom as youths had fought against the Communists and others of whom had fought alongside them, upbraided the New Left for being soft and sentimental toward Soviet "imperialism," while the New Left attacked those of the New Right for being cold warriors and imperialists.

The intellectual and policy disarray within Democratic Party and liberal-left ranks was somewhat reduced as the neo-conservatives deserted their old combat posts and moved into the intellectual and political orbit of Reaganism. Their desertion of the Democracy left the Democratic Party more united only for a time, however. The old-time dispute between the moderates and the liberal-left in the party intensified doctrinally, even while the New Right tended to unite them politically. The King-of-the-Rock showdown between Kennedy and Carter in 1980 was the most significant manifestation of this struggle. It persists today. In part the differences are quantitative, involving the extent of taxation, spending, social welfare, and hence are open to mediation by effective transactional leadership. Foreign-policy and some social-policy disputes—i.e., détente with Moscow and anti-crime policy—are issues of *kind* and not merely degree, and hence cannot so easily be composed.

Ronald Reagan's 1980 victory brought no truce between Democratic Party moderates and the liberal-left, no closing of the ranks against the common foe, nor unity within the Democratic Party. "Democrats must face the music," declared Ben Wattenberg, an able spokesman for neo-conservatism, a few weeks after Reagan's inauguration. "They are not in trouble because they have no money, organization, or unity. Exactly the opposite: They have no money, organization, or unity because they are in trouble. They are in trouble not because they stand for nothing but because they stand for two very different things. Some believe in the old Democratic beliefs (temporarily pilfered by Reagan). And some still believe in the new Democratic beliefs that got them into all the trouble they are in." The Democrats' choice was simple, Wattenberg concluded: "go left," or "go back to their roots."

In retrospect, Kennedy's 1980 campaign for the presidential nomination was widely and deservedly criticized for failing to come up with a comprehensive new vision, program, and set of policies for the decade ahead. His Georgetown speech, though exciting and courageous, failed to spell out more than a set of short-run emergency policies to meet the twin problems of inflation and stagnation. If he and his staff were not wholly receptive to new departures, it must be said that he did not receive a great deal of help from liberal and radical intellectuals, at least in the public prints. His longtime friend Arthur Schlesinger, Jr., was typically adroit and pungent in attacking the "shameless caricature of liberalism" constructed by neo-conservatives and Old Liberals. "A student of the writings of Irving Kristol, Henry Kissinger, Daniel Patrick Moynihan and Norman Podhoretz would gather, for example," Schlesinger wrote in *The New York Times Magazine,* "that a liberal is a person who believes in the perfectibility of man, who regards power as intrinsically evil, who is addicted to guilt, who is filled with 'self-hatred and self-contempt' (Podhoretz), whose favorite practice is 'self-flagellation' (Kissinger), who has an unrequited love affair with Marxism, who assumes what Bertrand Russell used to call (ironically) the 'superior virtue of the oppressed,' who advocates curing criminals at home and terrorists abroad by the 'therapeutic ethic' (Kristol)—i.e., compassion and the provision of social services—who is ashamed of America and supposes that 'third worlders stand closer to God' (Stephen S. Rosenfeld), and who abhors geopolitics, the balance of power and the idea of a national interest."

As a "bottled-in-bond" liberal, Schlesinger went on, he subscribed to none of these propositions, "nor do most liberals I know." But as for what *liberalism* should *do* at some future time when America in its great cycle of liberalism and conservatism girded itself up once again to face urgent domestic problems, he dealt only with the crises of inflation and energy. Intellectual leaders further to the left were hardly more forthcoming. Marcus G. Raskin in *The Nation* indicted the Right, Old and New, mainly for their "partnership" with Big Government and Big Business. But when it came to a positive program for the New Left, Raskin could only speak vaguely of fairness (progressive tax structure, common ownership of natural resources, etc.), economic security, cooperation as against competition, "economic democracy," and other shibboleths of the left. Indeed, he concluded his article by quoting Franklin D. Roosevelt's "second Bill of Rights" in its entirety. FDR's doctrine was magnificent for the time, but it is now forty years old.

Certain political leaders—often called "neo-liberals"—have been more daring than the intellectuals. Senator Gary Hart of Colorado has advanced a comprehensive agenda for the 1980s and 1990s, including a new definition of "standard of living" to include basic values "such as shelter, nutrition, health, education, and employment"; the financing of urban rebuilding through a "21st Century Cities Bank" capitalized by state budget surpluses and public employee pension funds; the encouragement of workers "to share in the ownership of production facilities through employee stock ownership plans or similar proposals." Senator Paul E. Tsongas, Massachusetts Democrat, has criticized liberals for "living off" traditional New Deal ideas such as pump priming, although he has come up less with an arresting new program than a moderate alternative to the New Left. Stuart E. Eizenstat, President Carter's special assistant for domestic policy, favors a "tax-based incomes policy" under which the government would grant tax credits to members of unions that hold down wages and to companies limiting price increases.

Promising though some of these proposals may be, they still fall short of confronting the most serious and intractable problems facing the country, in such areas as education, crime and justice, health, the environment, corporate power and poverty and inequality. They would not bring true equality of opportunity, economic, social, political, into the lives of tens of millions of Americans still inadequately nourished, housed, educated, motivated. Despite their global economic emphasis, they do not offer a strategy for a generation-long quest for peace. Above all, neither the neo-liberals nor the mainstream Democrats nor the New Left seem to comprehend the major changes that must be made in the governmental and political system if any of their more serious proposals are to be enacted and executed.

Can the New Left offer a striking new program that would learn from the errors and failures of liberalism of the recent past, win the support of a majority of the electorate, and serve as the programmatic foundation for a future government capable of overcoming long-term, entrenched domestic ills—and of making a breakthrough for détente abroad? Is there such a program on which Edward Kennedy or some other liberal-left Democrat could win? And if they won, could they *govern*, could they carry through their program, given the nature of the political and governmental system?

PART TWO

THE *Rise* OF

King OF THE *Rock*

FOUR

The Roots
of Leadership Failure

S HORTLY after Richard Nixon quit the presidency, with the statement that he no longer had a "strong enough political base" in Congress, the Washington *Post* headlined an AP story "Garbagemen rated over White House." That headline hardly raised eyebrows in the wake of Watergate, but the article itself reported that Americans placed equally little confidence in the police, press, church, law firms, and Congress. Only doctors rivaled garbagemen in public confidence.

This was no fly-by-night street-corner tally but a Louis Harris poll commissioned and paid for by a Senate subcommittee. Hence it received serious attention. Harris found that a majority of the public felt there was "something deeply wrong in America," as compared to the minority of state and local leaders who expressed such concern. Government officials also perceived a lack of confidence in government, but they tended to blame Watergate. Despite pessimism about government, cynicism about leaders, and alarm over the state of the nation, Americans remained confident "that the system can work."

I will contend that it is precisely the *system* that does not work, that what is "deeply wrong in America" is rooted more in institutional and intellectual forces than personal ones, that there is a wealth of potential leadership ready to burst through present constraints, and that no leader—no matter how charismatic or politically skilled—will be able to govern effectively given the existing constitutional framework and informal networks of power. Those who condemn current leadership often hark back to earlier days of "great leadership," when Presidents and famous legislators and judges were like giants against the sky. It is fashionable these days even for Republicans to resurrect Franklin Roosevelt and acclaim the glory days of the New Deal's first "hundred days." I believe, on the contrary, that we have had leadership failures almost from the start, that these failures have been increasing in frequency and seriousness, that they are now built into the system.

Personalizing our troubles is dangerous because it leads to scapegoating—a frantic search for the "bad guys" who are messing up an otherwise fine system. Or to "stupidity" explanations, which plausibly feed off the blunders and miscalculations of foreign and military policy, moral failures of the Watergate enormity, gross self-deceptions such as the notion that Latin Americans and other peoples are waiting for "liberation" by outsiders. Or to "confusion" theories— the idea that the problems are too complex and the future is too uncertain for long-range planning. Therefore, we must settle for coping, just plodding ahead from day to day.

I believe that our troubles go far deeper. Both conservative and liberal leadership have had their innings for years at a time in Washington and state capitals during this century without overcoming deep-seated problems in the areas of poverty, crime, health, environment, productivity, immigration, social equality, and economic justice. The failures have not been only those of particular leadership, but of leadership in a broader sense, and of the *system* that supports and fragmentizes it.

In short, our problem is not a new "blundering generation" like that set of leaders who allegedly plunged us into the Civil War. Our failures may take the form of crimes, blunders, and stupidities, but they arise more often from ill-defined purposes, murky values, confused priorities, incoherent programs, inconsistent policies, lost directions, and they manifest themselves in economic and social outcomes irrelevant to original moral and political purposes. But the root of the problem—the system itself—goes back a long way, to the work of the greatest collection of leaders that this nation—perhaps any Western nation—ever had, to a group of leaders who performed a supreme act of transforming leadership, but left a set of institutions that have bedeviled and frustrated American leaders ever since.

TRANSFORMING THE SYSTEM

The essence of transformational leadership is the capacity to adapt means to ends—to shape and reshape institutions and structures to achieve broad human purposes and moral aspirations. The dynamic of such leadership is recognizing expressed and unexpressed wants among potential followers, bringing them to fuller consciousness of their needs, and converting consciousness of needs into hopes and expectations, and ultimately into feelings of entitlement that can be transmuted into demands on the political system, including the original leadership. The secret of transforming leadership is the capacity of leaders to have their goals clearly and firmly in mind, to fashion new institutions relevant to those goals, to stand back from immediate events and day-to-day routines and understand the potential and consequences of change.

The supreme act of transforming leadership in American history was performed by hundreds of persons during the period from the Revolutionary days of the 1770s, through the nation-building period of the late 1780s and 1790s, to the establishment and effective operation of an opposition party and alternative government in the first years of the nineteenth century. The vital moment in this work of two generations came in the summer of 1787, when less than three score men—most of them politicians who were also planters, lawyers, and businessmen—hammered out the constitutional and political structure of a new national government. Their leadership was not only political, it was intellectual—that is, informed, analytical, reflective, creative, as in Richard Hofstadter's definition, "the critical, creative, and contemplative side of mind. Whereas intelligence seeks to grasp, manipulate, re-order, adjust, intellect examines, ponders, wonders, theorizes, criticizes, imagines."

Critical and creative—those words sum up the feat of the Founders. Because they could stand back from the existing political system and examine it critically, because they were not content to patch up the existing Articles of Confederation, because they could rise above the usual level of pragmatic brokerage, transcending their immediate interests even while powerfully motivated by their educational, social, and economic background, they brought off a striking act of creative leadership as they reshaped the constitutional and political leadership of which they were a central part.

We cannot fully understand these men, their leadership, and their *ideas* of leadership—especially at the point when they were about to reshape their political system—unless we think and imagine our way back into their political and public worlds. Ideally, we would sail with Charles C. Pinckney from Charleston, talking politics and philosophy with him between his bouts of seasickness; or listen to Connecticut's William Samuel Johnson over the rattling of his carriage as we made our way down the Boston Post Road; or even ride up from Mount Vernon with George Washington himself, in his coach. But we would have done best to journey with James Madison, perhaps stopping off with him at Princeton on his New York–Philadelphia trip, hoping that his memories of college days there would start him talking about the great political thinkers whose works he had read. For this son of Virginia gentry was as mighty in intellect and insight as he was slight and undistinguished in appearance. While he was only the first among equals at the convention, he was a prototype of those who wanted a strong, balanced, and national government. Others might have been more eloquent, polemical, and philosophical, but among a group of men who had a clear idea of their goals for the new nation and how to achieve them, Madison had the most carefully thought-out strategy of the relation of means to ends.

What were those ends? No one could doubt the Founders' central belief—Liberty. It was to secure liberty as well as life and the pursuit of happiness that they revolted against Britain; it was to secure the Blessings of Liberty as well as a more perfect union, security, and justice that they would "ordain" the new constitution. For American leaders of this day, liberty—or freedom, a word they used almost synonymously—was a palpable possession, a living, breathing entity they could seize and hold, safeguard and cherish. They wanted many kinds of liberty—of conscience, person, religion, speech, press, assembly, property. The Founders also believed in some kind of equality, proclaimed in the Declaration of Independence though not listed in the Preamble to the Constitution. They recognized that people were not equal in ability or virtue, nor need they be equal in condition, but they were equal in the sight of God and in their natural rights to life, liberty, and the pursuit of happiness. Just how these rights could be fulfilled was left open.

Loving liberty, the Founders hated Tyranny in any and every form—religious, kingly, mob, economic, governmental. Government, in particular, was a source of tyranny, so they would guard against it whether in the executive, the legislature, the judiciary, whether in the majority or in the minority. Of the need of government, they had no doubt, because only through collective action could they ward off external dangers and overcome internal unrest; without government, private forms of tyranny would crush liberty. Still—and here was the rub—government itself could be the most tyrannical force of all. The Founders were not so simplistic as to think that some autonomous mechanism called "government" itself was the source of tyranny; it was *people*—majorities, minorities, factions—working in and through government that were the threat. But equipped with the powers of the state, these forces could be formidable.

If the Founders had been setting up a monarchy, the solution would have been relatively simple—hire a suitable king, devise a method of succession as fail-safe as possible, endow the monarchy with the necessary legitimacy, authority, and armed strength, provide parliamentary and other restraints on the Crown, and hope for the best. But they were setting up a *republic*. While some of the Framers flirted with the idea of a hereditary upper house or even a monarchy, virtually all were committed to representative institutions—to legislators, executives, and judges whose obtaining and staying in office would depend, directly or indirectly, on the people's suffrage and sufferance. Thus they faced the daunting problem, awesome, perplexing, portentous, that confronts us today: how to create and maintain a government powerful enough to meet the needs of the American people for life, liberty, and justice, but not so powerful as to deprive them of those cherished values. In a popular government, how to represent people in a way that does not *mis*represent people.

Clearly they must—in a republic—depend on the people themselves. This idea neither delighted nor discouraged the Founders, for they were neither illusioned nor disillusioned about the people. On the one hand, they felt that popular government, more than any other kind, called for qualities of private and public virtue—patriotism, selflessness, honor, decency, industry—widely distributed throughout society. But no one had to tell these veterans of colonialism, war, faction, and tragedy that people also exhibited other qualities—greed, ignorance, corruption, aggressiveness, intolerance—and that all these qualities, good and bad, manifested themselves in varying degrees at varying times under varying circumstances.

And if the Founders had forgotten these hard facts, two incidents during the months before the convention would have brought them back to reality. Led by a man called Shays, western Massachusetts farmers struggling under crushing debts and taxes had taken to arms, closed down courts, and even attacked a government arsenal before they were dispersed. "What, gracious God, is man!" George Washington had written to a friend, "that there should be such inconsistency and perfidiousness in his conduct? It is but the other day, that we were shedding our blood to obtain the [state] Constitutions of our own choice and making; and now we are unsheathing the sword to overturn them." If government could not check these disorders, he wrote Madison, "what security has a man for life, liberty, or property?"

Madison shared his fears; liberty-loving men should use ballots, not bullets. But then came the second incident. The defeated Shaysites *did* turn to ballots after their defeat. And by using ballots they won what bullets had not: they replaced an unpopular governor with a more populistic one and picked up seats in both houses of the legislature.

So a representative republic was not enough; people could make wrong decisions with their ballots, just as rulers could with their power. How to represent in the new republic people's instincts for liberty, justice, and order; how to suppress their tendencies to tyranny and disorder?

Here the Framers demonstrated their consummate talent for choosing the best among hard alternatives. Clearly they could not set up a system requiring complete consensus, Quaker-style, because as realists they knew that any system would be rife with conflict over domestic and foreign policy. Nor could they establish a two-thirds or three-fourths requirement for passing laws, for this would have allowed *minority* tyranny. The Framers had little regard or even knowledge about another method—direct governmental action by the people through plebiscites, referendums, straw votes, or the like. They would have had no use for "direct democracy" on a national level.

All this left one alternative—rule by popular majorities through elected representatives. It was an alternative the Framers both feared and considered natural—natural because rule by the majority seemed only fair and just, worrisome because majorities themselves might become unreasonable, overbearing, oppressive, unjust, selfish, turbulent, "leveling." So the Founders would not flatly adopt majority rule, nor could they reject it. Rather they would *refine* it by filtering majority impulses through institutional sieves that would screen out the follies and impurities and irrationalities and passions and leave a residue of calm, deliberate, seasoned wisdom, to be reflected in leaders very much like themselves.

Time was a key filter. If you required that a popular majority first win a majority in the House of Representatives, then wait two years before it could win the Senate and the executive, you might stall hasty action and allow popular passions to calm down. The Framers went further. They carefully divided up legislative, executive, and judicial power into little parcels and distributed these among the three federal branches, so that it was difficult for government to act unless these different types of officials could work together. Finally—and the consummate act of genius on the part of the Framers—the three branches and officials within were made to be chosen by, accountable to, and in some cases dismissable by, diverse, conflicting, and overlapping sets of voters, *so that conflict would be permanently built into government, action could be taken only slowly and reflectively, and a majority of the people could not easily "gang up" on the people's liberties.*

No one led in the adoption of this system with more intellectual creativity and political dexterity than James Madison, and no one defended it more tellingly later. The great security, he wrote in the fifty-first Federalist paper, "against a gradual concentration of the several powers in the same department, consists in giving to those who administer each department, the necessary constitutional means, and personal motives, to resist encroachments of the others. . . . Ambition must be made to counteract ambition. The interest of the man must be connected with the constitutional rights of the place. It may be a reflection on human nature, that such devices should be necessary to controul the abuses of government. But what is government itself but the greatest of all reflections on human nature? If men were angels, no government would be necessary. If angels were to govern men, neither external nor internal controuls on government would be necessary. In framing a government which is to be administered by men over men, the great difficulty lies in this: you must first enable the government to controul the governed; and in the next place oblige it to controul itself. A dependence on the people is no doubt the primary controul on the government; but experience has taught mankind the necessity of auxiliary precautions."

Thus Madison would not rely on what he called "parchment barriers" that passionate majorities and ambitious factions and officials might smash through. He founded his barriers in one of the most enduring motivations among humans—ambition—and he channeled the powerful effects of ambition through a marvelous system of sieves and conduits so that power in government would be fragmented, balanced, and defanged. It was an idea, with its Newtonian mechanisms and balances, that had a wonderfully old-fashioned ring to it, but one so well conceived intellectually, so superbly contrived mechanically, that two centuries later it stares out at us from the front page of almost every newspaper as we read of the clashing ideas and ambitions of senators, representatives, presidents, judges, and bureaucrats.

PITTING AMBITION AGAINST AMBITION

Amid this symphony of intellectual leadership there occurred an occasional cacophony, as though the great orchestra had lost its place in the music. The problem was the presidency. Three months after the convention began the delegates were "again at sea" over this matter, as one of them admitted. The delegates were weary by now, having sat day after day in their woolen suits during the stifling Philadelphia summer, with the windows of the State House closed against the noise and flies outside. The delegates had laid out the architecture of the new system, but the shape and power of the executive were still in controversy. That there would be an executive branch, headed by a "President," was not in question. But how would he be chosen? For how long a tenure? Could he seek another term? How would the executive branch be related to the legislative? How much of a legislative role should the President be granted? Could he be impeached? On what grounds? And would it be "he" or "they"?—some delegates preferred a plural executive. (A "she" was of course unimaginable to this stag convention.)

The Framers were at a loss in part because they lacked clear intellectual guidelines in this area. The great philosophers who had dealt with the profoundest questions of individual liberty, representation, legislative power, the authority of the state—men like Locke and Hobbes, Hume and Montesquieu—had left a mixed intellectual legacy on the issue of executive power in a republic. The delegates liked to cite Montesquieu on questions of executive power, but the French thinker based his views largely on observation of British institutions that were undergoing fundamental change. There was much pointing to the lessons of "history," but history as usual was ambiguous. Its main impact on the Founders was to instill a fear of the Catilines, Cromwells, and other power seekers of olden and newer times who had usurped power.

Nor was their wealth of experience of much help to the men of '87. The older men present had not only observed the laboratory experiments in colonial executive-legislative relationships; they had taken part in them. Almost all had helped run the Revolutionary or post-Revolutionary state governments; and indeed, at the moment the convention met, according to Clinton Rossiter, more than forty of the delegates "were lending their energies to keeping the state governments from foundering." For decades colonial executives had jousted with legislators, under their own checks-and-balance systems, but these were typically *royal* governors, certainly not representatives of the people. Later, most of the states had weak governors and strong legislatures, but the Framers drew few firm conclusions from these experiments aside from their general fear of executive impotence, a sharper fear of legislative aggrandizement, and a general opposition to excessive power in *any* part of the government, executive, legislative, or judicial.

In effect, the Fathers in 1787 had to experiment with the executive as part of their larger constitutional venture, to *invent* the presidency as part of their larger creation. And in Philadelphia they went about it like experimenters and inventors, trying out this idea and that on one another, tinkering here and there with tentative arrangements, putting the issue aside until they could get a better sense of the overall shape of things. For some weeks the fate of the executive branch sat ignominiously in a Committee on Postponed Matters. Slowly they put the presidency together. A plural executive? Here both experience and common sense served as guides. As practical men the Framers knew that executive vigor required a single head, and they had seen enough of quarreling privy councils to know how ineffective they could be. One man would doubtless take over anyway, as in Rome; when two men ride on a horse, Hobbes had warned, one must ride in front.

How select a President, and for how long a term? These were far tougher issues. The Virginia plan and other plans that dominated the early weeks of the convention all presumed that the executive would be chosen by the legislature. While this move in effect would have established a parliamentary system, the Framers did not have a clear model of such a system. Anyway, they were thinking far less of grand strategy here than of finding a handy method of choosing the chief executive. As the deliberations proceeded and as the convention moved toward a checks-and-balance strategy, the idea of election by Congress—which would have made the President a kind of prime minister or first executive—gave way to arguments for either direct or indirect election by the voters. "If the legislature elect," Gouverneur Morris said, "it will be the work of intrigue, of cabal, and of faction: it will be like the election of the Pope by a conclave of cardinals; real merit will rarely be title to the appointment."

In a republic a simple presidential plebiscite might have seemed appropriate, but though the Framers feared power in legislative or other institutional form, they feared it even more as a solid entity in the hands of the masses. Only a few delegates clearly favored direct popular election of the President. Under the checks-and-balance strategy—that is, a strategy of "giving to those who administer each department, the necessary constitutional means, and personal motives, to resist encroachments of the others"—the solution was to put the decision into the hands of locally chosen electors in the states—into the hands, that is, of an Electoral College. It was expected that after the first election of George Washington—who was viewed as both the man who would be President and the *kind* of man who should be President—the Electoral College would not be able to agree on a candidate; so the Framers prudently provided for a decision by the House of Representatives if no candidate won an Electoral College majority.

The Electoral College was a fine solution for those who worried about popular distempers. Clearly the kinds of electoral passions that quickly might manifest themselves in Congress (and in state governments) would have ample time for cooling and refining and softening before they could touch the chief magistracy.

Should a President be able to succeed himself? This question provoked almost precisely the same debate in the 1780s as it does in the 1980s. Would the incumbent try to keep his post through force, fraud, and foreign influence—as Thomas Jefferson feared about an office he described as a "bad edition of a Polish king"—or would the hope of re-election make the President more efficient, honest, faithful, and responsible? And why be *forced* to drop a successful incumbent in favor of a new man who would have to spend time learning the job? These arguments carried the day. As for length of term, this depended largely on the manner of selection and the issue of re-eligibility. If the President could succeed himself, a shorter term seemed desirable. When the convention tentatively voted for legislative selection and non-re-eligibility, it voted also for a seven-year term. Why seven years? I do not know; an electoral span of seven years seemed to have a mystical attraction for Americans in those days as it does for French people and others today. Eventually the Framers settled on a four-year term and re-eligibility as a safe compromise.

The question of the President's *legislative* power caused less conflict among the Framers because the balance-of-power guidelines were controlling—powers must be distributed among the different branches and levels of government, with their diverse and conflicting constituencies. Also, a ready compromise was available in the modified presidential veto—a negative that Congress could overcome with a two-thirds vote in each chamber—as against either an absolute veto or no veto at all. Putting the shoe on the other foot, the two-thirds requirement for Senate ratification of treaties negotiated by the executive was another way to balance executive and legislative power. So was impeachment, which brought the House, the Senate, and the President into another kind of balance, presumably one of conflict.

I have been laying out these issues in an orderly, linear fashion, but this is not how the Framers went about their job. They were playing a gigantic game of jackstraws; every time they added or withdrew a piece from the pile of interrelated issues, they affected the shape of the whole thing. Well-balanced, essentially stable but subtly shifting coalitions among the delegates gave way to new alignments as they moved the straws back and forth. Great issues and interests— hardly spoken but evident to all—dominated the proceedings: western lands, slavery, commerce, taxation, banking, regional claims. The only way the Framers could achieve decision was through a series of ideological, economic, and regional bargains; the convention was a continuing exercise in transactional leadership. But the final product of the Framers—and the hundreds of persons who continued to shape the Constitution—was an exercise in transforming leadership that, paradoxically, produced enormous problems and potentials for the years ahead.

THE TAMED JUNGLE AND THE ROGUE PRESIDENCY

Two hundred years later we can rate the Founders' work as the most creative and durable piece of political planning in the history of the Western world. The men of '87 built a new national government that would stand the tests of war and peace and civil strife for at least two centuries. They left enough authority in the hands of the states to permit a persisting experiment in federalism on a continent-wide basis. Above all, they felt, they had tamed the savage jungle of power and ambition through the ingenious device of morseling governmental authority and distributing it among political leaders who saw that their own ambitions could be realized best if they responded to the needs and demands of their diverse and conflicting constituencies. And since the Framers had pitted faction against faction, section against section, interest against interest, liberty would be safe from governmental and political tyranny.

This charter had not been brought down by a Moses, as from Mount Sinai; it was the product of a remarkably collective effort. The Framers of '87 served but as the cutting edge for the thousands of Americans who had precipitated and conducted the Revolution, created new state governments, established the Articles of Confederation, and permitted, though with some reluctance, the constitutional convention to be held. Moreover, as the delegates crafted the charter in Philadelphia, they had to be conscious of the hundreds of local, grass-roots activists who would pass judgment on their handiwork. It was the fear of state and local politicos that compelled the Framers to leave considerable authority in the hands of the states. And it was in response to indignant demands in state ratifying conventions that the Framers promised—as the price of gaining ratification of the new charter—that adopting a strong Bill of Rights would be the first order of business for the newly established Congress. When the first Congress did promptly vote through the necessary amendments, which were soon ratified by the necessary number of states, the Bill of Rights became probably the most collective act of leadership in the whole founding era.

It was well that constitution making did not cease when Washington, Madison, and the other delegates left Philadelphia at summer's end, since much more building remained to be done. One obvious gap in the Framers' work was the extent of the power of judicial review of laws passed under the Constitution. Who would have the awesome power to strike down a government policy or action because it violated the Constitution? The executive and legislative branches could hardly be expected to pass neutrally on laws they had framed; besides, they were directly or indirectly elected by the people. The judiciary was the obvious place for judicial review. The judges were not implicated in the passage of legislation; they were removed from the passions and follies of the voters; they could act slowly and deliberately.

Few of the Framers doubted that the judiciary should exercise this kind of power; the major question was the extent of this authority. Clearly the judges should have the power to void actions that threatened their own independence; this was basic to the doctrine of separation of powers. Surely they should help define the dividing line between proper national and state action; who better could serve as the "umpire of federalism"? But could the Supreme Court strike down *policy* enactments passed by House and Senate and signed by the President? Or could it pass only on *procedural* aspects of national actions—that is, whether the laws had been properly legislated in Congress and administered in the departments.

How divided the Framers were over *substantive* judicial review was revealed in the struggle that broke out between Federalists and Republicans in the late 1790s over the reach of national authority. After Congress passed the Alien and Sedition Acts—precisely the kind of national assault on liberty that many anti-Federalists had feared—the Virginia and Kentucky legislatures declared the Acts unconstitutional. The Virginia resolutions even contended that states had the right and duty to "interpose" the execution of the evil Acts. Thus within a decade of the adoption of the Constitution two states, under the leadership of Jefferson and Madison themselves, were claiming that state legislatures, not the Supreme Court, should be the ultimate authority on the constitutionality of national legislation. Who then was the umpire?

Only a masterful leader could have pulled victory out of these troubled waters; such a leader was John Marshall. Not even a member of the Constitutional Convention, he had become the fourth Chief Justice, a post then lacking great prestige. Left holding the Federalist barricades after the Republicans' sweeping victory of 1800, Marshall knew that he could not defy President Jefferson by declaring unconstitutional an act passed by a Republican Administration and Congress. The President could counterattack—Jefferson had both electoral and real troops—or simply ignore him. What Marshall could and did was to wait for the opportunity to pass on an act of Congress that dealt with the court's own authority. He had not long to wait; in *Marbury* v. *Madison* he and his court ruled that a congressional action *granting* a certain limited power to the court was invalid. Jefferson was helpless; there was nothing he could do about the court's *self*-denial. But *Marbury,* ticking away quietly in the court's arsenal of precedents for decades, became the vital precedent for the court's voiding of a *substantive* act of Congress, in the Dred Scott case, which became in turn precedent for an even greater reach of judicial power in the next century.

Clearly the Framers had left a huge ambiguity in the Constitution's elaborate distribution of power. But even this vagueness dwindles in size and importance compared to the ambiguity over presidential power. The relatively brief treatment of the executive power in the second article of the Constitution, compared to the elaborate laying out of congressional power in the first article, symbolized the Framers' willingness to allow presidential power to respond to the play of events. And this it has done.

The President's stated veto power—so typical of the Framers' cunning in scrambling authority—left open some of the same questions unresolved in the delineation of the Supreme Court's unstated veto power. Did the President have the right to veto an act of Congress only to protect his own authority under the Constitution? Few would have questioned that right. Might he veto a bill that in his view violated the Constitution in a more general way? Some Founders would have said no. Did he have the right to veto on *policy* grounds? The Framers would have been quite divided on this matter, for it went to the heart of the whole issue of separation of powers and checks and balances. But the issue was left to Presidents to decide as they went along. Washington vetoed bills on both the second and third grounds above, but neither his Federalist successor, John Adams, nor Adams' Republican successor, Thomas Jefferson, vetoed a single bill on *any* grounds. Just when it seemed that the veto power might succumb to innocuous desuetude along came Andrew Jackson to veto policy bills left and right. And once the policy veto came to be accepted as a routine exercise of presidential authority, the *threat* of veto became another source of major—but ambiguous and unpredictable—presidential power.

It was in the fields of military and foreign policy, however, that presidential power was left most undefined—and most portentous. It was obvious, of course, that the executive must have extensive authority in these areas; that's what kings, prime ministers, and presidents were for. The great John Locke himself, as well as other political philosophers to whom the Founders had gone to school, argued for "Prerogative" empowering executives to cope with accidents and crises. Acutely aware, however, of the long record of kings and others who had plunged their nations into war without popular or legislative consent, the Framers tried to hedge in presidential war-making power as closely as possible. They proposed to grant him power to respond to surprise attack but deny him power to make war.

In that day as this, though, it was almost impossible to draw the line. Leaving the issue unresolved, the Framers took some comfort in the impeachment power of Congress. But this was chimerical too, for the Framers limited the basis of impeachment to "Treason, Bribery, or other High Crimes or Misdemeanors." Was it a "high crime" for a President to make war when he felt this was necessary to preserve the nation?

The chief executive's foreign-policy authority also was left unclear. That the vital treaty making was placed in the hands of both President and Senate was one more evidence of Madison's "partial mixture of powers" so necessary, in his view, to maintaining a "free government." Arthur Schlesinger, Jr., listed other matters on which the Constitution was simply silent: "among them, the recognition of foreign governments, the authority to proclaim neutrality, the role of executive agreements, the control of information essential to intelligent decision." The result, as he quotes Edward Corwin, was to make the Constitution "an invitation to struggle for the privilege of directing American foreign policy."

That invitation was accepted by Presidents, senators, congressmen, judges, bureaucrats, diplomats, scholars. Commenting on Macaulay's taunt, "Your Constitution, sir, is all sail and no anchor," Louis Henkin wrote that the real trouble was that from the beginning the "compromises, irresolutions, oversights, and intentional silences of the Constitution left it unclear who had sail and who had rudder, and, most important, where is command." Perhaps the profoundest problem of all, however, was that the Constitution provided an anchor for the Congress and a sail for the presidency. As the years passed, Presidents carved out huge areas of legislative as well as executive authority. Through a vast use of executive orders, they circumvented part of Congress's law-making power; through an extensive resort to executive agreements, which had the same force as treaties, they circumvented much of the Senate's foreign-policy-making power. And Presidents could make war, as Polk did in Mexico, pressuring Congress later into recognizing a state of hostilities.

It would take many pages to list the steps toward presidential foreign-policy and war-making aggrandizement even during the first seventy-five years after the drafting of the Constitution. Presidents seized almost full control of the conduct of diplomacy, tightened control over the sending of information to Congress, conducted numerous military operations against whiskey rebels, Indians, slave traders, smugglers, and the like without asking formal congressional authorization. Under presidential authority (usually), the Navy put down foreign brigands and upstart natives said to be harassing or endangering Americans in Africa and the Pacific. The acme of presidential power was reached under Abraham Lincoln, who as a young Whig had attacked presidential war making. During the early months of the Civil War, Lincoln put off convoking Congress while he expanded the armed forces, suspended *habeas corpus,* spent public funds, established a naval blockade of Confederate ports, and took numerous other actions without congressional appropriations or authorizations.

The problem was not that the presidency had become irresponsible or uncontrollable as an institution. Many Presidents behaved in just the manner the Framers had wanted and expected. George Washington was the very model of the President as vigorous executive but deferential to Congress, the chief magistrate who lent wisdom and experience and dignity to the councils of state, the ceremonial chief of state who liked to proceed through the capital in a glistening coach-and-four, with outriders flanking him. Jefferson took a broad initiative in acquiring Louisiana, but he brought Congress fully into the authorizing and appropriating process.

The problem was that in the midst of this new system with its exquisitely balanced powers, the Framers had created—or allowed to rise—an office that might not always be filled by benign supporters of the checks and balances. In the midst of a garden dominated by far-seeing lions and dexterous foxes, the Framers—and their successors—left open the possibility of a "rogue elephant" foraging on turf belonging to others and perhaps tearing it up. Much would depend on Presidents being able to build an independent political base of their own, and this is precisely what most Presidents did, after the Electoral College became an agency for ratifying a mass electoral decision rather than an independent entity.

Just as the Founders overly liberated presidential leadership, so they overly inhibited congressional. To move bills through Congress, legislative leaders had to win a majority vote from representatives elected a year or two before in small districts that typically forced them to take parochial positions in Washington. The leadership then had to gain a majority of senators, who had been elected at varying points during the last five or six years, together grossly overrepresented the less populated states, and loved and exploited the Senate tradition of individual senatorial independence. The leadership then had to adjust Senate-House differences in measures, which then had to run the gauntlet of possible presidential veto and judicial overturn. Since the states had essentially the same separation of powers and checks and balances—until Nebraska adopted its unicameral legislature many years later—leadership at the state level, and usually at the local level, faced similar difficulties.

The overall result was to cultivate leaders of a particular kind. Since the various decision makers were entrenched in their diverse and conflicting constituencies, there was no easy way to bring the leaders together, except perhaps in time of crisis. The only way leaders could produce results from the system was through a knack for endless negotiating, bargaining, accommodating, and brokerage. The men who made their way up through the leadership opportunity structure were those who learned to be "practical," "realistic," or—a word that became popular much later—"pragmatic." "Practicality" of course turned out often to be impractical, and "realism" unrealistic, but there was no other way. Transactional leaders thrived in this environment.

Except for one person—the President, the politician-in-chief. Presidents too had to be brokers in order to work with legislators, bureaucrats, and judges, but as a result of their prestige, visibility, nationwide power base, and enormous, undefined constitutional and other resources, they could rise above the level of transactional leadership to that of transformational. Two systems of government seemed to exist side by side in Washington. One had infinite tendencies toward gradualism, delay, compromise, deadlock, the other toward decision, action, miscalculation, and catastrophe. Thus the original source of leadership failures, as well as leadership potential, lies in the tendencies built into the system constitutionally toward an oscillation between stasis and spasm.

THE PATH NOT TAKEN

Europeans were perplexed by the hybrid American system of leadership. Envoys to Washington reported back that they had met important officials but could not find a government. Most of the parliamentary systems they knew seemed simpler: a supreme or symbolic executive, who might be king or president; a legislature, more or less representative; a Cabinet to unite legislature and executive; and a prime minister to serve as political and executive leader. Moreover, most Western democracies were unitary systems—that is, the central government in London or Paris or elsewhere was constitutionally supreme over regional and local governments. A central government of delegated powers, with reserved powers remaining with the "sovereign states," was a system that Europeans associated principally with small confederacies.

The British system was the great model for Western Europe, even when the other parliamentary systems renounced royal authority. In something more than a fit of absentmindedness, but without the concentrated political leadership and planning that characterized the founding era in the United States, Englishmen had built, piece by piece and century after century, the essentials of a parliamentary democracy, though far from a complete or perfect one. During the seventeenth century one British king lost his head and another his throne while Englishmen fought to assert parliamentary authority. The eighteenth century was a time of Cabinet building, as kings and queens, now tamed, learned the advisability of choosing their advisers from Parliament, especially from parliamentary majorities. During the nineteenth century, parties were built and the electorate expanded, creating a democratic base for the apparatus of Parliament and party. During the twentieth, the House of Lords was converted from a relatively strong upper chamber to a relatively weak legislative body.

The result was a system that gave tremendous scope to leadership—whether the Cabinet leadership of a Robert Walpole in the 1720s and 1730s, the party and parliamentary leadership of Disraeli and Gladstone in the Victorian era, or the policy leadership of David Lloyd George, Winston Churchill, Clement Attlee, and Margaret Thatcher in this century. Once a parliamentary leader commanded a majority in the House of Commons, he (or she) could expect to be made prime minister by the king; after which he would appoint his Cabinet, present his financial and other programs to the House, and expect them to be voted through. Prime minister, foreign minister, and Cabinet were given special leeway in foreign policy. But leadership was held accountable, through the strenuous question period in the House, the need to mobilize parliamentary majorities on major bills, and ultimately the obligation to hold the confidence of an electoral majority and of the nation as a whole.

By mid-nineteenth century, nations choosing constitutional and political systems had two leadership "models" to choose from, the British system of unified powers, the American system of divided. The French were in a position to make an informed choice in 1870. In the past century they had experimented with absolute monarchy, bourgeois revolution, left-wing terror, a five-man Directory, a dictator—Napoleon—arising out of that Directory, an Empire under Bonaparte, a restored monarchy after his overthrow, a constitutional monarchy under the "citizen king" Louis Philippe, a Second Republic after his dethronement, and a Second Empire under Louis Napoleon. Divided though they were over many constitutional questions, the Frenchmen who established the Third Republic after Louis Napoleon's overthrow seemed to have little hesitation in choosing the parliamentary model. A Chamber of Deputies would be chosen by universal suffrage and a Senate indirectly by elected officials. The premier and other ministers would be collectively responsible to the Chamber and the Senate. With the consent of the Senate, the President of the Republic could dissolve the Chamber of Deputies before its four-year term expired. As in Britain, the Cabinet or ministry must keep the confidence of Parliament, or both would shortly have to face the voters together. Thus France rejected the American model in favor of the British, just as Americans had earlier rejected the British model in favor of its own unique arrangements.

Decade after decade foreign leaders and publics rejected the American presidential-congressional-judicial checks-and-balance system in favor of the unified Cabinet-parliamentary system. "Rarely has an attempt been made to adopt the American system in its entirety," concluded the noted political scientist Carl J. Friedrich. Was there a message in this for Americans?

FIVE

The Rise and Fall
of Party Leadership

Some eight weeks after the Constitutional Convention adjourned, James Madison sat down in his Manhattan lodgings to write a newspaper essay on the most formidable question the Founders had confronted. In a political system devoted to the goal and ideal of liberty, and operated by the processes and standards of liberty, how could factional leaders act freely as representatives of conflicting interests without producing "instability, injustice and confusion"—the "mortal diseases under which popular governments have everywhere perished"? One method—removing the causes by "destroying the liberty which is essential to its existence"—he rejected out of hand. It would not be a "less folly to abolish liberty, which is essential to political life, because it nourishes faction, than it would be to wish the annihilation of air, which is essential to animal life, because it imparts to fire its destructive agency."

So what could be done to curb the "mischiefs of faction"? The problem would not disappear under the new republic, for the "latent causes of faction" were "sown in the nature of man." A zeal for political and religious ideas, "an attachment to different leaders ambitiously contending for pre-eminence and power," above all conflicting economic interests—especially between those who held and those who did not hold property—involved faction in the operations of government.

Nor would Madison comfort himself with the pious thought that good men would adjust the clashing interests for the public good. "Enlightened statesmen will not always be at the helm," he wrote in the essay, which would become the most famous of Federalist papers, the

120

tenth. The *causes* of faction could not be removed in a free society, he concluded: the solution was to control their *effects*.

Madison especially feared leaders of popular majorities who might arouse hosts of poor people with a "rage for paper money, for an abolition of debts, for an equal division of property, or for any other improper or wicked project." He feared minority factions too, but after all, the minority could always be outvoted by the majority. But who or what would control majority rulers in a representative republic? Again and again in this essay he returned to his main concern—demagogic and even despotic leaders who might mobilize debtors, the propertyless, the small taxpayer eager to shift his burden to the rich and to trample on the rights of property. And he began to develop his strategic solutions—to "refine and enlarge" popular views and passions by "passing them through the medium of a chosen body of citizens"; "extend the sphere" of the republic and devitalize every strong faction by placing it among a "greater variety of parties and interests"; above all, to separate power among diverse leaders responding to diverse and conflicting interests.

By the time Madison had finished writing this three-thousand-word newspaper column and sent it off to the *Daily Advertiser,* he had achieved an act of both moral and intellectual leadership. Moral, because he refused to subordinate his ideal of liberty to the political system he favored; rather he advanced ends to which he adapted his means. Intellectual, because he had brilliantly analyzed the human, or psychological, underpinnings of factional leadership, and had begun to lay out the grand solutions that he would complete ten weeks later in what would become the fifty-first Federalist paper.

FISSION OR FUSION?

One effect of the new constitution was to inhibit the rise of strong political parties. Whether the Framers were diabolically clever in their anti-party strategy or whether they frustrated parties merely as part of their broader effort against factions in general, the effect was the same—radically to alter the balance of fission and fusion in American politics. And if the Framers were masterly and farsighted in their constitutional strategy, within a few years they would find their party strategy in ruins.

That the Founders feared and loathed something called party is not in doubt. This feeling emerged partly from their English heritage, from their reading in the political violence that had racked the mother country. "Conspiracy and rebellion, treason and plot," according to J. H. Plumb, "were a part of the history and experience of at least three generations of Englishmen." David Hume, a thinker who had a marked influence on American leaders (especially Madison), wrote of "Parties in General" that the "founders of sects and factions" ought to be "detested and hated." When men acted in factions, he said, they were apt "to neglect all ties of honour and morality, in order to serve their party." Yet he reluctantly accepted parties under a free government. It was not always clear whether English thinkers loathed both faction and party or just party. For some party was simply a big, bad faction. "Faction is to party what the superlative is to the positive," wrote Bolingbroke; "party is a political evil, and faction is the worst of all parties."

American leaders inherited both the sentiments and the confusion. Parties, wrote John Adams in his earlier years, "wrought an entire metamorphosis of the human character. [They] destroyed all sense and understanding, all equity and humanity, all memory and regard to truth, all virtue, honor, decorum, and veracity." Years later he was still railing against people drinking and conspiring in smoke-filled rooms. The Founders feared that parties would spawn disunity, ignore the interest of the whole for the sake of the part, arouse base emotions among members and supporters, lead to greedy, brutish behavior, reward cunning, and ultimately produce disorder and tyranny.

Yet it was never clear in the American setting where factions left off and parties began. Americans feared parties in part because they *were* larger; factions could be controlled through elaborate institutional arrangements, like those embodied in the Constitution, while parties seemed likely to heat up popular passions rather than refine and soften them. Indeed, by establishing a new national government, the Founders had themselves created hundreds of new factions surrounding the legislative, executive, and judicial positions newly created under the Constitution. Around each of these positions—even lowly ones like postmasterships—there would spring up little circles of influence, perhaps consisting only of the incumbent, his friends, his family, and tiny bands of supporters, and of another set of persons trying to take his place. Some of these personally led factions would be immense, of nationwide scope, as Presidents and presidential contenders organized their followings.

The dividing line between faction and party evidently was not so much size as it was content or character. What the Founders feared above all, as we have noted, was a popular, egalitarian movement led by a "demagogue" who might get control of government and threaten people's liberty and property, as many a firebrand had done in history. They knew that conflict was inevitable—had they not set up a system that pitted leader against leader?—but they wanted it to be conflict among respectable leaders, not rabble-rousers. They knew that leadership was inevitable and even desirable, but they wanted it to be a leadership by gentlemen like themselves. The Framers have been accused of being elitist, and they were, but they were as concerned about how government operated as about what government would do.

Not one of the Founders came up with a theory of party—of fusion—that rivaled their theory of diffusion and checks and balances. In England, as Hofstadter noted, Edmund Burke "went beyond Hume's acceptance of party as a necessary evil to defend it as a necessary good," and in the most sophisticated terms, but there was no American Burke, at least among the top leadership cadres. Significantly, the Americans during the eighteenth century who had some comprehension of the role of parties in a republic tended to be obscure writers and politicos. A *New York Gazette* writer argued that parties served as a check on one another and thus served to protect "public liberty." Others made the same point in newspapers and at the state ratifying conventions in 1787–1788. "The object of a free and wise people should be so to balance parties," declared a Maryland anti-Federalist, "that *from the weakness of all you may be governed by the moderation of the combined judgments of the whole, not tyrannized over by the blind passions of a few individuals.*" No one could have made the point better than this Marylander—especially in the words he emphasized—but nobody of importance seemed to be listening.

It would be easy for us to jump to the next logical step—that the elitist Founders had conceived a system to break and control the power of big factions, especially majorities, and hence to prevent leaders of the masses from gaining control of government for egalitarian purposes. It would seem reasonable to assume that popular or demagogic leaders were hoping to build a unified nationwide party able to articulate popular needs, unite government behind clear and comprehensive goals, and produce government policies and programs for the benefit of the masses. But history is not always "logical." The nonelites were often as fuzzy about the relation of party and faction as were the elites. Far more important, the populist leaders saw government not as a means of collective action and self-betterment but as a threat to their liberties. Like the elites, they wanted to get government off their backs.

If neither elites nor masses wanted political parties, how did parties get started? Reluctantly, cautiously, by the "first cadre" of national leaders in Congress and the Administration. Gropingly, enthusiastically, by a "third cadre" of local activists and grass-roots leaders. The first cadre built from the top down, the third from the bottom up; a second cadre of local politicians, organizing mainly around state goals, played an indeterminate role.

It was a paradoxical situation in the nation's capital—men like Hamilton and Adams and Jefferson and Madison, who had unanimously condemned parties, reaching out for party support only a few years after the new government got under way. National party formations first developed in Congress, as Federalists and Republicans divided over Hamilton's economic policies, over John Jay's controversial treaty with Britain, over the proper stance toward revolutionary France, and over the burning issues of states' rights, tax and spending policies. The first national party was the Republican Party in Congress, headed by Madison, organized around Republican members of Congress and candidates for Congress, disciplined in formal and informal caucuses, reaching out to embrace networks of second- and third-cadre activists in the states and districts. The Republican thrust naturally produced some counterorganization on the part of Hamilton and his followers. In the capital each party had its own press, headed by the Federalists' *Gazette of the United States* under John Fenno and by the Republicans' *National Gazette* under Philip Freneau.

Party formations were developing at the grass roots too. As anti-Federalist feeling intensified throughout the country, especially during the euphoria of the early 1790s over the French Revolution, a score or so of Democratic or Republican societies sprang up in Pennsylvania and most of the other states. These societies often met in taverns and other low places; they were composed of county politicians, mechanics, country yeomen, tavern keepers, lawyers, local newspaper editors, but they were by no means mass organizations. Local party leaders denounced Washington's and Hamilton's economic and foreign policies; the President and his treasury secretary considered them dangerous and even diabolical.

The national and local leaders of the party "hooked in" with each other enough to strengthen their mutual effort against the common party foe. But the two levels, national and local, never meshed enough to create a party system or durable party structure. The politics of the 1790s was still largely a politics of deference, family-centered, clientele-oriented, patronage-motivated, a politics of aristocratic families, local elites, patron-client dependency. The principal difficulty was still intellectual. The elites of the day, however much they might *practice* party politics, considered it not wholly legitimate and even morally tainted.

Once again it was the third cadre of local activists who went about the business of building political societies that could provide a political base for national politicians. One of them, a tavern keeper named William Manning in a small town north of Boston, even wrote a tract calling for a national society—in effect an organized national party—to fight for the rights of the poor against the entrenched upper-class power of merchants, lawyers, ministers, and doctors. Organized on a town, county, state, national, and even international basis, the new movement would mass its power at the polls against the elite. The "ondly Remidy" against existing evils, Manning wrote, "is by improveing our Rights as freemen in elections."

But the national leaders did not hear such voices; indeed, Manning's was silenced, for the editor of the Boston newspaper to which he sent his tract was arraigned for seditious libel under the Sedition Act and died before his trial. Still, the national party leaders accomplished one momentous feat—a change of regimes without civil war or bloodshed.

Today, looking back, it seems wholly natural that one party would give way to another as part of the natural alternation of the ins and the outs. But if we recall the fateful experience of new nations created in the twentieth century—the seizure of power by revolutionaries of the right or left, their equation of their own rule with patriotism and virtue, their view of the new opposition as not simply opposing a party in power but as attacking the nation itself, and their suppression of that opposition as disloyal, diabolical, traitorous—we are reminded how difficult it is for many peoples to accept the concept of the "loyal opposition." And if we think our way back into the environment of the 1790s, we will see that Americans came closer than has generally been recognized to sharing the one-party destinations of more recent revolutionary movements.

Political conflict had been subdued during the early 1790s under the benign and magisterial rule of George Washington and in the absence of deep and bitter class conflict. As controversy heated up over foreign and economic issues during mid-decade, however, the Federalist and anti-Federalist factions hardened in their opposition to each other. Consensus disintegrated during Washington's second term—a development that helps explain Washington's bitter remarks about the "baneful effects of the Spirit of Party, generally." All combinations against the execution of the laws and the "deliberation and action" of the constituted authorities, said the old general, "serve to organize faction and give it an artificial and extraordinary force; to put, in the place of the delegated will of the Nation, the will of a party; often a small but artful and enterprizing minority of the community; and . . . to make the public administration the mirror of the ill-concerted and incongruous projects of faction, rather than the organ of consistent and wholesome plans digested by common councils, and modefied by mutual interests."

Federalist and Republican feelings rose to white heat during John Adams' presidency. Federalists tried to stifle dissent through the Alien and Sedition Acts. Republicans responded with talk of interposition and even secession. Some leaders must have wondered whether a presidential election would even take place in 1800, or at least must have feared that the outcome had been predetermined by the Administration. But the holding of the election was never really in doubt. Despite the fierceness of their rhetoric, essentially moderate and responsible men headed both parties. Increasingly they were embracing the notion that the answer to the "tyranny" of an Administration or the "treachery" of an opposition was neither secession nor suppression, but to fight the question out at the polls.

When the Jefferson Republicans bested the Adams Federalists in the election of 1800, again some wondered whether the "ins" would allow themselves to be ousted by the "outs," but again the matter was never in real doubt. John Adams knew how to take a licking. That Americans were not immune to the possibility of settling issues by force was indicated, however, when Jefferson and his Republican running mate, Aaron Burr, won the same number of electoral votes, and Federalists had enough leverage in the House of Representatives to throw the election to either man. As balloting and jockeying continued over an anxious twelve weeks, and as tempers and fears rose during the deadlock, Republicans talked of bringing in state militias from Virginia and Pennsylvania if the Federalists persisted in balking the public will. Only an ingenious, last-minute compromise, giving the election to Jefferson but enabling the Federalists to save face, averted a grave crisis.

Clearly 1800 was the most critical year in the early history of the new republic, both because the Republicans took over, ending twelve years of Federalist hegemony, and even more, because a *party opposition* took over. Americans seemed to have mastered the crucial art of shifting power from ins to outs without violence. They had dramatized another crucial liberty—the liberty of the opposition to oppose, to survive, to win, to govern. Not only was this a signal to the world; it was a signal to future opposition party leaders at home that they did not need to indulge in coups or flirt with violence, but rather could and should appeal to future electoral majorities.

The events of 1800, moreover, legitimated a whole new vocation of leadership at home—that of the responsible opposition party leader. Thus it became a priceless source and sustenance of an essential element of American leadership. But the leaders coming into power would have to work within the structure of fragmented power and checks and balances, which raised the question of whether the alternation of ins and outs in America would be as clear-cut, representative, responsible, and democratic as would be the case in some parliamentary systems abroad.

The thrust of party rule, party opposition, party alternation was toward the fusion of leadership, just as the thrust of checks and balances was toward its diffusion, or fission. Party strategy would require leaders at all levels to band together in factions big enough and organized enough to bid for electoral majorities—that is, in parties. The checks-and-balance strategy, its supporters contended, made for balance and moderation, for representative and responsible government, because leaders of factions and constituencies would have to broker their differences and arrive at a responsible consensus. What could be claimed for party strategy?

In the first place, party defenders answered, each party would monitor the other. Jefferson, who increasingly during the 1790s came around to comprehending the role of the party, noted that "in every free and deliberating society, there must, from the nature of man, be opposite parties, and violent dissensions and discords; and one of these, for the most part, must prevail over the other for a longer or shorter time." He added: "Perhaps this party division is necessary to induce each to watch and relate to the people the proceedings of the other."

Party defenders—majoritarians—had another argument that was both more powerful and more subtle: that under a system of party ins and outs, opposing sets of party leaders would have to remain representative and responsible in order to appeal to the great middle elements that might hold the electoral balance of power in America. Significantly, the statement of this case was made best not by a celebrated national leader of the first cadre, but by a South Carolina congressman of the second, Robert Goodloe Harper. Two opposing parties struggling for power in government were like performers competing for a prize, Harper said. "The public is the judge, the two parties are the combatants, and that party which possesses power must employ it properly, must conduct the Government wisely, in order to insure public approbation and retain their power. In this contention, while the two parties draw different ways, a middle ground is produced generally conformable to public good."

PARTY LEADERSHIP—
THE VITAL BALANCE

Thomas Jefferson's inaugural address in March 1801 showed how far he and other political leaders had come in understanding the grand strategy of parties as well as the grand strategy of checks and balances. "Every difference of opinion is not a difference of principle," the new President said to the crowd straining to hear his low, flat delivery. "We have called, by different names, brethren of the same principle. We are all republicans; we are all federalists."

Having made his tribute to unity, he made one to liberty. "If there be any among us who wish to dissolve this union, or to change its republican form, let them stand undisturbed, as monuments of the safety with which error of opinion may be tolerated where reason is left free to combat it."

All Republicans and all Federalists! Some scoffed at the moderation promised by this alleged atheist and radical. Others assumed, on the other hand, that the new Administration would offer moderate, consensual, bipartisan government. Both views were wrong. Jefferson had no desire to work with the Federalists; rather he hoped and expected that the Federalist Party would die. He still thought of extreme Federalists as liars, slanderers, potential tyrants, witch burners. He had a far bolder strategy than simple cooperation with his party foes.

Rather, he would seek to draw moderate Federalists away from their conservative, "monarchical" leaders; to isolate and kill off High Federalists as a political force; to forge a new majority coalition of

Republicans and moderate Federalists behind his program and policies. Did Jefferson then want a one-party government, the tragic destiny of so many revolutionary movements? Not at all; he was too much a democrat and libertarian for that. What he hoped and expected was that a new opposition leadership would rise out of the ranks of the broadened Republican Party.

"We shall now be so strong that we shall split again," Jefferson said; "for freemen thinking differently and speaking and acting as they think, will form into classes of sentiment," but no party would take on the name Federalist, he said, for that party was discredited.

What Jefferson both foretold and favored, then, was two rival parties operating within the broad Republican stream, offering meaningful but not extreme alternatives to the voters, each uniting President and a majority of Congress in a common team effort. The majority party must not and would not become tyrannical or extremist, in part because civil liberty would prevail. "All, too, will bear in mind this sacred principle," he had said in his inaugural address, "that though the will of the majority is in all cases to prevail, that will, to be rightful, must be reasonable: that the Minority possess their equal rights. . . ." Even more, the majority party leadership would necessarily reflect so many diverse interests, sections, and attitudes, in a pluralistic society, that the majority must pursue a moderate and balanced program in order to stay in office or even to put through its policies.

Thus Jefferson in effect called for two sets of leaders: one of a majority cohesive enough to govern, the other of a minority strong enough to keep the rulers on their toes and to offer an attractive alternative program to the electorate. Certainly the President personified the first half of this proposition. The man who had proclaimed once that if he "could not go to heaven but with a party, I would not go there at all" became as President one of the most astute party leaders in American history. He chose a Republican Cabinet, headed by James Madison as secretary of state; for his appointments—"appointments and disappointments," he called them—he picked Republicans after sacking some Federalists; and he gave a fine demonstration of collective party leadership by sharing decision making with department heads. He also worked closely with congressional leaders, "embodying himself in the House," meeting with them often to discuss policy, analyze problems, and mobilize support among state party leaders. The fact that Jefferson did not veto a single congressional measure reflected not only his distaste for this kind of presidential authority but his close collaboration with congressional Republicans during the bill-writing process.

The party Jefferson headed was still mainly organized from the top down. It was not a mass party in the modern sense, with several cadres of leadership pyramiding up from an organized, grass-roots party membership, through county and state organizations to the national. Even in Washington, where the national government was now located, the Republican congressional party lacked formal party organization, such as regular caucuses and openly elected leadership. It was largely a personal and even elitist party, led by men who had long worked together, shared a broad ideology, and almost revered their leader in the White House. It was a party strong enough to support Jefferson in his purchase of Louisiana and other creative acts of statesmanship during most of his eight years in the presidency.

Despite Jefferson's hopes and predictions, however, the Federalist party did not rapidly die away, nor did the Republicans split into two parties. Old party leaders linger on; old party memories die hard; old party support persists in the electorate. Federalism did not receive its political deathblow until the leadership took the "unpatriotic" side of the War of 1812–1815. Lacking the kind of opposition that might have unified it, the Republican Party split not into halves but into fragments under Presidents Madison and James Monroe. The result was not an era of "good feelings," nor really of "one-partyism," but of a multitude of minority factions and small conflicts. It took years for a new minority party to pose a challenge to the dominant Democratic Republicans, more years before it was strong enough to win an election and take over the presidency. This was a time for transactional leadership and brokerage politics.

Great conflict makes for great leadership. A young French visitor, Alexis de Tocqueville, had observed in 1831 that America "swarms with lesser controversies"—but this was before Andrew Jackson's dramatic veto of the United States Bank recharter. That veto was a catalyst for countless Americans who could not follow high policy but could understand a political shoot-out between Nick Biddle and Andy Jackson. Jackson's emergence on the national scene and his controversial Administration coincided with a rising ferment among the populace. Women leaders were becoming conscious of female rights, especially to the ballot; labor unions were forming in the larger cities; religious fervor and disputes were intensifying; men and women were being swept up in reform, radical, communal, and millenarian movements. More people—including those with little or no property—were claiming and exercising the right to vote.

State and local parties were a natural vehicle for political action at the grass roots, since parties influenced nominations, handed out patronage, welcomed adherents, and took positions on major issues. America's enduring party system was built during the 1830s and 1840s, built mainly by local leaders and activists meeting in caucuses and taverns and smoke-filled rooms. Half consciously these local leaders "framed" what I have called a second, or "people's," constitution. Whereas the first constitution—that of 1787—was shaped by elitists and patricians, according to a clear intellectual concept and constitutional strategy, and under the most respectable and even celebrated sponsors such as Washington, the "party" constitution after Jefferson was framed by leaders of the second and third cadres, attacked by many of the more respectable persons of the day, and viewed as illegitimate if not subversive by the political Establishments of Washington and the state capitals.

Above all, the party constitution differed from the checks-and-balance constitution in its prime effort to supply teamwork and support collective leadership between the state and national levels of government and the three branches of each level of government. Thus vertical and horizontal party unity offset to some degree constitutional fragmentation between and within levels of government. The major expansion of party during the Jacksonian era occurred in the states, with New York serving as the bellwether. Down-state Virginians had taken the leadership in shaping the first constitution; upstate New Yorkers took the lead in shaping the second, or party, constitution.

And the man who took the lead in New York party building—and one of the most unsung heroes of American democracy—was the bland, inconspicuous-looking Martin Van Buren. With his fellow Bucktails, William Marcy, Azariah Flagg, Silas Wright, and others whose names hardly trip off the lips of American schoolchildren, Van Buren built what came to be known as the Albany Regency. This was a disciplined party organization in which leaders made collective decisions, members—legislators, bureaucrats, editors, and others—were expected when necessary to put loyalty to the Regency over individual advancement, and all joined ranks to establish a common front against the opposing party. These men acted on common, not always articulate, assumptions: that competition between two strong, disciplined parties was vital to democracy; that not the presence but the *absence* of parties would sap the foundations of liberty, especially freedom of press, association, and speech; that party spirit and interparty competition stimulated popular interest and participation; that a party system—a governing party monitored by an opposition party—served as a vital, extraconstitutional set of checks and balances.

As the New Yorkers and their counterparts in other states built their party organizations, they reached downward to recruit activists from the enlarging electorate, outward to join hands with fellow partisans in other counties and states, and upward to build national party organizations. The great instrument for deepening and broadening the party was the convention. Party caucuses, shaped during the era of deferential, exclusive politics, steadily gave way to more representative party gatherings made up of delegates chosen at the grass roots. These conclaves, with their rows of straw-hatted delegates, with their stentorian, spread-eagle speeches, earsplitting demonstrations, jubilant parades, and all the inevitable heat and stink, the nobility and dignity of democracy, became also the great, representative decision-making institution of the party, especially for nominations.

The crowning glory was the national convention. The Democrats staged their first national convention in 1832 in Baltimore, for the renomination of Andrew Jackson and, even more appropriately, the nomination of Martin Van Buren as his running mate.

Of the fierce hostility to Jackson and his "despotic" and "monarchical" ways a new party had been born, the Whigs. Taking their name and symbolism from the English who fought royal authority under the banner of liberty, the American Whigs developed their own party organization and nominated their own military hero in General William Henry Harrison, who defeated Van Buren in the turbulent "log-cabin" campaign of 1840. By the late 1830s, Americans had created a party *system,* with an impressive array of leaders in both great national organizations. Parties at the various governmental levels, from national to ward, were linked through a pyramid of local, county, and congressional-district conventions in turn sending delegates to state and national conclaves. Cadres of party leaders were active and organized at almost all levels, though varying widely in strength from state to state. Not only were the parties well balanced against each other nationally, but also in most of the states.

The essence of this system, and its justification, was an *active balance* between parties—a continuing, competitive, dynamic equilibrium between two mass-elected, cadre-led organizations competing with each other over policies, patronage, and principles as well as candidates. Under this system, the parties would offer voters meaning-ful alternatives; they would cleave toward the center in order to appeal to the great "middle elements" among the electorate, but not become so centrist as to alienate more ideologically minded voters ranging toward the end of the party spectrums. Each party would serve as a watchdog against the other, publicizing corruption and threats to the liberties of the people. Such a system called for leaders who were skillful party brokers but who were able also to transcend short-run political and personal interest and to demonstrate aggressive, creative, and even transforming leadership, in contrast to the enormous empha-sis on transactional leadership implicit in the constitutional system of fragmented power.

Party balance between the ins and the outs—so crucial to both the vitality and moderation of the second constitution—would seem to be so natural as to be self-maintaining. If the government party became bloated or top-heavy with support, you would expect, political loaves and fishes would have to be divided among a larger number of persons, some would feel cheated or left out, and some supporters would defect to the opposition, thus restoring the balance. Several circumstances, however, constantly threatened the two-party balance. Rapidly shifting economic, social, and military developments could shake the pendulum of parties so hard that the two-party balance might be upset for decades. The same forces might throw the party balance in the states out of harmony with that of the nation; for example, the parties might be evenly matched in Congress or in the presidential vote, but so imbalanced in some states as to give way to virtually a one-party system. And the 1787 Constitution, by pitting leader against leader, interest against interest, and agency against agency, tended to divide and unbalance the parties even as parties tried to unite the branches of government. It was possible for a party to win Congress but not the presidency, or one house of Congress but not the other, or governorships but not state legislatures.

Despite all these obstacles, during much of the late 1830s and 1840s, the Democrats led by Van Buren & Company, and Whigs led by the likes of Daniel Webster and Henry Clay, maintained a fine party competition, with the two sets of leadership alternating in power. The Whigs, however, never fully established themselves as a grass-roots organization with strong national-state-local linkages. Much of their philosophy was negative, rooted in anti-Jacksonianism. And they had bad luck; two generals they put up for the White House died there, and a third never got there at all. Would the demise of the Whigs in the early 1850s be followed by another long period of one-partyism and no-partyism, as occurred with the decline of the Federalists earlier? The Republicans answered this question by building a party strong enough to challenge the national Democracy in 1856 and to win the presidency with Abraham Lincoln four years later.

The Civil War was an even harsher threat to two-party balance. Lincoln formed an amorphous "Union Party" to bring sympathetic War Democrats over to the Administration, while the Democratic Party took on an unpatriotic odor as sympathizing with the South and secession. But so strong was the two-party tradition by now, and so entrenched the Democracy even in the North, that the Democrats mounted a powerful challenge to Lincoln during the war, carried the House of Representatives within a decade of war's end, almost won the presidency in 1876 in the famous disputed election between Hayes and Tilden, and did seize the White House with Grover Cleveland in 1884.

During the 1870s and 1880s, as the two parties achieved this dynamic electoral balance, leaders of both parties showed their talent for maintaining a strong two-party system despite intense and rapid changes in the social, economic, and political environment. Party leaders had to deal with an immense expansion of the electorate (almost doubling during this period); welcome, recruit, and assist millions of immigrants; hold third parties in check; cope with crusades of prohibitionists, woman suffragists, labor militants, reformers and radicals, Populists, currency reformers, and a host of other movements. Voter coalitions were highly stable during this period, Richard Jensen notes: "Normally fewer than 5 per cent of the voters changed parties between elections, or split their tickets to vote for candidates of different parties." The press continued to be partisan and polemical. People listened attentively to party orators who would spend an hour or so getting into the meat of politics, policies, and personalities. By the 1880s some presidential elections were drawing around 90 percent of the (white, male) electorate. Politics had become a mass sport.

It was, in many ways, a rather crass politics, occupied with economic issues like tariffs, fierce fights over patronage, old and new ways to make legal and illegal money. The two-party balance in presidential and congressional elections concealed a good deal of one-partyism in the states, as memories of old Civil War issues lingered on; both in the North and the South voters were urged to "vote as you shot." But on the whole, parties served a democratic, positive, and even creative role, recruiting candidates, mobilizing voters, unifying the efforts of legislators and administrators, and to some extent overcoming the constitutional fragmentation inherent in checks and balances and in federalism. Local parties often acted as service organizations, especially for immigrants and other poor city dwellers.

The machine, noted the English writer Denis Brogan, "gave some kind of coherence to a society in perpetual flux, in which even the natives were bewildered by the new problems of urban life in cities growing like the prophet's gourd." He listed the bosses' activities: providing quick naturalization, jobs, social services, access to authority, deference to ethnic pride, and charity in the form of coal and food, excursions and booze—charity, moreover, without lecturing or hectoring. The welfare services of the machine have doubtless been exaggerated—a lot of people were left out—but those services were triply important in an age without social security, minimum-wage legislation, or federal relief and welfare programs.

It was a grand age for local party leaders. Men could attend national, state, and county conventions and actually choose the party's nominees, amid great suspense and hijinks. Party leaders could directly or indirectly influence government policy, and if they were often no more pure of heart than Presidents or senators or other officeholders, at least the party leaders tended to think in terms of maintaining the standing of their party over the long run and not just winning the next election. Above all, party leaders were recruiters of people—of followers, voters, candidates, party lieutenants. In this respect the average district leader like George Washington Plunkitt was of far greater significance than the more publicized and venal Boss Tweeds. "There's only one way to hold a district," Plunkitt told a young reporter. "You must study human nature and act accordin'. You can't study human nature in books. Books is a hindrance more than anything else. . . .

"To learn real human nature you have to go among the people, see them and be seen. I know every man, woman, and child in the Fifteenth District, except them that's been born this summer—and I know some of them too. I know what they like and what they don't like, what they are strong at and what they are weak in, and I reach them by approachin' the right side." And Plunkitt described how he reached young people through his glee club and baseball club.

The enduring party system had been formed by average men and a few women working in the rural towns and city precincts. It had been maintained by grass-roots cadres of leadership that understood the wants and needs of the people around them. As the nation's elite celebrated the centennial of the formal Constitution in 1887 with pompous and self-congratulatory speeches, it seems unlikely that even ward leaders and county courthouse politicos stopped to realize that the second constitution was now half a century old. But as long as they maintained the vitality and popular participation and essential democracy of the party system, the two constitutions could work together in creative tension.

Then, in the 1890s, began a series of shocks that upset the party balance, disrupted the equilibrium between the two constitutions, and started the party system on a long slide toward impotence.

HOW TO DISMEMBER A PARTY

What triggers a massive political transformation? The upsetting of the party balance in 1896 probably had its roots in the economic and social disarray of Cleveland's second term—panic on Wall Street, spreading financial fear, industrial failures, soaring unemployment, widening strikes and violence. Farmers had been suffering for years from falling prices, tightening credit, high interest rates, and exploitation by shippers and wholesalers; now the economic crises brought long-simmering feelings to a boil. The political result was a crisis within the Democratic Party as the conservative Cleveland, who once had denied federal funds to send seed corn to Texas after a drought, refused now to take strong action in face of economic want, except of course on behalf of capital. The aroused populist and labor leadership in the Democracy struck back against Cleveland in 1896 with the nomination of William Jennings Bryan.

The candidacy of the Great Commoner precipitated the first ideological confrontation in American presidential politics for decades. Never mind that Bryan was a social conservative, anti-urban, anti-cosmopolitan, anti-immigrant. To the men who controlled the Republican Party Bryan was anathema—a threat to credit, capital, and Constitution. Bryan "would steal from the creditors of the nation half of what they saved," Theodore Roosevelt ranted. Republican newspapers labeled him an anarchist, assassin, revolutionary. At the same time the Republican nominee for president, William McKinley, showed a fine talent for coalition building as he united eastern and northern capital and agriculture and labor, Civil War veterans and

Negroes, Republican liberals and conservatives, against the populist threat from West and South.

The outcome was a vast imbalancing of the national two-party balance, as McKinley swept the North and East. The Republicans carried even the urban counties of New England and won every northern state east of the Mississippi. It was the lopsided state results that were crucial, for this was the most sectional of elections. Eighteen ninety-six brought not merely a shift of the pendulum, one that would swing the opposite direction in the next election. The pendulum would not shift for a long time. McKinley won again in 1900—the only man who could stop him was not a Democratic candidate but an anarchist with a gun—and Republicans Roosevelt and William Howard Taft came along to win the next two elections.

Thus the decade of the 1890s witnessed, in Paul Kleppner's summary, "an abrupt, massive, and durable shift in the competitive balance between the nation's major parties, ending two decades of partisan stalemate in which neither major party regularly commanded the allegiance of a majority of the nation's voters." This was not only more than a pendulum swing. It was more, even, than a realigning election, or realigning era, in which the long-term strategic relationships of parties are changed. The 1890s brought a *structural* or *institutional* change that profoundly affected the future of political parties and American politics in general. The 1890s elections were so sectional that the one-partyism in northern and southern states, which had long existed to some degree beneath the surface of national two-party politics, intensified and reacted back on national politics. State legislatures dramatically reflected the imbalance. For decades after '96 hardly more than a few Democrats made their way into the upper or lower houses of Vermont or Pennsylvania or Michigan; for decades only handfuls of Republicans could gain seats in the Alabama or South Carolina or other southern legislatures. And by the same token, northern delegations to Congress were heavily Republican, southern delegations even more heavily Democratic.

This was one-partyism with a vengeance, and meant that many states lacked a healthy, competitive party balance. And it had massive and enduring consequences. The health of the party system—its vitality and stability and justification—had lain in that party balance. Now, in state after state, one party could always expect to win, unless it nominated Caligula, and the other party could expect to lose, even if it nominated Cinderella. The pressure on party leaders to perform—to offer good candidates and programs, to govern wisely and compassionately—fell off. If you always would win, why make the effort? Or if you always would lose, why make the effort?

Party leaders, whether local bosses or national chairmen, had long been attacked in press and pulpit as venal, arbitrary, and incompetent. Party leadership had been strong and competitive enough to withstand these assaults. Now, after the turn of the century, political moralists and purists renewed their campaign, and now they had a far better case. What had happened to the opposition party as watchdog? they could ask. They painted lurid pictures of party bosses meeting in smoke-filled rooms and handing out nominations to henchmen who were entirely unfit for the offices they sought, but who would win because of one-party control. Middle-class moralists, most of them white Protestants, had long detested the vulgar, lower-class types who ran the parties at the grass roots. Often they found themselves at the polls choosing between unsavory types from both parties. Now they seemed vindicated.

How combat the heightened corruption, incompetence, and autocracy in party? Middle-class reformers had the solution: more democracy, participation, and representation within the parties. And they had the devices—the initiative, referendum and recall, and direct primary—that could purify and democratize the government. Civil Service reform was another means of striking at boss control.

The primary was by far the most powerful of these reforms, for it struck at the heart of party power, the nominating process. The essence of the role of party leader had been his influence over the choosing of party nominees. The unique role of party had always been its control of nominating; interest groups, reform organizations, mass movements, could affect the outcome of elections, but they did not have that precious and unique authority, safeguarded by state law, actually to put the names of nominees on ballots. In the early years of the new century, state after state, responding to the iniquities of boss-controlled conventions in particular and to the moral force of progressive, middle-class reformers and "muckrakers" in general, adopted party primaries, along with the initiative and referendum and recall. These reformers were protesting against the party "machine" that had allegedly monopolized politics just as they had turned against the corporate machines that had allegedly monopolized meat packing, utilities ("Trusts"), steel, and oil.

The revolt against party leadership—not just against the Democratic or Republican party leadership but against *party leadership as such*—manifested itself most dramatically in Congress. In the House of Representatives, Speaker Joseph G. Cannon had been acting virtually like a prime minister, controlling the order of business, committee and chairmanship appointments, procedure on the floor, until he was challenged by a young insurgent, George W. Norris, and stripped of much of his power. In the Senate, Robert La Follette of Wisconsin led the fight against "Aldrichism"—Old Guard control of the upper chamber by Senator Nelson Aldrich of Rhode Island and his cronies. La Follette was less successful than Norris, but reformers' and liberals' indignation over the conservative Senate oligarchy helped lead to passage of the 17th Amendment, shifting election of senators out of state legislatures and placing it directly in the hands of the voters. Perhaps it was fitting that the place where national parties were first established—in Congress—was the place where the start of their decline was first evident.

It was in state and congressional politics, though, that the disintegration of party leadership was most evident. There the direct primary fundamentally altered the relationship among party leaders, party nominees, and voters in ways that on balance continued to cripple parties not only in their nominating role but in other functions. Much has been made of the decline of local parties as service and welfare organizations—a result, it is said, of the rise of the New Deal welfare state. But that decline was probably as much a result of parties' earlier organizational erosion as a cause of it. Party "bosses" were able to extract services for their people (and boodle for themselves) out of government because they had held a central role in the "hiring and firing" of city officials. Once they lost their candidate-choosing power, much of their clout was gone.

The rise of "direct democracy" and the decline of party were not dramatic. These alterations in the political system, moreover, proceeded at an uneven pace from state to state. California, under Hiram Johnson and other progressives, took the lead in dismantling the state parties, not only by establishing primaries but also by making city and county elective posts nonpartisan, introducing cross-filing (through which candidates could run for more than one party's nomination), and discouraging straight-party voting. New York, on the other hand, retained significant party conventions and machinery, which for a time heavily influenced even primary outcomes. Hence it was not wholly surprising that New York continued to produce strong state party leaders—Democrats like Al Smith, Franklin D. Roosevelt, Senators Herbert Lehman and Robert Wagner, Republicans like Henry Stimson, Charles Evans Hughes, Thomas E. Dewey, and Nelson

Rockefeller. Most of these men, whatever their individual strengths and failings, had a sense of the need for collective leadership, teamwork, and responsibility.

As the collective leadership of party declined, the individual leadership of candidates and officeholders flourished. As parties came to be less effective in furnishing votes and political money to their nominees, office seekers increasingly built their own personal organizations independent of party. A spiral of weakness developed as individual politicians grew increasingly dependent on their own political resources, with parties increasingly cut off from those resources. More and more politicians played King of the Rock as five or ten or more aspirants plunged into primaries, fought for money and publicity, and won or lost on their own, while the party leadership stood by passively, forced to be neutral.

All this had crucial implications for government; it meant that officeholders responded more to diverse and shifting constellations of money givers, organized interests, single-issue groups, and ideological movements than to party programs, interests, and memberships. Teamwork among officeholders, unity across branches of government, collective responsibility and accountability—all these suffered. As the force of the party constitution dwindled, the problems of the first Constitution intensified.

Perhaps the oddest aspect of the wasting away of parties was the general unawareness of it. Enfeeblement seemed to proceed in the dark. State party leaders grumbled privately about their frustrations but took no significant action, issued no summons to arms or even call for help. National party chieftains basked in the limelight and enjoyed their status, even while the power of the national party chairman dwindled dramatically from the time that a Mark Hanna could talk with Presidents almost as an equal. A group of academics in the American Political Science Association warned of party fragmentation and put forth a powerful case for a more responsible party system. Headed by a scholar-practitioner, E. E. Schattschneider of Wesleyan, whose fundamental premise was that "political parties created democracy" and were indispensable to it, the political scientists suggested some significant institutional changes, but neither press nor public nor politicians were listening, many scholars opposed the proposals, and the Schattschneider committee recommendations, controversial though they were within academia, fell short of the drastic remedies that seemed increasingly necessary to cure parties of their debilitation.

Once again, as in the 1890s and after, it was a condition of intense social and political conflict that reopened the whole issue of the role of parties and the need for change. Tension and tumult over civil rights impacted directly on the party process in 1964 when the Mississippi Freedom Democratic Party challenged the national convention credentials of the all-white regular Mississippi delegation, charging that it was disloyal to the national party and excluded blacks from the ballot box and party meetings. No one attending that Democratic convention in Atlantic City—at the height of Lyndon Johnson's popularity and prospects—will easily forget Fanny Lou Hamer, mild in appearance but mighty in her indignation and determination, detailing the experiences of black Democratic activists in Mississippi before hostile and skeptical onlookers.

The compromise worked out in the convention was a weak one, granting the Freedom Party two delegates, but still it was an important milestone for the civil rights movement, in Carol Casey's view, and was to have an even greater party significance because, for the first time, "the national party established standards that state parties would have to observe in selecting delegates to national conventions."

Even before the searing conflict over Vietnam turned Chicago and the 1968 Democratic convention into another battleground, presidential politicians had run into pitfalls in the selection of convention delegates, amid the pressures of activists mobilized over intervention in Southeast Asia. In the snows of New Hampshire Eugene McCarthy scored a media triumph over Johnson by benefiting from a loophole in the state's presidential-primary law that awarded him more votes than the winner of the primary. When LBJ withdrew from the contest at the end of March, Hubert Humphrey learned that the filing deadline for entering presidential primaries had passed in all but two states. Bobby Kennedy found many obstacles in the path of translating public support into delegate votes because so many states had in effect chosen their convention delegates well before he entered the race. By convention time a group of "concerned Democrats" formed an ad hoc commission on the Democratic Selection of Presidential Nominees. Chaired by Harold Hughes, then governor of Iowa, the commission concluded that both the delegate-selection system and convention procedures displayed "considerably less fidelity to basic democratic principles than a nation which claims to govern itself can safely tolerate."

For Democrats this effort was the start of an intensive and unprecedented series of self-investigations and self-evaluations, headed by leaders of the caliber of George McGovern, Donald Fraser, and Barbara Mikulski. The investigators dealt with some of the most perplexing questions in politics and political science—questions of participation, representation, majority rule, minority rights, due process. Titanic struggles and bitter debates erupted over issues such as quotas for women and minorities, proportional representation, national party law versus state party law, and above all, representative versus participatory democracy. Some of these are vital issues for party government and leadership (we will return to them in later pages). But the most significant aspect of the work of these commissions—like Sherlock Holmes' dog that did not bark in the night—was the issue that received little attention as such.

That issue was the strength and survival of the Democratic Party as a national organization. Probably ten times as much thought and debate were devoted to the question of how the Democratic Party should nominate Presidents than of how the party could become strong enough to *elect* Presidents, how to help them (and Congress) formulate party programs in national and state capitals, and how to get those programs legislated and administered. The party did take one or two steps toward party renewal, and not just reform, most notably in adopting a party charter that established a National Midterm Conference. But with its usual capacity to move a large step back for every two forward, the party had no sooner suffered its shattering defeat of 1980 than it installed a new chairman who in effect moved to eviscerate the Midterm Conference.

The central organizational question facing the Democrats was that of party leadership. But this question was typically misconceived and misstated. Great debates broke out about the relative powers of grass-roots activists, especially those representing women and minorities, as against the regular, old-fashioned, established leadership, but this was merely an important side issue. The real question affecting party was the relative power of party officials chosen, dominated, and dismissable by *candidates* and *officeholders,* as against the power of party leaders *elected by and responsible to rank-and-file members of the party.* Nearly two centuries after Madisonians and Jeffersonians and Jacksonians and Van Burenites undertook the long process of converting the (then) Republican Party from a personalistic and elitist network into an organized national party with durable structure and grass-roots membership, the Democrats still lacked the intellectual leadership necessary to solve their organizational leadership problem.

With their somewhat more established party leadership, Repub-

licans have been content to concentrate more on nuts-and-bolts organizational problems than on grander questions of representation and
democracy. The GOP's 1972 convention improved and somewhat
liberalized some internal party processes and encouraged state parties
to "take positive action to achieve the broadest possible participation
by everyone in party affairs, including such participation by women,
young people, minority and heritage groups and senior citizens in the
delegate selection process." These proposals emerged from a Committee on Delegates and Organization, generally referred to as the
"DO" committee, and labeled the "DO-nothing" committee by its
critics, until it came out with these proposals, many of which were
approved by the 1972 convention.

Still, the Republicans were sufficiently dominated by their leadership in office—President Ford and his Administration—to be able
to overcome the pro-Reagan rank-and-file leadership in the 1976
convention. Four years later, after capturing the hearts and souls of
the grass-roots Republicans in the presidential primaries, and then the
presidency itself, Ronald Reagan was being scrutinized for his own
party leadership. A significant test arose early in the Reagan Administration over his courtship of several dozen conservative Democratic
representatives—the "Boll Weevils"—in the budget fight. If Reagan
was willing to offer them recognition and jelly beans in exchange for
their votes, GOP stalwarts wondered, what about the Republicans in
those districts who were hoping to run against those Democrats in the
next election? What about the grass-roots party organizations that
were trying to develop Republican Party support for such persons?
Who, in short, was thinking of the long-term interests of the party and
its program and not merely of the next budget fight?

Even more important, who was thinking about the health of the
party system as a whole?

RETHINKING PARTY

Not often has there been such a gap between informed thought
and final action as in the case of party decline and renewal. For years
some of the leading academics, journalists, and political leaders have
been warning about the implications of the broken party mainspring
for American democracy. Thus the sagacious and controversial Committee on Political Parties of the American Political Science Association more than thirty years ago reported:

The first danger is that the inadequacy of the party system in sustaining well-considered programs and providing broad public support of them may lead to grave consequences in an explosive era. The second danger is that the American people may go too far for the safety of constitutional government in compensating for this inadequacy by shifting excessive responsibility to the President. The third danger is that with growing public cynicism and continuing proof of the ineffectiveness of the party system the nation may eventually witness the disintegration of the two major parties. The fourth danger is that the incapacity of the two parties for consistent action based on meaningful programs may rally support for extremist parties poles apart, each fanatically bent on imposing on the country its particular panacea.

This warning has been repeated hundreds of times, especially since Watergate. It has been little heeded.

Parties never fully marshaled their intellectual defenses against the heavy blows dealt to them in the Progressive Era when much of their power—particularly their determining role in the nomination of their own candidates—was stripped from them in the name of "reform." Perhaps more seriously, they never overcame their public relations problem: to this day, many voters perceive political parties as corrupt machines to be shunned by any self-respecting American—or if not corrupt, as irrelevant because parties have failed to adapt to changing economic and social conditions. As an increasingly educated and economically affluent electorate replaced the politically untutored, mass-immigrant base upon which parties depended in days of old, and as the government itself usurped the patronage function of parties, new incentives for affiliating with the parties did not emerge. As the nature of political campaigning in this country changed with the enactment of campaign finance laws, the development of more sophisticated campaign techniques, and the rise of the media as the most important communication link between the candidates and the voters, the parties failed to find innovative ways of supporting their own candidates in a manner that would ensure that those candidates would also support the party, once elected.

But most important and with few exceptions, parties failed to do their own thinking. They showed little capacity to develop cohesive, consistent policy programs around which to mobilize the voters and to create within the electorate some realistic belief that party office-holders would work in unison to see that program enacted. Nor did they seem to pose real alternatives. "There's not a dime's worth of difference between the parties" is not a new refrain, but a slogan too often heard and containing more than a kernel of truth. The Reagan Administration is an exception—one in a series of signs that a re-surgence of party is not only possible but may indeed be under way.

Another problem was the failure to join the issue within the academic community. Some political scientists denigrated the APSA committee report because it had a slightly Establishment flavor, others, perversely, for the opposite reason that it argued against the old Pro-gressive, intellectual bias toward political reform, anti-bossism, anti-centralization, grass-roots participation. Central issues tended to dis-appear during this kind of debate.

Another difficulty has been lack of intellectual daring since the original APSA parties-committee report. To be sure, its recommenda-tions for a more nationalized, programmatic, structured, participa-tory, and—above all—responsible party system still serve as the intellectual framework for party-reform discussions. The political science community has continued to evidence its concern about parties through an ever-growing variety of vehicles. Private "think tanks" such as the Brookings Institution and the American Enterprise Insti-tute for Public Policy Research, as well as educational facilities like the Kennedy School of Government at Harvard, the Eagleton Institute of Politics at Rutgers, and the American Assembly of Columbia Uni-versity, have stimulated public debate by organizing research studies, sponsoring forums in which academics, politicians, and political com-mentators can exchange views, and publishing books and articles. But conceptual confusion over parties persists.

Perhaps the most unnecessary intellectual failure in party re-building was the confusion of party renewal with party reform. Some of the reform proposals of the McGovern and other commissions—especially proposals for more grass-roots participation in better-orga-nized local parties—might have served to strengthen the parties, but other reform proposals were irrelevant or even hostile to better-led and organized parties. It was partly for this reason that politicians and academics in both parties joined in 1976 to set up the Committee on Party Renewal. Without money, staff, or public attention, the commit-tee has propagandized for party reinvigoration, testified before congressional committees and party commissions, and encouraged the formation of similar committees on a state level—from Connecticut to California—to speak out on the need for state party renewal.

Many of the proposals from both practitioners and scholars have not, however, broken through the crust of conventional thinking. Today, any project considering party reconstruction or major change should be enjoined at the start: "Be bold, because only strong, even dramatic proposals will interest a press and public bored by too many lackluster, consensual commission reports. Be bold, because as you stake out major long-run potentials, you immensely expand the short-run possibilities of incremental improvement. Be bold above all because the seriousness of the situation demands it."

But there was little boldness. By the mid-eighties the Democratic Party leadership was still in intellectual disarray, the Republicans still facing the old leadership problems that had plagued the American party system from the start and had never been resolved. The issue was still the balance and tension between the individualistic, personalistic, bargaining, fragmented leadership politics of the first Constitution, and the collective, unifying, programmatic, and sometimes transforming politics of the second. By now, however, that balance was increasingly threatened by the power, real and reputed, of another force in American politics, the media.

SIX

The New Leader:
King of the Rock

I<small>N</small> the old days, gaining your party's nomination was both a boon and a burden. It meant that throughout your election district, hundreds of activists would automatically rally to your support. State or local party committees would probably give you campaign money. Perhaps you would find your name, along with others, on party billboards, matchbook covers, posters, radio ads. True, you might not like some of the candidates you were teamed up with; you would have to listen sometimes to some pretty awful party rhetoric including your own; you might wonder where some of the party money came from; and being identified as a Democrat or a Republican might hurt you in some places. But the boons usually far outweighed the burdens. Most important, you knew that thousands of people would vote for you just because that little (D) or (R) was next to your name.

I enjoyed some of these benefits when I became the Democratic candidate for Congress in my western Massachusetts district some years ago. That (D) brought me thousands of votes in the few Democratic cities, and the backing of party stalwarts. Prominent Democrats as diverse as Senator Paul Douglas and Speaker John McCormack journeyed to my district to speak for me. Jim Farley himself, though long retired as head of the national party during the FDR years, wrote for me a letter signed in his famous green ink. Still, the party benefits were rather meager. By the late 1950s party organization and activism had declined in my district as in others. There were few party billboards or other advertising. I got practically no money from the national, state, county, or local parties. Once, on accosting a party chairman, I had hardly opened my mouth to ask him for a contribution when he got *his* mouth open first and asked me to "help out" his party committee. The candidate supporting the party!—it was all topsy-turvy.

I was not surprised by all this. As a longtime local and county party leader myself, I knew that we party people were not doing our job. Too many factions and divisions; too much concern with trivia rather than issues and organization; too little money, spirit, and activism. What *did* surprise me was the effect on my own outlook and behavior, as a candidate. Lacking party help, I proceeded to beef up my own personal campaign organization, raise my own money, take out my own ads, put out my own campaign literature (mentioning only me, of course). Previously, I had yielded to no one in my party devotion; I had served in party leadership posts; I had written copiously on the need for greater party organization and responsibility; and I have never changed my views. But in the campaign crunch, I felt that if the party could not support me adequately, I must run on my own.

As I fell back increasingly on family, friends, neighbors, and unorganized Democrats and fellow liberals throughout the district, I developed something of the loneliness and the psychology of the long-distance runner, or at least of the single-minded political entrepreneur. If I had won, I would have felt loyal to my personal coalition, not to a party. In Congress, I would have felt little obligation to the Democracy, though doubtless I would have voted with it out of conviction. Certainly my successful Republican opponent seemed to have no sense of obligation to *his* party, since he proceeded to wander back and forth across party lines in his own congressional voting.

All this reminded me of a game I played as a schoolboy, King of the Rock. One of us would clamber up on a large, smooth boulder that protruded from the playground, taunt all around us, and fight to remain king until the others pulled us down, and someone else struggled to the top. It was all against all. So later, in the fall campaign. We Democratic Party nominees rarely campaigned as a team. Members of the personal organization of one Democratic candidate would often vote against another Democratic candidate, just as Democratic voters themselves split their tickets. Indeed, every Democratic candidate knew that if he or she alone should win office in the heavily Republican area, it would be enormously beneficial because of the press attention and the enhanced prestige for future contests. All against all.

THE MEDIA: PACK LEADERSHIP

A personal organization is no substitute for party in large constituencies, as I discovered in a small way and Jimmy Carter discovered in a big way. After all the work that Anne Wexler and other political lieutenants did—inviting local and interest-group influentials by the thousands to the White House for a presidential handshake—and after the President's hundreds of telephone calls to the grass roots, he had built perhaps the largest personal organization in the nation's history, but it was buried in the tens of millions who turned out on election day. For his 1936 re-election campaign Franklin Roosevelt had set up a personal organization of his own, the Good Neighbor League, bringing together a coalition of religious, civic, labor, and women's leaders. The League, however, merely supplemented the main effort of the Democratic National Committee (which indeed financed it), for the national Democracy was still thriving in FDR's day.

Without a national organization, without cadres of leaders and grass-roots membership, how does a leader reach millions of voters? Only through the mass media. But to appeal to the people "directly" through the media, rather than "indirectly" through party, is not to bypass politics. The mass media have their own internal leadership, organization, and constituencies, just as parties do. But the politics of media is far different from the politics of party, with some profound consequences for the American polity.

The problem is not simply that politicians "exploit" the media, or that the media "exploit" the politicians—this has been going on since ancient times. Pundits who wax euphoric or hysterical about the latest media blitz or Reagan public relations ploy would do well to study the 1840 campaign of William Henry Harrison, the first presidential candidate really to run for office rather than merely to stand for it. Harrison had not really planned to campaign actively—it was considered undignified—but once he started speaking more or less extemporaneously from the steps of the National Hotel in Columbus, he seemed to fall in love with campaigning. On he went to Cincinnati and other Ohio towns, drawing huge crowds and denouncing "King Mat" (Van Buren) for setting up a "practical monarchy."

Harrison and his managers also pioneered in "campaign hype." Though born to a genteel Virginia family and raised on a plantation, he was packaged as a man of the people, a "hero ploughman" seated in front of the log cabin in which, it was claimed, he had been born. Whig entrepreneurs hawked "Old Tip" lithographs, canes, miniature hard-cider barrels, whiskey bottles in the shape of log cabins. Whig media experts pioneered or perfected transparencies, floats, campaign hats, placards, banners, transportable log cabins filled with coonskins and barrels of cider. Issues were virtually ignored as the campaign turned into a media extravaganza and ultimately into an "exhibition of abuse, evasion, misrepresentation, and irrelevancies," in Richard B. Morris' view, "on a scale unparalleled in U.S. history up to that time." The Democrats responded in kind, even trotting out old General Jackson to show what a real hero looked like, compared with the Whig-fabricated one. But the Whigs had the most media muscle and they won.

We find it hard to realize today that nineteenth-century campaign media was largely party controlled. It was the local party that organized the parades and mass meetings, decked out the storefronts in bunting, brought in the delegations and crowds from the hinterland. In any decent-sized city or town at least one party newspaper helped rally the faithful and belabor the opposition. Of about 1,700 newspapers in the 1850s, more than 1,600 were party-affiliated. A century later the ratio was about reversed. Why this turnabout? Mainly for commercial reasons, according to McClure, since partisanship increasingly antagonized both advertisers and subscribers. Too, journalism became increasingly professionalized, dedicated in an age of "objectivity" and "rationality" to rise above crass partisanship in reporting the "truth."

Parties identified popular wants, defined popular needs, channeled popular hopes and aspirations, organized voters' expectations and demands. So do the mass media today, but in so different a manner as to have helped bring about a transformation of the American political system.

The striking characteristics of the parties during their long heyday were their durability and continuity, their leadership cadres, and their entrenchment in the minds and hearts of tens of thousands of party activists and millions of partisan voters. Their best campaign tactic was repetition, arousing in election after election people's loyalties to party ideas and symbols handed down from parents to children. They fostered a two-party conflict between the good guys and the bad guys—a conflict that aroused the mass electorate, provided cues and reference points, and ultimately left governing in the hands of the "ins" and opposing in the hands of the "outs." This conflict struck deep into the popular mind and psyche; it is fascinating, in going through raw public-opinion data of an earlier day, to find uninformed and almost illiterate voters who still had a glimmering of the fundamental difference between Democratic and Republican Party philosophies.

It has been fashionable to say that a one-party press, in the form of a monolithic mass media, has replaced the old two-party division. This one-party control is liberal or conservative, depending on the point of view. In a fundamental sense the media, being composed almost wholly of commercial news-purveying and attitude-influencing organization, express and defend the interests of a system of private property and profit. If the existing socioeconomic system were in peril, they would almost unanimously rally to its defense. The crucial aspect of the media, however, is not their alleged monolithic nature, nor a substantial and lasting bipolarity between Democrats and Republicans, or between conservatism and liberalism, but rather the opposite. The media are so multipolar, pluralistic, and volatile as to reflect the central leadership problem in America—its personalism—rather than moderating it or overcoming it.

The United States has never had an establishment press, like the London *Times* and the papers that followed its lead, or an anti-establishment press, such as the left-wing newspaper network of many European democracies. In a continental nation, we have had too many establishments and anti-establishments for that. To be sure, the press has been heavily conservative and Republican, and still is to a significant degree, at least on its editorial pages. But American conservatism as an ideology has been too pasty and "pragmatic," and Republicanism as a creed too variegated and opportunistic, to serve as a guide to political thought and action. Hence political leaders and media leaders divide with one another and among themselves over a vast grab bag of more or less trivial issues rather than posing clear alternatives over central, strategic, principled questions of ends and means. Thus, when Senator Kennedy gave his Georgetown University speech calling for gasoline rationing and wage controls, the three television networks played down the policies and issues in the address and concentrated on the immediate campaign effect. Thomas Patterson of Syracuse University has called this typical of television's absorption in "the game, winning and losing, appearances and hoopla."

Neither conspiracy nor confusion theories explain this kind of reporting, and much like it in the print media. It does not emerge from ideological thinking, or even from mild liberal or conservative bias. There is about as much ideology in the average Washington reporter, David Broder observes, as there is vermouth in a good martini. According to a study by Stephen Hess, the Washington press corps is youthful, more conservative than liberal but essentially apolitical, highly involved with prestige and careers. Their reporting tends not to probe beneath the surface or to reflect intellectual depth and sensitivity, but rather overplays personalities—especially glamorous or "powerful" ones—surface events, immediate breaking news, day-to-day happenings, spot items.

The organs of mass media play their own version of King of the Rock. Network competes with network, newspaper with newspaper, journal with journal, reporter with reporter, and all these with one another in a vast and intricate struggle in a highly competitive marketplace. But what stakes are involved that are any greater than one brand of soap over another? The kind of "pack journalism" that Timothy Crouse has pictured as purveying a uniform picture of presidential politics across the country is by no means unknown in other segments of the media. Political and media leaders intertwine in quick, superficial embraces of consensus. "Nearly all of our political comment originates in Washington," John Kenneth Galbraith notes. "Washington politicians, after talking things over with each other, relay misinformation to Washington journalists who, after further intramural discussion, print it where it is thoughtfully read by the same politicians. It is the only completely successful closed system for the recycling of garbage that has yet been devised." But the problem is not only misinformation but pseudo-information.

In the absence of true party conflict, it is proposed, the mass media could serve as the loyal opposition. Journalists have such a fine reputation for skepticism, cynicism, and negativism that an adversarial role might seem appropriate. I dissent. An effective opposition leadership must be consistent, collective, continuous, committed, in contrast to media leadership, which tends to be volatile, individualistic, episodic. In the game of King of the Rock, no one rules, and no one opposes, for more than a moment.

What kind of leadership, then, emerges from a personalistic, fragmented politics intertwined with a multipolar, volatile mass media, both operating in a highly competitive, widely accessible, socioeconomic marketplace? The kind of leadership I have called transactional, in which bargaining power is widely (though not necessarily equally or fairly) distributed among many actors and access to the political marketplace is relatively open. Bargainers seek to maximize material and psychic (self-esteem) returns through never-ending exchange of goods and gratifications. Transactional leaders, both electoral and media, seek to maximize their economic and psychic income through trading and brokering in a rather restricted arena. This is the politics of arithmetic, adding and subtracting political debts, exchanging such political goods as access and favors for rewards that media leadership can offer, such as recognition.

This system has its formidable defenders. Transactional leadership is seen as the leadership we exercise in our normal lives from day to day: incremental, gradual, adjusting. Recognizing the limitation of the human mind, the inability to plan far ahead as compared, say, to a chess master, the wayward and unpredictable factors that affect all good plans, and the role of chance and serendipity, transactional leaders make short-run plans, adjust to other leaders' needs and decisions, adapt their hopes and aspirations to existing conditions, bargain and compete and maneuver in a continuing series of accommodations. This kind of leadership can be compared to an alternative form, which I have called transforming, in which leaders seek to engage with not only passing and relatively superficial desires of followers but with their most fundamental wants and needs, which in the interaction of such leaders and followers are converted into hopes and aspirations and ultimately into expectations, entitlements, and demands on leadership.

This is not the place to debate these alternative forms of leadership, but two cautionary notes are in order. There is no hard-and-fast line between the two types of behavior; transforming leadership usually involves much bargaining and accommodation, and some transactional leaders may have transformational instincts and even outcomes. And the kind of leadership necessary or even possible in a given society will depend heavily on the existing organization of power, the structure of government, the present wants and needs of the people, the extent to which these may be mobilized, and the social and ideological temper of the times. In the American context, the presidency as a potential leadership institution embodies or reflects many of these variables.

PERSONALISMO:
THE ROSE GARDEN PRESIDENCY

During the past decade or so a profound, perverse, almost revolutionary change has occurred in the way we choose our Presidents.

Not only has the number of presidential primaries radically increased, from seventeen of them electing 40 percent of the national convention delegates in 1968 to thirty-five primaries picking more than 80 percent of the delegates in 1980. Not only have all the old problems endemic to primaries intensified—fragmentation of candidate attention and vote impact because of a swarm of entrants, the virtual abdication of party leadership, emphasis on personality rather than issues, superficial press coverage, heavy campaign spending. But all these problems have been enormously enhanced in presidential primaries because of the rapidly tightening interlock between the defects of primaries and the faults and frailties of mass media—especially television—coverage.

Adding a gloomy and portentous cast to the whole situation is our awareness that a *President* is being chosen—the man who, we are endlessly told, holds the nation's security in his trigger finger, who makes the economic decisions that affect our daily lives, who makes the "historic" judgments that shape the lives of our children and grandchildren. All this poses the most serious question of all: What relation does the manner of electing Presidents have to the way they *govern?*

These questions were not new, but they took on new urgency during the past decade, as academic and other analysts—with the use of the latest techniques of content analysis, in-depth panel surveys involving repeated interviewing, random selection of thousands of news stories in all the media, and comparative analysis of different kinds of media and different kinds of communities—heightened some of our worst fears about electoral and media developments.

An obvious problem was the sheer cost of campaigns—about half a billion dollars in 1980 for the federal (presidential and congressional) offices alone, including nomination races. Campaigns for the senate and for governorships are now typically running into the millions, sometimes several millions. Congressional candidates are spending several hundreds of thousands, sometimes a million or so. Campaign costs have escalated—from $4,800 for a one-minute television commercial on a prime-time Boston show in 1976 to $7,400 in 1980, from less than four cents apiece for a one-page campaign flyer, triple-folded, in 1976 to more than six cents four years later. Television networks and major newspapers continue to pour enormous sums into their coverage of presidential nominations and elections.

In analyzing media coverage the analysts were especially struck by the "horserace" phenomenon—media emphasis not on what candidates were saying about issues and policies but on who "is winning and losing, on conducting polls and touting their significance, on the strategies and tactics associated with the 'election game,' and on the immediate circumstances surrounding the horserace—the next motorcade, the next primary, and the current 'campaign issue,' " in Robert McClure's words. Sometimes—especially in presidential primary coverage—television newspersons would spend twice as much time commenting on trivial personality and tactical matters as on substance. Further investigation indicated that viewers were temporarily intrigued by these tidbits, like spectators watching a performance, but found them eminently forgettable within a few hours.

Media coverage focused on campaign ephemera. Newspeople were fascinated by little blunders—Gerald Ford bumping his head, someone else confusing the town he was in with another place, Ted Kennedy stumbling over some words. Since these were matters essentially lacking in any intrinsic substance or significance, it was easy for the media to put their own gloss on them. Thus Senator Muskie's teary talk in New Hampshire, in which he vented his feelings about his wife's treatment by a particularly unfair and fanatically right-wing editor, might have been perceived as the authentic feelings of a compassionate man who, along with his wife, had been wronged; it was perversely covered as some kind of weakness. It is evident in many of these cases that viewers are not especially affected by the incident when reported "straight"; only when the media itself selects it for special attention and distortion does the matter become a minor *cause célèbre*.

Even more perverse is what I will call the "Double-X" phenomenon—exaggeration and expectation. The best example of the former—indeed, of an incident that had historic consequences—was the media's conversion of Lyndon Johnson's primary victory in New Hampshire in 1968 into a victory for his challenger, Eugene McCarthy. McCarthy did remarkably well, of course, against a President, but he did not *win*. It is the expectation-raising game, however, that I find the most remarkable example of media *chutzpa*. A newsperson will report, on the basis of obscure and perhaps flimsy evidence, that "it is expected" that Candidate A will win by 10 percent next Tuesday, and Candidate B will lose by 8. As it turns out, Candidate B wins by 9 percent and Candidate A loses by 12. Then comes the "10 o'clock surprise," as the media report this remarkable comeback or reversal or "upset." Nothing is said about the *real* story—the media's earlier misreporting of the election situation. It would be hard to imagine a more perverse example of an institution not only disguising but benefiting from its own error.

Perverse, superficial, unfair, often biased—these failings of media coverage have been endlessly discussed, especially in the mass media itself. I consider them only minor or secondary problems. Candidate "hype" by the media or by the candidates themselves is such an old story in this country that most voters guard against it. There has been much talk of intensifying video domination of campaigns, but selling a presidential candidate over television is not as simple as selling cornflakes. John B. Connally based his 1980 presidential primary effort almost wholly on television, with convincingly negative results. Many voters have caught on to the "Double-X" phenomenon and protect themselves against it. As V. O. Key, Jr., perhaps the ablest political theoretician and analyst of this century, concluded a searching study of public opinion, "Voters are not fools."

Nor do I see campaign money as the central problem. Clearly, some campaigns cost too much money and some candidates spend a lot more than others, hence there are gross inequalities and inequities. A candidate without money is virtually doomed. Dollars are not automatically convertible into votes, however, and the federal government and some states have made considerable progress in "sanitizing" campaign finance through limitations on the giving, receiving, and spending of political money; forced disclosure of the sources and uses of campaign funds; and subsidies of campaigns in order to produce more equity among candidates. Congress typically has left gaping holes in the regulation of its own campaign money, but with pressure from the public, mobilized by reform groups like Common Cause, we can reasonably expect that senators and representatives will finally get around to equalizing their own campaign spending. At the moment, admittedly, the problem is outrunning the reforms.

What *does* deeply disturb me is the long-run effect of all these political forces—the reinforcement of tendencies toward electoral disorganization, political disintegration, mass spectatorship and passivity, opinion volatility and superficiality, and, above all, leadership personalism or *personalismo,* already present in our political arrangements. In short, these tendencies undermine effective, committed, collective, and durable leadership in politics, with dire implications for governance. The late-twentieth-century presidency poses these questions most urgently.

The television news system, Michael Robinson has observed, develops a "symbiotic relationship with the strong institutions and a parasitic relationship with the weak." Perhaps the weakest of our major electoral institutions is the presidential nominating system, based in complex and shifting arrangements of bewildering diversity in more and more states. Its weaknesses are numerous. Because most presidential primaries have a dual role—testing a candidate's popularity in a "beauty contest" and choosing delegates to the national convention—voters are typically not clear about the relation, if any, of the two voting decisions, that is, voting for presidential *candidates* and voting for convention *delegates*. Typically these primaries are divorced from other electoral decisions, from nominations for senator or representative or state posts. And the party stands by, helpless and useless, while its most important decision is taken over by the "people," most of whom are neither active party members nor politically knowledgeable.

Gradually, the media have imposed a relationship on presidential primaries—a relationship both parasitic and exploitative—such as virtually to dominate them. And since the final convention decision has come to be largely decided in the primaries, in effect the media dominate the convention as well. Yet the convention is a potentially strong institution with which the media could establish a symbiotic rather than parasitic relationship. For the convention is an old and established institution, as regular and predictable as presidential elections, acceptable and understandable to the press and public, with focused activity, a schedule determined by the party, and active and visible party leadership. The media—especially television—could do a superb job of covering a wide-open, rip-roaring convention: moving into caucuses, spotlighting debates on the floor, picking up quiet meetings among competing managers that might portend shifting coalitions, highlighting dramatic roll-call votes—in short, converting the convention not only into great theater but meaningful political drama. As it is, media leaders have had the audacity to complain about the dullness and indecisiveness of presidential conventions—after television itself helped turn presidential primaries into a series of beauty contests that in effect robbed the "nominating" convention of its essential *raison d'être*.

Because of the perverse relationship between mass media and presidential primaries, those who would be President play the ultimate game of King of the Rock. They must exploit the media in order to reach a mass public without being chewed up in the internal processes and mechanism of the media. Since they will largely bypass party leadership and organization, they must build their own following on a continental scale. They must deal with a volatile, badly informed, largely apathetic electorate, cut up into big and little segments that become relevant on a series of dates from February to June. Above all, because the pack of candidates within the party may not fundamentally disagree on issues, or may prefer to conceal what disagreements they have, they tend to play down policy questions and build personas for themselves that will entice the media and set the candidates apart from one another. It will be personality over policy.

How relevant is all this to the job of *governing?* A case can be made for it. Overcoming a series of presidential-primary hurdles will test a candidate's resilience, agility, resourcefulness, commitment, tenacity, unflappability. These qualities are not irrelevant to those needed in the White House. The presidency can also call for a continuous and massive public relations effort, on issue after issue and in crisis after crisis, not unlike a presidential-primary campaign. Then too an effective presidential candidate must mobilize a sizable cadre of full-time aides and supporters, and a much larger "third cadre" of grass-roots activists—together making up a personal constituency of leaders and followers that could mobilize even broader support for him in the presidency.

It is hard to push this case much further, however, because public relations is only a minor part of the job of the President. What is the *essence* of the job of the President? Opinions vary, of course, but I believe there would be wide agreement on the following, on the part of both Presidents and President watchers: The essential job of the President, and the classic test of his greatness, is to mobilize support within government—and especially with his fellow policy makers in House and Senate—behind a program that would realize the broader purposes and principles on which the President campaigned for his office. While such a President naturally would hope for grass-roots popular support, if only to help put pressure on Congress, this is not his first need, and hence he does not become preoccupied with television news programs, polls, mail, and the like. His first concern is concerting the effort of many other political leaders with diverse constituencies behind *policy.* This calls less for public relations gimmickry than for establishment of clear priorities, intensive consultation with congressional leaders, willingness to compromise within the perimeters of the program, an understanding of when *not* to compromise, and the capacity, both intellectual and institutional, to follow through after decisions are reached.

Our presidential nomination system favors qualities more opposite than apposite to these. The presidential hopefuls shun cooperation with one another—indeed, they keep their distance from one another —because each is playing King of the Rock. Presidential candidates pay little attention to members of Congress and congressional candidates because legislators typically have a minimal role in presidential primaries; many of them prefer to stay out of the pre-convention brawl. Hence during the campaign few coalitions are forged that might carry over into government. In the absence of strong party organization or sentiment, there is no vehicle to tie candidates to a common constituency or to one another. Even candidates who win the presidency by massive popular majorities, such as Johnson in 1964 or Nixon in 1972, lack today the kind of "coattail" influence that binds congressional candidates more tightly to them. In King of the Rock, it is all against all and devil take the hindmost.

The upshot is for more a politics of personality than of policy, program, authority, governance. It is a politics that by no means ignores the attitudes of the public—its electoral support after all is crucial— but seeks votes by appealing to short-run, superficial, and narrow needs and hopes. No one has stated the problem better than Senator Nancy Landon Kassebaum. The essence of leadership, she says, is the identification of mutual values, needs, and goals. She deplores the "media-ization" of politics that fosters a governmental view of citizens as mere consumers. "We are replacing the Madisonian conception of government as the careful arbiter of a large and diverse nation with a Madison Avenue conception of the state as responsive to the sundry appetites of our citizen-consumers." Defining the fundamental needs, as against the "appetite" needs, of the people should, of course, be at the heart of meaningful party and electoral combat.

We have in effect created a plebiscitary presidency under which the incumbent seeks to retain power and influence policy through his direct—that is, media-dominated—relationship with the public. Plebiscitary leadership is classically short-run, unstable, ineffective, irresponsible. In the absence of solid policy linkage with voters and with other leaders, and in an effort to maximize his influence, the plebiscitary President is tempted to "rise above politics," transcend partisanship, and seek, as "President of all the people," some kind of electronic pulpit that would enable him to draw people across party lines. Any kind of "loyal" but authentic opposition would hardly find footing in such an artificial atmosphere.

Ultimately the President embraces his role as chief of state, "adjourning politics," evading the mean problems created by the separation of powers and checks and balances, and creating a relationship with the mass public based on symbol, myth, and ritual. The relationship could be relatively benign, helping produce a Rose Garden presidency consisting largely of pomp and circumstance. Or it could be malign, moving us toward a plebiscitary, imperial, or even Caesaristic presidency.

VOTERS ADRIFT:
THE DECLINE OF FOLLOWERSHIP

When leaders fail, they are tempted to make scapegoats of their followers. Jimmy Carter, in decrying the loss of "unity of purpose" and the "erosion of confidence," was not the first President to attribute failure to the people; Harry Truman, for example, fumed about Americans giving in to "the powers of selfishness and greed." If the American voters are unduly criticized, however, it is in part because they are unduly burdened. Even before the rise of the presidential-primary system, no polity on earth put such civic demands on its citizens as did the American.

From the very start, the national Constitution required voters to choose among candidates at three levels of government, and state constitutions compelled them to choose among numerous candidates at the state and local levels—among contenders for governor, state senator, and state representative, among other aspirants, and for a host of county and local posts. Today voters typically mark a ballot or pull a lever for candidates at the local (town or city), county, state, and national levels, making a total of at least thirty or forty decisions. Often voters will find on the ballot an awesome array of other contests, for a variety of state and local authorities, commissions, and functions, representing a bewildering variety of overlapping districts. Then there will be the referendum questions—perhaps a dozen of them, in their fine print and opaque language. To cap it all, most of the general election contests will have been preceded by primary balloting, that might make voters choose among half a dozen primary-election aspirants to each office. No wonder voters grow weary of those repeated trips to the polls, to face a baffling selection among candidates they hardly know, running for offices whose duties they may hardly understand.

All power to the people! was the war cry of American political reformers as well as Bolshevik propagandists. The latter never delivered; the former succeeded so well as to create a decision overload. The extraordinary demands we make on voters are a major, and somewhat neglected, cause of the political malaise in America today, that is, of the failures of rational and democratic decision making, leadership and followership, effective and responsible government. We have only to contrast the electoral duties of the voter in a parliamentary democracy—to vote (typically) for one member of parliament once every four or five years, and once or twice for a city or county (equivalent) councillor—to see how enormously the job of the voter is simplified and clarified in those nations. And the primary is hardly known there; the task of nominating candidates is handled within the party organizations.

It is above all the decline of party in the United States that has made the citizen's task so overpowering. In the last century the Democrats, Republicans, and third parties took over the whole task of nominations with their caucuses and conventions. The party designation or even symbol—the eagle or the star or the hammer—supplied voters with the instant information they needed to make at least a rough judgment about candidates. Especially for the "average man," the party "ticket," listing candidates neatly grouped by their party designation, was in fact a ticket of admission into the electorate on reasonably knowledgeable terms. Educated men and (later) women could bone up on candidates and issues, listen to the speeches, read the editorials, and intelligently pick and choose among parties and party factions. But the low-income voters, lacking schooling and often even much reading ability, were able to mass their weight at the polls on the basis of simple notions of the parties' positions on slavery, the tariff, currency, labor, monopoly, and the like.

Under the overload of ballot decision making, lacking the moorings of party, and in a mass-media context, American voters today exhibit typical symptoms of people under stress: withdrawal, irresolution, instability, volatility. Nonvoting is one of these symptoms. It has been suggested that a "reservoir of perennial nonparticipants may be a benign indicator of good times," at least in the short run, but most students of voting turnout take a less benign view. Nonvoting results both from institutional barriers such as irksome registration requirements and from "psychological" factors such as apathy, alienation, and anomie; apathy is perhaps the most important of these, especially when voting choices seem of little importance, controversy, and excitement. When almost half of the potential electorate fails to vote even for President, and two-thirds fail to vote on important state and local offices and referenda questions, the mass electoral base radically shrinks, drastically reducing the electoral foundations of national democratic leadership. Most important, the erosion of voting intensifies at low levels of income and education, so that families in the higher socioeconomic levels are grossly overrepresented among the ranks of those who do show up at the polls. Nonparticipation becomes malignly unrepresentative and inegalitarian.

Those who do vote seem today to be more uncertain and volatile in their ballot decisions. Voting straight party tickets, which was running at more than 60 percent in the 1950s, dropped to about half that percentage in the following decade. Some of this decrease may result from responsible voters thoughtfully picking and choosing the best from both or all parties; most of it is due to the fading away of party and ideological cues. The more tickets are split, in general the more party leaders in office will be split, as mayors of one party confront city councils controlled by another party, Democratic governors have to deal with Republican legislatures, Republican Presidents face off against a Democratic House and/or Senate. Ticket splitting, in short, fosters government splitting.

Split-ticket voting is part of a more fundamental political development that specialists like to call the decomposition or even disaggregation of the American electorate. Parties "decompose" as voters increasingly split their tickets, shift back and forth between parties on the basis far more of candidate personality than party position on issues, discontinue their party registration, consider themselves as "independents." Parties decompose organizationally as formal membership declines, membership dues and other sources of grass-roots financing dry up, local and state and national parties become ideologically and structurally at odds with one another, party leadership is subordinated to governmental officials (i.e., the party national headquarters becomes increasingly a staff arm of the White House).

Electoral disaggregation is a less visible but even more significant process. Voters, finding few party cues, have inadequate guides to policy issues and candidates. Issues lack coherence or patterning; they not only cut across party lines but cut across one another. To be "liberal" on domestic policy, for example, may put one at odds with "liberals" in such areas as foreign policy or civil liberties. "Social" issues cut across "economic" issues. As party and ideological guidelines weaken or entangle with one another, voters are thrown on their own; they may respond by searching for personalities or by retreating into tighter embraces with single-interest groups.

Sometimes these trends are hailed in the press as proof of a growing and healthy independence in the American electorate. Certainly the number of self-styled "independents" has been swelling in the voting surveys of recent years. They surpassed the Republicans in numbers and later—in some surveys—topped the Democrats. They have been called in the press the "biggest party"—except that they are not a party. Rather, independents comprise a formless mass of people. A large number are partisans who for business or other reasons prefer to style themselves as independents. (Pollsters occasionally come across the man who styles himself "independent" but when asked how he has voted for President over the last three decades answers, "Stevenson, Kennedy, Johnson, Humphrey, McGovern, Carter.") The independents also include voters who approach candidates and issues on a case-by-case basis. Other independents are among the most uninformed persons in the electorate. But the vast majority of independents break away from party or ideological ties only to fall into other dependencies, on their interest groups, ethnic affiliations, race, religion, personality cults, or—and above all today—the media.

The result of these trends is the spectacle of voters adrift. Lacking the moorings of party or the anchors of ideology, Americans, or at least those who bother to turn out on election day, tend to be volatile, shifting from party to party and candidate to candidate as they try out the offerings on the ballot like goods in the supermarket. Many independents, like many partisans, do the best they can, searching for qualities in candidates of "temperament, competence, and stability," in James Sundquist's words. But many more, in my view, are tending to be less participants than mere spectators, cut off from the public decisions that affect their lives. Stimulated by the media, they like to play "political horse race," becoming more absorbed in day-to-day tactics, episodes, gamesmanship, and showmanship than in the serious candidate and party alternatives facing the country. Above all, this tendency encourages a personalism among voters as it does among candidates, resulting in an emphasis in voting on superficial aspects of candidates' personalities rather than their potential ability to respond to the essential needs of the electorates. Followers' *personalismo* matches leaders'—and enormously encourages it.

Is all this so serious? Is not "independence" precisely the quality we want in voters to insure that they pick and choose freely and rationally? Is not "volatility" simply another word for the voters who will give parties and officeholders a chance to show their stuff and quite properly dump them when the voters conclude that the stuff is not there? Certainly there are healthful aspects in some of these tendencies. But the overall result is damaging to both leader and follower, both official and citizen.

The notion that the great mass of citizens can make rational and independent decisions if only they are exposed to the "free market" of ideas and electoral competition is a carry-over from eighteenth-century theories of individualism and representation. Liberate good citizens from their ignorance, their parochialism, their family and geographical blinders and you can expect them to make as sensible and calculating a judgment as they would in the marketplace and stock exchange. We know today, however, that the great number of voters neither wish to, nor would be able to, cleanse themselves of family, neighborhood, ethnic, occupational, religious, and interest-group influences. Nor need they; a representative democracy assumes that these are authentic human interests and affiliations and must be reflected in the actions of governments.

The test for citizens is not whether they can exorcise such interests and affiliations but whether they can transcend them when events call for a more general, national, even international conception of the public interest. Such events need not call for a suppression of individual and group interests but some modification of their expression, or postponement of their satisfaction. Such a transcendence can be encouraged by an ideological movement, by a revolutionary ideology, by a national leader of the Churchill stamp, or by a political party. The last is the most effective, dependable, and long-lived instrument for such transcendence, because no other instrument is designed, in credo and organization, to meld group and individual interests more justly and democratically with general and national ones. Ideological leaders may suppress "special interests" in a fanatical pursuit of their transcending cause. National leaders, even with benign aims, may suppress valid groups, as in Franklin Roosevelt's relocation of Japanese-Americans in concentration camps in 1942. Party leaders, however, must be sensitive to that delicate balance between national imperatives and partisan interest over the long run.

Citizens may well join other national groups, such as liberal or conservative reform or policy groups. But the point is this: The great "mass public" must find some vehicle to reflect its organic, corporate, combined interests. This kind of collective action is quite opposite to the ephemeral, volatile, personalistic, "independent," media-dominated King-of-the-Rock politics that we have been discussing.

Indeed, it is its best antidote. Only as voters organize into coherent national groupings, representing diverse political thrusts in a competitive national political arena, will the common interests of great numbers of voters gain effective representation.

This is a matter not merely of national power but of rational collective action. A political party is a communications and educational system as well as a structure of influence. It serves as a means of informing, educating—sometimes even in party schools—and instructing party members in their voting and other political acts. This job is undertaken by party activists, teachers, publicists. Ideally, party members delegate to grass-roots cadres the task of following political events, presenting policy alternatives for party platforms, and articulating party programs. This would be a dangerous delegation if the activists were arbitrary, dishonest, or out of touch with the rank and file. But in a democratic context the party leadership at all levels must stay reasonably representative or it will give way to competing factions in the party, or to competing parties outside.

There is, in short, an art of followership as well as of leadership. Good followers do not try to comprehend the whole political world and all the policy alternatives; they have other things they prefer to do. But they believe in certain ends, in accordance with certain values; and their main task is to find the political vehicle in which they will invest some time and money and effort. Once they have done so they will not lead in the usual sense; they will not take the initiative; they will not be activists. But they *will* respond to the call of party leaders when they are needed, speak up at an important party meeting, make a financial contribution, or go to the polls on election day. And they have a duty to keep an eye on their chosen political vehicle—to criticize it, even to desert it when the party loses sight of its public goals.

Some party followers may serve as experts on certain matters, while depending on fellow members in other areas. Thus good followers seek advice from their comrades-in-arms. Let me describe my own plight as a kind of reverse example of this state of affairs. As a professional political scientist and an occasional political activist, I keep in close touch with national politics and, to a lesser degree, with the problems and crises of the Commonwealth of Massachusetts. In these areas I might on occasion take a small role as leader. But on the affairs of my community, Williamstown, I am almost a total ignoramus. I find its governmental collection of boards, authorities, and commissions as bewildering as the national and state governments must seem to some of the local activists. Worse, I don't know most of the local candidates for the fifteen or twenty elective town offices. So what do I do? I turn for information and counsel to people who share my political philosophy and know about town affairs—friends in the League of Women Voters or American Legion or education groups. I would prefer to turn to my local party committee, because I know I share their views. But town officers are not elected on a party ballot, so I cannot benefit from the old practice that would be most useful—party endorsements. Hence I join the ranks of the "independents and the spectators, the ephemeral and the volatile, the disaggregated and the drifting." I cast my ballot more for personalities than for policies. In town affairs I am not a good follower, because I am deprived of the cues that a good follower needs.

What does good followership have to do with good leadership? A great deal. Good followers are not passive citizens who can be ignored, manipulated, exploited. Forming the membership foundation of organizations, they actively respond to leadership guides and initiatives, provide vital support as needed, vote with their ballots on important issues and with their feet—that is, they desert the party—on more important ones. They may follow the party line at the moment, but as a whole, and in the long run, they have a vital role in shaping it. Leaders in turn benefit from the durable institutions of the party, its dependable support over the years, its vital role in mobilizing votes and money for candidates, its up-to-date party platforms and manifestos.

Well-organized followers thus supply the electoral foundations for coherent, consistent, comprehensive leadership. From them are recruited future leaders, just as present leaders may return to the ranks of good followers. The result is a dynamic engagement between leaders and led that can make government and politics more participatory, can make conflict sharper and more meaningful, can make policy and program more coherent and consistent.

Parties are not the only institutions that can combine good followership and good leadership in creative partnership. A mass movement, or all-embracing labor federation, or national reform organization, might do the same. But party has two vital distinctions. No political group can be as widely embracing, as reflective of an enormous variety of interests, as the major political party. And only the party can formally nominate candidates for office. Hence, as long as parties are in disarray, leadership and followership will be in disarray.

PART THREE

THE *Reshaping*
OF *Power*

SEVEN

Reorganization:
The Politics of Tinkering

MOST of the problems we have been considering—the collapse of popular confidence in our political system, the deep-seated historical and institutional sources of fragmented and unstable government, the perverse relationship between media and the nominating system in which each brings out the worst qualities of the other, the recurring deadlock within the national government and between the nation and the states, the continued lurching of the system between "spasm and stasis"—are not new in American life. They have been diagnosed, discussed, deplored for most of this century. Has the system, then, not changed? It has, in fact, been immensely democratized, as men without property won the right to vote early in the last century, and women and blacks in this; as political parties fostered grass-roots leadership during the 1830s and 1840s and party reform broadened political participation during the 1960s and 1970s.

Still, confidence in the system dwindles and criticism mounts. The last decade has brought an avalanche of proposals to reform, reorganize, or reshape virtually every part of our political system. While some of these proposals have been adopted—centralizing the budget process, for example, and creating the Senior Executive Service—the structure remains essentially unaltered as we approach the two hundredth birthday of the Constitution. How could there be such dissatisfaction with government, so many proposals to improve it, and so little change? Mainly because the system so artfully withstands significant alteration, but largely too, I believe, because the countless reformers, rejuvenators, and reorganizers have not agreed on their central goals and have not mobilized popular support for them. What do they want?

More authority in government—at least enough to re-establish legitimacy and popular respect, and enable government to *govern?* "There is a crisis between the functions of the American people and the functions of the American Government," James Reston wrote during the 1980 elections. "The people have acquired the power to nominate Presidents and even to determine foreign policy they know very little about. The Governments they elect have in the process lost the authority needed to govern. . . . The crisis of leadership is not merely political but general in America. It cannot be resolved by just another guy or another party. . . ." But strengthening the authority of government raises old and unresolved problems of the imperial presidency and arrogant, insensitive rule.

"Good government"—is that the supreme goal? It is the most commonly expressed aim, and the vaguest. Typically, it means honesty and economy, but both of these are such minimal and unexceptionable goals as to invite a radical lowering of expectations of government. Yet these goals are also heavily value-laden and, if realized, would have varying impacts on the government and the governed. The age-old campaigns for "honesty in government" may have cleansed Congress and courthouse and bureaucracies of some of their rascals and sinners, and doubtless saved upper- and middle-class taxpayers some money, but those campaigns also damaged party organizations as dispensers of jobs and help and as formulators and energizers of programs. Economy, as a weapon against welfare and other entitlements, can threaten the use of government as a means of income redistribution— an outcome that some reformers would favor and others would rue.

Majority rule? The Constitution thwarted this goal from the start, through checks and balances in the national government and separation of powers between nation and states. Political parties have rarely been able in this century to overcome these governmental fissures, which are intensified by the political and social fragmentation of the country. Government seems to respond to coalitions of upper- and middle-income voters, as in the late nineteenth century. Only fleetingly, as in FDR's "second hundred days," does it respond to majority coalitions of low-income and lower-middle-class voters, perhaps because the poor and the low income need so much from government but expect so little from it.

Better representation, fuller accountability, clearer responsibility? These are vital goals in a democracy but again raise hard questions. Representative of *whom*—of "all the people," of the majority, of minorities, of single-interest groups? Accountable *how*—through elections, public opinion, referenda, polls? Responsible to *what*—the "people," the public interest, the national conscience, the next generation, the verdict of history?

Let us start with a reasonable goal, one that would win overwhelming approval from a wide spectrum of Americans—achieving far greater efficiency and economy in government (whatever its purposes) through more unity and consistency of purpose and program, more coordination of policy making within and between the executive and legislative branches, greater concert in carrying out legislative measures and executive decisions. In short, teamwork. Conservatives like teamwork because it implies greater effectiveness in achieving conservative goals of economy and "leanness" in government, large or small. Liberals like teamwork because it implies greater force and effectiveness in government in carrying out new and comprehensive programs that put heavy burdens on the state. Each side may be deluding the other—or itself—but the breadth of support makes the idea of adopting teamwork proposals not wholly utopian.

Real teamwork also means genuinely collective leadership—a sharing of planning, program setting, decision making, and outcome supervising by all the members of the leadership team. This does not bar leadership within the team, of course; there must be captains and quarterbacks. But within the leadership hierarchy there must be a meaningful exchange of ideas, proposals, information, criticism, assessments, and audits; a continuing dialogue among the leadership elements; and full opportunity for subleaders to offer initiatives, and to "vet" and contribute to the proposals of top leaders—that is, of the President of the United States, Speaker of the House, majority leaders in House and Senate.

Transcending all these considerations is the moral or ethical factor, the notion that genuine teamwork implies leaders' *answerability* for policy to the majority that put the team into office, *accountability* to the nation for the moral and efficient conduct of high office, and *responsibility* to the ever-changing "bar of history" through the leaders' capacity to engage with followers by responding to their deepest and most durable needs, hopes, and expectations. But let us begin modestly with the simple and sensible goal of efficiency through teamwork. And let us begin with the first branch of government.

CONGRESS: MESS OR MESH?

Congress is made up of 535 individualists, most of them of the rugged variety. Typically these men and women are experts at King of the Rock—organizing personal followership back in their state and district, gaining a party nomination with no help from a political party, winning an election with little help from that party, and then, in Washington, developing a personal standing, a circle of friends and allies, and a zone of influence in House or Senate. To be sure, they develop many dependencies—on organized interests in their constituencies and in Washington, on the President, on the legislative party leadership, on informal leadership and influence groups in the chamber. Ultimately, however, senators and members of Congress are politically fixated on one target—the present and potential followers they hope to mobilize in a particular geographical area on a predictable November day against an unpredictable adversary.

So we start with diffusion, not teamwork—with hundreds of men and women fighting separately for their political lives. This competitive individualism has long been institutionalized in the structure of Congress. The most dramatic example remains the filibuster, which continues to give one senator the power to delay action in the upper chamber and hence to give him or her both positive and negative influence. In both houses too the committee and subcommittee structure reflects and enhances the power of the individual legislator. Members of Congress continuously work together, of course, in shaping and enacting and amending and defeating measures, and they all operate in a vast arena of brokerage and give-and-take, in a system of transactional leadership. Still, when the chips are down, they are feudal chieftains, seated in their tiny baronies.

This was the system that a young scholar named Woodrow Wilson denounced as "government by the Standing Committees" and labeled a "disintegrate ministry." Few have recognized this atomization of power in Congress more acutely or apprehensively, however, than members of Congress themselves—especially leaders of Congress, who must, in Paul Appleby's apt phrase, try to make a mesh of things. Congress has occasionally reorganized its committee systems in order to make them more relevant to broad policy areas. Probably the most ambitious attempt came in 1946, in the Legislative Reorganization Act that regrouped a large number of specialized committees into a smaller number with wider policy scopes. In a typical two-steps-forward-one-back shuffle, the act exempted the big taxing and spending committees from reorganization.

The most visible result of the 1946 act was the spawning of a host of subcommittees and hence, on balance, further fragmentation of the legislature. By 1980, 210 "separate legislative entities" could be identified in the House alone. Subcommittee staff members proliferated as well, from about 6,600 in 1960 to about 17,700 twenty years later. Subcommittee chairmen had never had it so good, or had so much. Out of three hundred or more Democratic senators and representatives, almost all were chairpersons of some committee or other "unit." A rookie congressman of the majority party could look forward to presiding in a year or two over a three- or five-person subcommittee.

"If the trend is not reversed," declared Peter Rodino, chairman of the House Judiciary Committee, "the day is not far off when every majority member will head a subcommittee. Then we will have no leadership, and no 'followership.' Everybody will be a boss."

Coalition making and majority building—and hence teamwork—inevitably suffer from this kind of fragmentation. "There has to be a way," concluded the Panel on the Electoral and Democratic Process of the President's Commission for a National Agenda for the Eighties, "of melding the members into a policymaking body; there has to be a way to encourage them to compromise some short-term interests for the long-term interests of the nation. If Congress is to develop national policies and to reconcile seemingly irreconcilable interests (such as the opposing interest groups involved in the abortion issue), countervailing pressures to local or special-interest group demands are needed to build decision-making majorities." Yet the Panel grants that coalition building has become far more difficult because of the proliferation of subcommittees and other atomizing tendencies.

On several occasions during the last two decades the House has tried to renew the unfulfilled effort of 1946. Special House committees have repeatedly proposed substantial committee reorganization, but to little avail. The Senate has been more successful in modernizing its committee structure, but the power of the independent committees remains. Why is it so hard for Congress to put its own houses in order? Primarily because each committee and even each subcommittee operates as a little barony and fears that in any reorganization it may lose power and independence. Behind the committees and most of the subcommittees stand potent interest groups that sound the alarm throughout the country and rally their lobbyists in Washington whenever "their" committees are threatened. The "iron triangles" of mutually supportive committee, interest group, and federal agency remain hard and obdurate under their rusty exteriors. Congress as a whole fears that wholesale reorganization, merely for the sake of efficiency, is hardly worth the inevitable power fights.

Can Congress fundamentally reform itself? Probably not, except under extraordinary circumstances. Consider the efforts of Congress to regain the "power of the purse," a power granted mainly to the legislature by the Constitution. By the end of the New Deal and World War II years the "colonizing presidency" had largely taken over the budgetary process just as it had most of the other crucial functions of the federal government. The crisis came, though, with a Republican President, Richard Nixon, and even before Watergate. During 1972, the last year of his first term, Nixon was pushing the presidential right of impoundment to a new extreme. For years Presidents had been selectively stretching out or delaying the spending of funds appropriated by Congress; now Nixon, asserting he had a constitutional right to bury funds, carried both the scope and volume of impoundment "far beyond the actions of any previous President," according to James Sundquist, and in doing so collided head on with an aroused—and Democratic—Congress.

Incensed by the President's withholding of urban, farm, environmental, rural electrification, and other types of funds, Congress passed the Congressional Budget and Impoundment Control Act of 1974, which drastically limited the President's right to impound by requiring, in effect, congressional permission. Even more significant were the budget provisions of the act. After having become almost wholly dependent on the President for budgetary leadership, Congress in the 1974 Act sought to establish coherent congressional control of the whole process. A Congressional Budget Office, with a staff of budgetary and fiscal experts, was established under a new permanent budget committee for each chamber. The two committees separately review and evaluate the President's proposals, propose alternative fiscal directives, activate Congress to set fiscal guidelines for the regular authorizing, taxing, and appropriations committees, take the lead in congressional adoption of the fiscal plan, all for the sake of more integrated budgetary policy making by Congress. At the advent of the Reagan Administration, while congressional fiscal leaders were congratulating themselves on having reclaimed their constitutional authority over federal spending, the White House asserted extensive influence over legislative budget making during Reagan's first year in office, though Congress regained some influence during his second and third years.

The legislative branch has not been able to establish counterpart machinery to the executive in an even more crucial area—foreign policy. When Congress established the National Security Council to unify presidential policy, it provided no comparable machinery for itself. Following the new congressional assertiveness over Vietnam, and rising distrust of the White House, Congress tried to enlarge its influence over foreign policy, but its individualistic organization produced near-chaos. "Various committees in the two houses went their separate ways, and the committees themselves were fragmented," according to Sundquist. "Leadership began to come from almost anywhere, inside or outside those committees, unpredictably. On a series of critical issues—aid to Vietnam, the Greek-Turkish clash over Cyprus, intervention in Angola, Jewish emigration from the Soviet Union, the Rhodesian chrome boycott—Congress took it upon itself to reverse the presidential policy. Yet it did so on a piecemeal basis, emotionally, under the pressure of constituency groups at home, sometimes almost whimsically, rejecting presidential strategy without the benefit of any substitute global strategy of its own. . . ." On other vital policy areas the congressional leadership is equally fragmented.

Can Congress through internal reorganization re-establish its general and positive legislative power under the Constitution? Skeptics are doubtful. Yet Congress has shown an impressive capacity to reorder its internal power structure in the past two or three decades. Forty years ago, when I first worked on Capitol Hill, Howard Worth Smith of Virginia was considered the most powerful man in the House, and the barony over which he reigned—the House Rules Committee—the most powerful single entity. Many years later Smith was defeated, and then his barony was reduced. The unwritten seniority rule for choosing committee chairmen was considered all but sacrosanct. That rule has been considerably modified. The filibuster was considered part of the very life and soul of the Senate. It has been tamed to a degree. Ironically, though, most of the reform measures, rather than shifting power to central, representative leadership, have scattered power into a labyrinth of committees, subcommittees, committee staffs, individual legislators, and their assistants. Can Congress, having overcome the big barons, now curb the power of the little ones?

One way to shift authority to elected policy-making leadership, some urge, is through better staffing of the central legislative offices. "While Congress is all but overwhelmed by its own *specialized* staffs," Steven Bailey noted, "key areas of legislative policy lack sophisticated *generalized* staffs directly responsible to congressional leadership. The speaker and the Senate majority leader, and their ranking minority counterparts, need small but highly capable substantive staffs, familiar with the general fields of national security (and its domestic connections), the economy (including energy and environment), and critical areas of human development (e.g., youth employment, health care). These leadership staffs should supplement the present services of the Congressional Budget Office and help top congressional leaders to work on policy analysis in consensus-building terms. . . ."

Given the fragmentation of Congress, however, it would be difficult for even central staffs not to become atomized. That has been the experience of regular committees with expanded staffs. In 1975, during a vast expansion of committee staffs, junior senators gained the right for every member to hire one staff member for each of his committees. Minority party members also have "their" staff experts. Soon senators were complaining that committee staff members were "each going their own way, without any responsibility to their respective committees," that the staffs were making Senate business more demanding and complex. The House had a parallel though less serious problem on this score. In an individualistic environment, stronger central staffs might quickly be colonized by powerful members of House and Senate.

A standard response to the problem of policy diffusion is to urge an up-to-date, logical regrouping of policy committees. Both houses, according to the Panel on the Democratic Process, should reorganize so that similar issues are handled within one committee, committees should parallel more closely the functional structure of the executive, the total number of subcommittees should be limited, and the number of subcommittees on which members serve should be slashed. The Panel also recommended that the House curb the practice of referring bills to more than one committee at the same time, or of splitting up bills and sending parts to separate committees. The Health Services Bill of 1979, for example, was referred to nine standing committees simultaneously. Such proposals, however, assume a coherent, centripetal structure in Congress that simply does not exist.

Inevitably, those who seek to unify legislative decision making turn to the devices of policy committees, steering committees, and caucuses. Here the leaders and members of the majority party and, separately, the minority, meet together to counsel. In the House, the Speaker, majority leader, minority leader, and majority and minority whips; in the Senate, the Vice-President, the president *pro tem,* majority and minority leaders and whips, provide the structure for collective leadership. But leaders cannot lead if followers will not follow, and that is the case on critical issues in both houses. Thus Speaker O'Neill, despite valiant efforts, could not rally his whole flock of Democrats in 1981 to stop President Reagan's budget and tax bills in the House, or in 1983 to head off Reagan's tax reduction for the affluent classes.

The elected leadership in Congress can draw on a few power resources, such as influence over committee appointments and chairmanships, choice of junket participants, advancement in the leadership hierarchy, allotment of the limited House patronage, and prized assignments to serve as party spokesperson on television. But these are woefully feeble in the face of the centrifugal force of state and local constituencies, single-interest groups, and the myth of independence and individualism.

"You have a hunting license to persuade—that's all," said House Democratic leader Jim Wright. A congressman agreed: "You know, there is nothing the leadership can offer me, really nothing."

THE PRESIDENCY:
WHAT PRICE TEAMWORK?

If legislators can differ sharply over both the desirability and practicability of unity within Congress, leaders of the executive branch seem to agree on the need for teamwork in the White House. Legislatures, after all, are classically given the right to deliberate, dawdle, and delay, but executives are supposed to produce speedy decisions and concerted action. This has been the very articulate major assumption of the executive mind from the start. In March 1788, in the *New York Packet,* Alexander Hamilton called for a "vigorous Executive" on the ground that a "feeble" one implied a feeble execution of government. Essential to vigor, he declared in the seventieth Federalist paper, was unity, followed by durability and competent powers. Beginning with George Washington and ever since, Presidents have fought to establish and maintain control over the executive branch.

Their frustrations as "team leaders" have expanded about as fast as the executive branch itself. Throughout this century, presidential commissions, scholars of the presidency, and management experts have been urging a more unified executive. The Brownlow Committee of the late 1930s, on the proposition that the "President needs help," urged a compact executive team designed mainly to enhance the chief's ability to oversee and coordinate the executive. The Hoover Commissions during the Truman and Eisenhower Administrations endorsed a strong presidential staff and incidentally legitimated the kind of presidential power that conservatives had associated with the New Deal. Later advisory groups even more forcefully called for more presidential control as well as coordination. Most recently, in urging better policy coordination, a President's Commission (1980) listed shortcomings that well summarize the standard indictment of presidential disorganization: "severely limited ability to anticipate trends, events, and problems; policy formulations which are narrow in scope, or if broadgauged, often hortatory and unrelated to purposive action; difficulty in integrating policy across functional lines and consequent difficulty in coordinating programs of action; lack of a sense of history or an institutional memory; and a dominant style which is reactive. Because people at high government levels are chronically overworked and are forced to spend most of their time in 'firefighting,' they lack the opportunity to engage in thoughtful reflection about what they are doing and why, the kind of reflection which might enable them to ameliorate some of these problems." The commission recommended a special staff for unified, long-range policy analysis under the President.

White House watchers have come up with a plethora of other proposals to unify and invigorate the presidency. A favorite idea— once proposed by ex-President Gerald Ford himself—is to appoint the Vice-President as a powerful chief of staff. A variation is a powerful but dispensable chief of staff presiding over a set of reorganized staff offices—one for foreign affairs, perhaps, one for domestic, and the third for economic. White House reorganization ideas usually founder on the hard fact that Presidents will structure their office as they see fit, adapting and readapting it to political and administrative exigencies as they come along. As for the Vice-President becoming top staff man, this idea usually fades when someone recalls that Vice-Presidents are usually chosen to balance tickets, not to run complex decision-and-action machines—and besides, veeps cannot be fired.

The Cabinet—the most disappointing single entity in American government—has long attracted the solicitude of the reorganizers. "The Cabinet must be reorganized and given more authority," urges *Time*. Regroup seven existing departments into four (Human Resources, Natural Resources, Economic Development, Community Development), proposed a 1971 presidential commission headed by Roy Ash of Litton Industries. Revamp the Cabinet to align departmental jurisdictions with congressional committee domains, suggested Walter Mondale. View "the Cabinet secretaries as crucial links in an attenuated and vulnerable chain of command that extends from you down to career civil service managers in the bureaus and sub-bureaus of the major departments," two old Washington hands advised the "next President." Cabinet members, concluded the President's Commission (of 1980), should be seen as specialists running their own departments and carrying out presidential policies in their areas.

Others have given up hope that American Cabinets could ever resemble their European parliamentary counterparts, as truly collective decision-making units under the premiers. "The Cabinet is one of those institutions in which the whole is less than the sum of the parts," said George Reedy, one-time LBJ aide. "As a collective body, they are about as useful as the vermiform appendix." To others the Cabinet is worse than useless; it is dangerous. Cabinet members, who are initially presidential friends and indeed creatures, become presidential enemies as they fall into the magnetic field of the iron triangle. Rather than radiating the President's ideas and dynamism out into the departments and the whole Washington political arena, Cabinet officers often carry messages and pressures from their constituencies into the White House.

Finally, there is the bureaucracy, extending from the White House office into the executive office of the President, the departments, and out into the bureaucratic hinterlands. Americans have never known quite what to make of the federal civil service—whether to honor and elevate it, as in Sundquist's proposal to create a corps of professional government managers; or to despise it as a haven for graft, nepotism, make-work, and incompetence; or to reform and purify it. "What America needs," wrote political scientist and former Cabinet member Robert Wood, is "a better bureaucracy, not less of one, disciplined bureaucracy, not amateurs run riot." The upper echelons of the civil service might have been invigorated to some degree by the Civil Service Reform Act of 1978, which established a top civil service meritocracy whose members could be moved from agency to agency, provided firmer protection for the employment rights of federal personnel, and gave the President more power to hire and place political appointees in key agencies. Rather than revitalizing the federal service, or even moderately enhancing White House capacity to develop teamwork at the upper echelons, the effort encountered the contempt of the Reagan White House for the federal bureaucracy and lies in limbo.

The question remains: What kind of presidency do we want, for what purposes? The deep popular ambivalence toward the American federal executive continues to haunt any discussion of the office. Specialists in the presidency no sooner have proclaimed some fine new methods of unifying and invigorating the White House office than other—and sometimes even the same—specialists are lamenting the extent of presidential power, the excesses, secrecy, and manipulations of the strong President. Fear of presidential power is as old as the office, beginning with attacks by Jeffersonian Republicans on the "dictatorial" Washington and Adams, continuing through the Whig counterattacks on the Jacksonian presidency, the Populist fears of centralized executive authority, the Republican complaints about FDR's executive "usurpations," Vietnam-era attacks on the "imperial presidency," and manifested most recently in Democratic ire over Reagan's "ramming" budget and tax bills through Congress.

Inevitably, critics divide as well over proposals for containing presidential power, especially over the question of whether to curb it from within the executive establishment or from outside. The "internalists" propose such measures as a legislative limit on the number of White House assistants and a ban on White House assistants holding Cabinet office—the latter an evocation of the grim shadow of Henry Kissinger reaching from White House to State Department. To curb "excessive personal loyalty" to the President on the part of the White House staff—shades here of Watergate—some have proposed a broadened ethics-in-government act covering presidential assistants. Arthur S. Miller has advocated a public ombudsman within the executive branch and especially within the Executive Office—"an *advocatus diaboli,* who, in combination with a truly open government publicized by the media, could then operate as an internalized check upon an *excès de pouvoir. . . .*"

The "externalists" would rely more on reorganizing the pressures from outside the presidency—especially electoral restraints—in order to curb power grabs and excesses. One of the oldest proposals in this respect is the single six-year presidential term. Such a term was considered in the Constitutional Convention and has been proposed in Congress at least as far back as 1821, and innumerable times since. Practical men of affairs have renewed the idea, especially since Watergate.

"I can readily testify," wrote Jack Valenti, a top aide to Lyndon Johnson, "that no sooner does a president enter the White House than he begins his re-election campaign," which meant plunging again into "politics in the raw, jungle-smell aspect of the word." Another frequenter of the White House, former Secretary of State Cyrus Vance, contended that the "virtues of a single, six-year term are that a President could devote his full attention to national needs, rather than spending much of his energy on trying to win re-election; the paralysis in decision-making that grips the executive branch during the long primary campaign could be eliminated, and a single-term President would be less inclined to use his office for the purpose of courting voters to win re-election. . . ." It has also been argued that four years is too short a time for a President to put his program through Congress and the bureaucracy.

It is remarkable that such a proposal would achieve such durability among political leaders of a system founded on the principle of elections as means of hiring and firing leaders. Over and over again proponents of the single six-year term have been asked how they would feel around the middle of a six-year Buchanan or Harding or Nixon term if they knew that they had to suffer another three or four years under the man—and that even then the voters could not render their verdict on the incumbent. "A president whose term was limited to one six-year stretch," George Reedy points out further, "would be a president who could command about two years of enthusiasm, two years of acquiescence, and two years of obstruction." (I would change these numbers to one, two, and three.) Above all, as Richard Neustadt has suggested, a six-year term would make the presidency less accountable to the people.

How account for this continually surfacing proposal for a six-year term, for this "idea that will not die," in a democracy, especially in the light of its lack of popular support? The idea battens off our ambivalence over leadership and accountability. On the one hand, we want a President who, transcending politics, is able to resist improper party and interest-group pressures, even brave enough to court defeat for re-election, ready to soar above the raw politics of the jungle. On the other hand, we want a President who will carry into office a mandate from the people, who will need to maintain popular support from the people, and hence must play politics, and who must at a stated time regain a mandate from the people. We want a President, in short, who is above politics and yet also in politics.

Some of those who favor a more accountable and "politicized" presidency have their own remedy: repeal the 22nd Amendment, the constitutional barrier erected in 1951 against a presidential third term. Proponents of repeal do not contend, of course, that Presidents should, or would, typically seek a third term if the amendment should be repealed. They recognize that only the rare President would be able to govern effectively for more than eight years. What they want, however, is to compel second-term Presidents to face the fact that they *might* want another term, and hence to be compelled to maintain their standing with the electorate, and to strengthen a president's hand during Term II by warning rival politicians that there *might* be a Term III.

On this issue too the American people have shown their ambivalence over the decades, and nothing better symbolizes that equivocalness than the attitude of the men closest to the problem—past, present, and prospective Presidents of the United States. Harry Truman—to whom the amendment did not apply—had favored the two-term limitation in 1940 but exempted Roosevelt from it; in 1947 he seemed to support a *three*-term limitation, but he switched back to his earlier anti-third-term view in the early 1950s, only to come out flatly against the 22nd Amendment in 1959. Dwight Eisenhower seemed to disfavor the amendment toward the end of his first term, perhaps out of fear that the third-term limitation might reduce his influence during his second term, but on balance he seemed to favor the limitation toward the end of his second term. John Kennedy as a young congressman had voted for the amendment in 1947 and continued to favor it as President, though he worried that if he completed two terms he could not serve another, and hence would be at "the awkward age—too old to begin a new career and too young to write my memoirs."

Lyndon Johnson advocated a single six-year presidential term, and he never appeared to waver from that stand. Richard Nixon during his presidency seemed to favor a single six-year term, although he evidently encouraged the activities of an organization opposed to the 22nd Amendment. Gerald Ford as a congressman had voted for the amendment, and he adhered to this stand. Jimmy Carter originally seemed to support the third-term limitation, but toward the end of his term he told a group of visiting journalists that he had changed his mind and now favored a single six-year term, and he stuck to this position when I interviewed him fifteen months after he left office.

CONGRESS AND PRESIDENT: WEDLOCK OR DEADLOCK?

The oldest and toughest problem of our governmental system is the relationship of President and Congress. In no other area has there been greater intellectual confusion. The very term that schoolchildren learn for that relationship—the "separation of powers"—causes mental mischief, for nowhere else in the constitutional separation did the Framers more artfully *intermix* power than in the legislative-executive connection. Congress could pass laws, President veto them, Congress pass them over his veto. The President could draw up treaties, one-third plus one of the Senate could veto them. The President could nominate executive heads, the Senate could veto them by majority vote. Legislative and executive power has become even more scrambled in the two centuries since the Philadelphia convention as Congress made huge delegations of power to the executive branch, the President accumulated vast authority over foreign and military policy, and Congress in recent years seized much of the executive-appointment power and retrieved some of its authority over war making, the budget, and administrative organization.

But if the Framers required some kind of holy wedlock between the legislative and executive departments in the practical, mechanical, day-to-day handling of public affairs, at least for an activist government, they built powerful tendencies toward unholy deadlock in the very foundations of the political system. Nowhere did they apply Madison's strictures more craftily than in the different modes of selecting and empowering President and legislators—Madison's strictures, we recall, that the "great security against a gradual concentration of the several powers in the same department, consists in giving to those who administer each department the necessary constitutional means and personal motives to resist encroachments of the others," that "ambition must be made to counteract ambition," and that the "interest of the man must be connected with the constitutional rights of the place."

So, when we call for more teamwork between President and Congress, we cannot pretend that we are trying to bring together two disciplined armies and hence need only work out agreement on issues between the leaderships of each. Rather, we are seeking to unify a considerably decentralized executive army with a collection of guerrilla militias in the legislature. We might as well try to coordinate quicksilver. Greater unity between and *within* Senate and House, moreover, often produces greater *dis*unity between legislature and executive. Thus Presidents have often been able to marshal much more support in faction-ridden Congresses, where the "chief legislator" could exploit weak legislative leadership in House and Senate and play faction against faction, than in more centrally led chambers. On the other hand, on occasions when legislative leaders did have considerable power, and when that legislative leadership supported the President, as before 1910, he could maximize his influence in that kind of situation as well.

So the question of presidential-congressional teamwork is really a set of questions: Are we talking about an equal and creative partnership between the leaderships of the two branches—the kind of partnership ritualistically acclaimed at both ends of Pennsylvania Avenue but rarely put into practice? Or are we really talking about the kind of "teamwork" that results when one side dominates and directs the other—when the Congress exerts mastery over the presidency or vice versa?

Each side can marshal a formidable battery of powers against the other, when so minded. Congress not only possesses the basic legislative and fiscal authority; it has developed—as part of the *intermixing* of powers—a number of extraconstitutional or de facto powers. One of these is influence over the Administration through legislative oversight. In passing laws or appropriations, Congress can narrow the discretion it grants administrators, consult with administrators as to future plans, and threaten legislative retaliation if certain policies or procedures are not followed. Congress may even prescribe systematic oversight in the authorizing law itself. After a law is passed and its administration established, Congress may review, probe, and assess, with an eye to interesting the media and arousing a critical public opinion. At any point Congress can expose, harass, praise, threaten, coax, browbeat in trying to influence administrative policy and action.

Overall the results are mixed at best. I refer to the oversight of "Congress," but in practice oversight breaks down into numberless committees, subcommittees, and individual senators and congressmen engaged in numberless small fishing expeditions, hearing-room tussles, publicity campaigns, and even genteel blackmail, as they seek to gain some influence over the vast federal bureaucracy. But, as Sundquist points out, the result is often frustration: legislators "cannot ordinarily anticipate, and so take measures to forestall, administrative actions of which they disapprove; they lack information and authority to intervene while the action is going on; and while they can punish administrators afterwards, and propose corrective legislation, by then the damage will have been done." The fundamental problem is the diffusion of power in Congress itself, with the result that would-be "overseers" intervene here and there, in a spasmodic, ad hoc, uncoordinated, and often undisciplined manner, with little of the steady, comprehensive, continuing, and balanced examining and assessing that true oversight demands.

A more formidable congressional weapon for confronting the executive was the legislative veto, until its recent evisceration by the Supreme Court. The term itself reflects the swing of the pendulum from legislative to executive power and back. The Constitution of course gave Congress the positive power of lawmaking and the President the negative veto power; in this century the President usually acts as the policy formulator and Congress exercises the veto power by the simple device of voting against the President's proposals, or simply refusing to act on them. And just as the President for decades has employed the *threat* of veto to extract legislative concessions from Congress, so the legislative vetoers use this weapon against the White House.

Today the "legislative veto" refers typically—and in these pages—to a narrower congressional power: the right to review and disapprove specific actions proposed by the executive. This form of legislative veto, as set forth by Congress in the basic act, could be exercised by a majority vote in both houses, or by a two-thirds vote of one house, or even by a two-thirds vote of both houses; and the veto power may in effect be delegated to committees, subcommittees, or even a committee chairman, depending on the importance of the measure being considered for disapproval. In the past half century more than one hundred laws were passed—the great bulk of them in the latter part of those years—embodying some kind of legislative veto.

The legislative veto is now crippled, but not necessarily gone forever. Many congressional leaders would like to retrieve this power; most Presidents would radically limit it. Depending on the political state of executive-legislative relations it could, if re-established, benefit either side—benefit the President by enabling him to win laws he wants by accepting a built-in legislative veto, benefit Congress by giving it considerable influence over implementation of its legislation. A long period of congressional resurgence probably would bring back the legislative veto, though in modified form.

On the most crucial matters of all—war making and peace making—the partnership between President and Congress is more rhetoric than fact. From the start Congress has conceded the primacy of the President in precipitating as well as conducting hostilities. As wars have dragged on, senators in particular have become clamorous in their demands for more consultation between executive and legislature during the "road to war," but earlier, amid the precipitating crisis, members of Congress have tumbled over themselves to rally around not only their flag but their President. After World War II a series of controversial presidential interventions—Cuba, Dominican Republic, and especially Vietnam—produced a hostile reaction in Congress, culminating in passage of the War Powers Resolution of 1973; under its terms the President, in committing armed forces in a national emergency resulting from an attack on the United States or its military, must report the facts at once to Congress and consult with it. Within sixty days the troop commitment must be ended unless Congress declares war, or otherwise indicates its concurrence in continuing hostilities. The President is allowed another thirty days to withdraw troops if they are in jeopardy. The resolution further provided that after ninety days Congress, by concurrent resolution not subject to presidential veto, may direct the chief executive to withdraw the troops, but the constitutionality of this provision is now in doubt.

President Nixon vetoed the resolution, labeling it an unconstitutional intrusion into presidential authority and an action that would seriously undermine the "nation's ability to act decisively and convincingly in times of international crisis." Congress passed the resolution over his veto. Other Presidents besides Nixon have opposed congressional restraint on their war-making (and war-preventing) authority, and their reasons, like his, have been as much practical as constitutional. If the White House is to consult with Congress, with whom does it consult? All 535 members? The several score members of foreign and military policy committees? The chairpersons of the same? The elected leaders of House and Senate? And how much delay and loss of secrecy can be tolerated in such consultation?

Gerald Ford, just after leaving office, described the problem of simply *finding* congressional leaders to consult with during the Danang evacuation. "Without mentioning names," he said later in a public lecture, "here is where we found the leaders of Congress: two were in Mexico, three in Greece, one was in the Middle East, one was in Europe, and two were in the People's Republic of China. The rest we found in twelve widely scattered States of the Union." Congress happened to be in recess, he granted, but added caustically, "events, especially military operations, seldom wait for the Congress to meet."

To organize consultative machinery for crisis situations, it has been proposed that each chamber select a key person to serve as contact with the White House, or that an ongoing committee, on the alert to meet at short notice and capable of keeping military secrets, be authorized to represent the whole Congress in crisis consultations with the President. But Congress, always fearful of "centralization," and even more respectful of established leadership, has failed to organize—or even reorganize—consultative machinery. In a situation where the President is left with—from the standpoint of Congress—a still one-sided War Powers Resolution, and Congress with its usual diffusion of power, teamwork lags.

A genuine, continuing partnership between Congress and President has been equally elusive in the day-to-day making of foreign policy and conduct of foreign relations. Each side makes pious espousals of the need for teamwork while finding the other impossible to collaborate with. The President could not speak authoritatively in foreign affairs, Gerald Ford protested in vetoing a foreign-aid bill that he felt "shackled" him unduly, if his valid decisions could be reversed by a bare majority of congressmen. For Congress to become a virtual "co-administrator" in operational decisions, he said, would cause inefficiency, delay, and uncertainty. "In world affairs today, America can have only one foreign policy" and that "must be certain, clear and consistent." After the usual honeymoon with Congress was over, President Carter complained that he was beginning to reflect on the ability of the government "to act promptly and decisively" to help countries facing possible aggression.

Congressional spokesmen have been equally remonstrative. They complain of executive secrecy, rash and headlong action, failure to consult, failure even to inform. They like to quote Senator Arthur Vandenberg's plea of an earlier day: "Let us in on the takeoffs if you want us in on the crash landings." To be sure, congressional leaders grant clear primacy to the President in foreign policy. "I recognize that the President is the chief architect of American foreign policy," said Senator Church, while warning against second-guessing the chief executive. The President must be the "ultimate spokesman of American policy," said House majority leader Jim Wright. Many rank-and-file legislators agree in rhetoric but not in practice. It was a congressman, not a President, who complained of Congress having "535 Secretaries of State."

The issue has boiled down to "consultation." What they want, say congressional leaders, is "participation" (Hubert Humphrey), "consultation and accommodation of views" (Representative John Brademas), "a genuine dialogue" (Representative Lee Hamilton), and "collaboration" and "cooperation" (everyone). But each of these terms has different implications, and that is the problem. What really is consultation? "Consult with whom?" asks Sundquist. "Participate and collaborate and cooperate: on what decisions? In what manner? And if, after all the consultation, views are not accommodated, what then? Who has the last word?"

As usual, the machinery reorganizers have some proposals for uniting executive and legislature in foreign-policy making. One is to add members of Congress to the National Security Council. Another is to create a legislative-executive council or cabinet that would encourage joint discussion of foreign policy and even joint decision. Other proposals would seek to unify congressional foreign policy before trying to collaborate with the executive—for example, by bringing all the international and military affairs committees of both chambers under a supreme "joint committee" to guide Congress and even to oversee the National Security Council. Hubert Humphrey even proposed that such a joint committee might serve as a congressional "crisis management team."

Once again we see the triumph of hope over experience. Congress has shown neither will nor capacity to unify itself for better foreign-policy making. It has rarely been able to formulate a grand design or comprehensive program in this field. And if it did, the result might be less rather than more partnership with the executive. Or the result might be to make Congress more subordinate to the President. The reorganization of budget machinery is a dramatic example of the latter. Conceived to rehabilitate congressional control of the budget, the machinery was turned upside down in the spring of 1981, becoming more a weapon of presidential authority than congressional. There was little consultation and even less "partnership" between President Reagan and Speaker O'Neill, but a great deal of "teamwork" between the President and a congressional majority of Republicans and dissident Democrats.

The conclusion is inescapable: It is difficult to reorganize machinery to create more partnership between the executive and legislative branches because of the diffusion of power in both branches, especially the legislative. It is almost impossible to centralize authority, and hence make it more accountable and responsible, in House and Senate. And even if machinery were changed, the pattern of political motivations, perceptions, ambitions, rewards, deprivations, and other behaviors surrounding that machinery could not so easily be transformed.

Congress, in short, can tinker with machinery but it cannot fundamentally reform or reorganize itself from within. This is also true of the executive branch, though to a lesser degree. Both are subject to the power forces, the political pressures, operating on them and through them and within them.

Let us face reality. The Framers have simply been too shrewd for us. They have outwitted us. They designed separated institutions that cannot be unified by mechanical linkages, frail bridges, tinkering. If we are to "turn the Founders upside down"—to put together what they put asunder—we must directly confront the constitutional structure they erected.

EIGHT

Taking
the "Path Not Taken"

As at present constituted, the federal government lacks strength because its powers are divided, lacks promptness because its authorities are multiplied, lacks wieldiness because its processes are roundabout, lacks efficiency because its responsibility is indistinct and its action without competent direction. These are the exact words—I have simply omitted the quotation marks—that Woodrow Wilson penned almost a century ago in concluding his masterwork, *Congressional Government*. A century before Wilson wrote this, other students of government with names like Madison, Washington, and Hamilton could have used almost identical words to describe the Articles of Confederation, which they shortly would be abolishing.

A century from now—in the mid-2080s—will students of government be using the same words to describe the federal government? Will there indeed be a federal government to criticize? Having survived, with all its failings, two centuries of enormous economic and social change, several world wars, and wrenching internal strife, our constitutional system might seem timeless, permanent, impervious to change. Yet when we contemplate the tensions piling up in this explosive, hate-filled world, the proliferation of weapons, the breeding of new fanaticisms, the population time bomb, and the dwindling resources, we must wonder whether a divided, cumbersome, ineffective government can long survive in the nation's third century, much less the Western world's twenty-first.

Later Wilson was chided for taking an elitist attitude toward the American governmental system, for ignoring economics and politics and favoring an intelligent, meritorious aristocracy. In fact Wilson's was a cry for *leadership,* a cry he would utter time and again in the forty years of academic and public life that lay ahead of him. That cry is more urgent and valid today than ever. What we will need, in all the interstices of politics and society and at the top, is a compelling and creative leadership that not only will meet people's collective wants but will raise their needs and aspirations to the highest levels of self-realization and fulfillment.

For there come times in the history of every people—of Russians in 1917, of Britons in 1940 and 1945, of mainland Chinese in 1949, of French in 1958, of Egyptians in 1978, to mention only a few examples in the modern era—when leaders must in the short run *mis*represent as well as represent their followers, must call for a supreme national effort, for a popular capacity to grasp the enduring stakes of the whole community, above all for a collective willingness to sacrifice comfortable intellectual habits as well as comfortable ways of life. Leaders evoked that kind of response from Americans during the founding days, and later in 1861 and 1933. It may have been a matter mainly of luck whether a Jefferson or a Burr, a Lincoln or a Benjamin Harrison, a Woodrow Wilson or a Henry Cabot Lodge, a Roosevelt or a Hucy Long, a Dwight Eisenhower or a Joe McCarthy, stood at the helm of state during critical times. But can we depend on such good fortune during our third century?

I am not referring to some mystic bond between a people and its leadership, some media hype emanating from a presidential Rose Garden, some plebiscitary device whereby an electorate plucks a farmer-statesman from his plow. I am referring to a governmental system that provides for reasonable teamwork and efficiency, to a party system that sustains majority rule, to a constitutional system that protects minority rights. I mean a polity that identifies, recruits, elevates, empowers, sustains—and constrains—the kind of rare and gifted leadership that lifts a people out of its merely parochial, short-run interests into its highest qualities of humanness—compassion, generosity, and public spiritedness, along with individual self-expression and self-fulfillment.

Hence our political system must be tested by exacting criteria:

1. Does it enable, indeed compel, public officials to provide economical, efficient, and effective administration of governmental services?

2. Does it sustain leadership in transcending, when necessary, special-interest demands and the surface eddies of public opinion; does it compel leadership to respond to the more enduring needs and

aspirations of the people, and to be accountable to popular majorities in competitive elections?

3. Especially in foreign and economic policy, does the political system make for greater coherence in planning and policy making, more firmness, consistency, and clarity in decision making, greater coordination within and among military and foreign-policy agencies, speed and decisiveness in times of crisis?

4. Does it enable leaders to respond to the inarticulate needs of persons who cannot provide political support in return—to the adult voteless, to the unenfranchised persons under eighteen, to future generations; even more, does it encourage leaders to recognize "claims without constituencies"—that is, to respond to the highest canons of duty, trust, honor, responsibility, to stand up proudly before the ultimate "bars of history," to exercise when need be a transforming leadership that adapts institutional means to the service of human goals and values?

Such a system would have to be versatile indeed, sustaining leadership able to meet intense, diverse, and shifting demands. During the two centuries of our nationhood, Congress and presidency have on occasion demonstrated such versatility while competing, sometimes cooperating, to provide effective, representative, and responsible government. Both those institutions, however, have lost that capacity today—the presidency because of deep popular distrust after Vietnam and Watergate (a distrust not overcome by the Carter and Reagan presidencies), the Congress because of the dispersion of power and leadership throughout its two chambers, multitudinous committees, and 535 tiny but fiercely independent baronies. What is to be done?

CONFRONTING A SACRED COW

The first question is what need *not* be done if we wish to go about the serious business of rejuvenating the American constitutional system. And the second is, if something needs to be done, *can* it be done, given the longevity of the system, its entrenchment and entanglement in our present society, and continuing Constitution worship on the part of some Americans who have granted the Founding Fathers virtual papal infallibility.

It is in part this sacred-cow view of the Constitution that leads some Americans to favor tinkering with the system without really challenging its essential structure. Because the Constitution separates the presidency from Congress, there is the notion that if only "com-munication" could be improved between the legislative and executive branches, more "teamwork" would ensue. Various gimcracks are pro-posed. One is to give Cabinet members the right to speak on the House or Senate floor, so that the two sides could directly confront each other. Another is that key Administration leaders meet with selected congressional leaders "around the table," in some kind of joint (but unofficial) executive-legislative Cabinet.

I call such proposals gimcracks because they would have virtu-ally no effect on the power system in Washington. That system is rooted in a structure of divided and competitive voting and interest-group constituencies that keep White House and Congress separated. The problem is not that the two sides fail to communicate; they under-stand each other only too well, through a hundred formal and infor-mal channels of communication. The problem is when they disagree—and our system fosters disagreement. Getting them around the table would produce only superficial harmony at best, lasting only until the parties returned to their conflicting power bases. These proposals would do no harm, I grant, except that they divert us from the serious business at hand.

Other proposals are by no means so innocent, though equally futile, in my view. They would tear chunks out of the constitutional system and revamp them. Perhaps the most popular proposal of this sort is the single six-year term for President, discussed in the last chapter. Along with its other dangers, this proposal violates one of our basic democratic criteria—the accountability of leaders to the elec-torate. On this test, it would be better to repeal the amendment—the 22nd—that bars third terms, not because most Presidents should have a third term, or would want to, but because the possibility that they might in the end seek such a term would have a chastening influence both on the chief executive and his rivals.

Some bold spirits would even challenge the division of power between the federal and state governments, a division long and mis-leadingly called "federalism." They would do so by shifting large slices of power from the national government to the states, or from the state governments to the national, or by setting up regional gov-ernments that might absorb extensive authority from both levels. Thus they would defy the ultimate godhead of American politics. Theirs would be a rightful cause, considering the social and economic crimes that have been committed in the name of "states' rights." But it would be a quixotic cause too, for the current era of protest against the "federal monster" is no time to be concentrating more authority in Washington. Nor on the other hand dare we decentralize governmentally at a time when we continue to centralize economically (conglomerates) and socially (demographics, media concentration). "Problems are *national* or *planetary*," Arthur S. Miller reminds us, "and have been at least since the promulgation of the sixteenth amendment. A nation with a central income tax cannot be truly federal. . . ." As for regionalization, this lovely old idea, even if adoptable, would tend more to compound fragmentation than to solve it.

Is the Constitution, then, still the "totem and fetish" that people believe to possess "supernatural powers," as Max Lerner pictured it almost half a century ago? And if it is, should we abandon any hope that the Constitution could be amended to compel and sustain more effective, representative, accountable, and responsible leadership?

A recent intensive study of public attitudes toward the Constitution indicated that a large number of Americans still hold a reverential view of the 1787 charter. They called it a "masterpiece," "an incredible document," written by Founding Fathers who were giants in the sky. One respondent seemed to view it as virtually a security blanket: "The Constitution stands between order and chaos, between organized government and chaos, between ruthless power and helplessness." Others who were interviewed in depth, however, saw the Constitution variously as weak, ineffective, inequitable, outmoded, and needing reform and modernization. One respondent mentioned "too many loopholes through which the oligarchic elite of this country can forever maintain their power system."

A third type of respondent took a mixed view, feeling that it performed vital functions, such as maintaining order and overcoming crises, and should essentially be preserved, but also that it "is merely the will of the strongest for the time being," discriminates against some while helping others, and has elitist or at least paternalistic aspects. Viewing the Constitution realistically as both benign and repressive, these persons reflect the attitudes of a large number of Americans who evaluate it on the basis of its practical, day-to-day effectiveness—and who would probably wish to amend the Constitution if it ceased to be functional.

Even aside from polls, common observation finds highly critical or mixed attitudes toward the Constitution along with the reverential ones. Criticism has become more respectable in recent years as a result of critical examinations of the Constitution by men with the stature of Senator Fulbright, Douglas Dillon, Thomas Finletter, Lloyd Cutler, of journalists like Henry Hazlitt and Richard Strout (*The New Republic*'s longtime TRB), of academics stretching from the young Woodrow Wilson to William Yandell Elliott of Harvard, New Deal adviser Rexford Guy Tugwell, and Charles Hardin, a University of California professor who has become the intellectual leader of constitutional reform.

But is the Constitution amendable in any major way? The history of our constitutional system is the history of structural rigidity. The Constitution (since the first ten amendments, the original Bill of Rights) has been amended to change the powers of the national and state governments, to add to the size and powers of the electorate (granting the suffrage to blacks, women, and eighteen-year-olds), to diminish the power of the electorate (inability to vote for a presidential third term), very occasionally to make substantive policy (Prohibition, and then the repeal of it). Only in very small ways has the *structure* of our political system been altered. The rugged edifice of the constitutional checks and balances stands hardly touched—the separation of powers among President, Congress, and judiciary, the division of powers between the nation and the states.

Not wanting their charter easily trifled with, the astute Framers made it amendable only through a complex combination of national and state action. Amendments can be initiated either by a two-thirds vote in both chambers of Congress or by a national constitutional convention called by Congress at the request of two-thirds of the state legislatures; proposed amendments must be ratified by legislatures in three-fourths of the states, or by legislatures in the same. It is much simpler and more realistic, however, to note how easily amendments can be *blocked*—by a few persons constituting a legislative majority in *either house* in thirteen states. As ERA proponents most recently have seen, a measure may have vast support in Congress, among Presidents (and their First Ladies), in both major-party platforms, and in the great majority of state legislative chambers, and still die in the anti-majoritarian amending process. While significant changes have been brought about through extraconstitutional processes, such as the rise of the party and presidential systems, the written Constitution (as interpreted by the judiciary) still serves as the supreme arbiter.

Why not hold a second grand constitutional convention—in Philadelphia in 1987!—and draft a brand-new twenty-first-century charter? This is not exactly a new idea; recently states have filed scores of applications for such a convention, usually, however, to fix in constitutional cement specific policies such as balancing the budget or banning abortions. Today the idea of a constitutional convention is both impractical and dangerous. Impractical because, such a convention never having been held, procedures are so uncertain that one senator warned that holding a convention would be like entering a "black hole in space," and a Congress hostile to a convention might strangle it in restrictions and red tape. Dangerous, because if a convention ever were to get under way, it might conceivably break loose from congressional controls and become a runaway horse, in which case we would have to depend on thirteen state legislatures to save us. In short, we know so little about the dynamics of a national constitutional convention that it might be either impotent or out of control.

And if a convention somehow did contrive to meet and consider a whole new constitutional structure or even just a few key amendments, who would play the part of a James Madison or an Alexander Hamilton, a George Mason or a James Wilson? And who could lend it the prestige of a George Washington or a Benjamin Franklin?

The Constitution, in short, exemplifies the cunning of history. It most likely will allow only those structural alterations that fit its philosophy of divided powers and checks and balances, and suffers only a handful of "process" and "policy" amendments to run and survive its gauntlet. Then why talk about any basic, systemic reformation? For three reasons:

First, profound constitutional change may come willy-nilly during some great domestic or world crisis of the future. Such a crisis will spur leaders to consider basic alterations in the constitutional system, just as the approach of the Civil War caused the leaders of the day, including both James Buchanan and Abraham Lincoln, to contemplate hastily contrived changes in the system of federalism. It will be of the utmost importance, if such a crisis descends on us, that Americans will have done their homework in the Constitution and constitutional change, that there be intellectual resources in the bank of ideas on which they can draw.

Then too, in thinking about any kind of modernization, it will help to take a "holistic" approach—that is, to look at the entire constitutional system in the light of the economic and social and world trends that continue to transform our society. In effect, we can consider the present Constitution as one "model" to be compared to a quite different model of what a new constitution might look like.

Whether or not we like either model, or *any* model, this form of broad and imaginative conceptualization is a useful guide to analysis.

Finally, this is the time for "going back to school in the Constitution." In 1987 we will commemorate its two hundredth birthday. A great charter of government that on the whole has performed well for two hundred years deserves reconsideration and perhaps revamping as it enters its third century. A large number of official and unofficial re-examinations of the Constitution are under way in an effort to cerebrate as well as celebrate the occasion. Can we *think* our way out of our constitutional bind?

KNITTING THE GOVERNMENT TOGETHER

Some analysts answer this question by working up "process" changes to the Constitution; let us call such critics "process changers." As a practical matter they note that Americans, for all their Constitution worship and resistance to major *structural* changes in the system, have been willing to accept major alterations in key aspects of representation and procedures—thus the 13th, 14th, and 15th Amendments limited the powers of the states; the 17th Amendment substituted popular election of United States senators for selection by state legislatures; the 12th Amendment altered the workings of the Electoral College; the 22nd limited presidential terms to two. Make further nonstructural changes of such importance, the process changers contend, and we can rejuvenate the constitutional system without alarming Americans who shy away from changes in the overall shape of the system.

One procedural change of the utmost potential importance— broadening the presidential impeachment power—might not even require constitutional amendment, some process changers believe. Thomas Jefferson so construed the Constitution, they point out, that Presidents (and other officials) in whom Congress had lost political and governmental confidence—even without any suspicion of wrong-doing on their part—could be removed by a majority of representatives and a two-thirds vote of the Senate. Since the Vice-President might need also to be removed (as might have occurred in the case of Richard Nixon's Vice-President, Spiro Agnew), Congress could change the procedures for establishing the succession. The Speaker of the House, for example, might continue as the first successor; since the lower chamber chooses its own Speaker, and hence can reselect one, the House could put a new President into office from its own ranks, and indeed a further President or two if the new incumbent also lost the confidence of Congress.

Many oppose such a change because it would tilt the balance of power too heavily toward Congress, which could get rid of a President whenever it fell into sharp disagreement with him. Former congressman Henry S. Reuss would answer this objection by allowing Congress to depose the President by vote of a 60 percent majority in both houses; but the removed President *plus all members of Senate and House* would then have to run for re-election. Thus Congress would not change Presidents without major reason or cause—would not do so for trivial or personal reasons, certainly—for it would have to consider both its own electoral situation and the likely nature of the presidential successor.

Recognizing that such a change would come close to major structural alteration, other process changers favor a much simpler reform: the four-year term for members of Congress, concurrent with the presidential term. Such a change would of course require a constitutional amendment, but proponents contend that public sentiment would favor it for practical reasons. It would cut down on the cost and burden of "congressmen constantly running for re-election," and it would subject congressional candidates to the larger voting turnout of presidential election years as compared with congressional "off-year" elections. Besides, many state senate terms have been shifted from two to four years, as have state governorships, so Americans are used to such changes.

Whatever its merits for efficiency and economy, however, the four-year term has fallen afoul of the politics of checks and balances. Several Presidents have endorsed the concurrent four-year term; most members of Congress have opposed it, largely because of the "concurrent" feature. This feature would be grand when representatives were running on the coattails of popular Presidents, but horrendous when the President lacked popular appeal—as has been so often the case in recent decades—or when they opposed a popular President. If they had to make a change, most congressmen would favor a *non*concurrent term; better to run on their own in the off year, they would calculate, than to risk joining fortunes with a presidential candidate of unpredictable popularity. But many representatives do not want any change at all, while senators turn red, white, and blue at the very thought of a four-year term for the Senate. And it is representatives and senators, not Presidents, who initiate constitutional amendments.

Another version of the four-year proposal is even more controversial, and would have far-reaching implications. This is the idea of a "team ticket" among President and representatives and possibly even senators. Under this proposal, "voters in each congressional district would be required to vote for a trio of candidates, as a team, for President, Vice-President and the House of Representatives," in Lloyd Cutler's summary of the scheme. "This would tie the political fortunes of the party's presidential and congressional candidates to one another, and provide some incentive for sticking together after they are elected. Such a proposal could be combined with a four-year term for members of the House of Representatives." The hope would be that after running as a team, President and congressman would govern as a team and stand accountable to the voters as a team.

Would such a change make partners of President and congressman? Long experience with the "team ticket" of President and Vice-President is hardly auspicious, since the two men have often gone their own way politically after being "teamed" on the ballot, as in the case of Franklin Roosevelt and John N. Garner. To become a member of the team ticket, congressional candidates would not need to agree on issues with the presidential candidate; indeed, the former might be nominated long before the latter, and in any event, candidates for President and for the House would typically have very little to do with the others' nominations. The congressional candidate would become a member of the team ticket entirely on his or her own, without obligation to, or perhaps any connection with, the head of the ticket. Both would either win or lose together, but if victorious, there would seem to be little more reason than at present for the two to cooperate. To be sure, each might be somewhat more solicitous of the other's political needs—the member of Congress in particular might try to "sell" the President in his or her district—but both in office would go their own way depending on their perception of their political needs for re-election. Presidents would continue to appeal to a national constituency, and their several hundred "teammates" in the House to local ones—and the total in politics, unlike mathematics, would not add up to the sum of the parts, under present political conditions.

The team ticket, in short, would bring President and congressman together in a quick election-day embrace and could not compensate for the absence in American politics of the kind of unity that a strong party could produce because of its power over the nomination and election of teams of candidates. The proposal, moreover, would not touch senators, unless they too were to be added to the team ticket. This might require four-year terms for them as well, and as Cutler adds, no one "has challenged the gods of the Olympian Senate by advancing such a proposal."

A very different type of proposal—also offered by the innovative Henry Reuss—would aim at the very heart of presidential-congressional deadlock by compelling or authorizing Presidents to choose at least half of their Cabinet from among their fellow partisans in House and Senate, *but allowing the "legislative" Cabinet members to keep their seats in Congress.* This is not simply another version of the old idea of a legislative-executive cabinet or council aimed at better communication and coordination between executive and legislature. The Reuss scheme would permit members of Congress to retain not only their seats and seniority but also, it is hoped, their influence on the Hill, and at the same time grant them formal (even paid) top-ranking positions in the Administration. Such a plan, according to advocates, would bring each side more intimately into the problems and politics of the other, extend legislative influence into the executive and executive influence into the legislature, foster between the two a genuine teamwork based on shared perspectives and even political interests, and develop a far greater sense of collective responsibility.

Unlike the simple "coordinating" proposals, the Reuss idea would require a constitutional amendment, for presently Section 6 of Article One forbids any "person holding any office under the United States" to be a "member of either house during his continuance in office." Would the potential benefits of such a change justify opening up the amending process? Certainly it gets closer to the heart of the problem than simple coordinating-type reforms. The "congressional" members of the joint Cabinet could bring back the President's proposals and needs to the Hill secure in their position there, no matter how unpopular the proposals. They could speak for congressional attitudes and interests in the executive branch secure in the knowledge that their status there was firm too; a President would think twice before sacking a joint Cabinet member who was both Secretary of the Treasury *and* chairman of the Senate Finance Committee!

Still, the reach of this reform would be sharply limited. If things began to fall apart in the White House, congressional members of the joint Cabinet would have to calculate where their future political interests lay. Typically, they would have built up loyal constituencies in their states or districts, as the foundation of their political power. If the joint Cabinet included, for example, a senator from an anti-civil-rights state working with a pro-civil-rights President, or a congressman from a poor, heavily urbanized district working with an economy-minded President, those Cabinet members would have to decide whether they could antagonize local interests by taking "national" positions. They might opt to support the President because the White House could help them in various ways, or simply because they felt that this was the right thing to do. But the leadership in the White House might not be there very long, and most senators facing a reelection campaign would rather be "wrong" than ex-senators.

Nor would Presidents have an easy time with such a joint Cabinet. They would have to deal with independent persons holding jobs in the White House but able to fall back on their congressional positions whenever they wished. The congressional members of the Cabinet might insert the politics of Congress and of special-interest groups too deeply into the President's own domain. It is hard enough to hold a group of proud, self-assured persons together even when they are on your own payroll. It would be supremely difficult to hold together a group of politicians, half of whom could easily, perhaps triumphantly or even vengefully, fall back on their own bailiwicks. Such a change might curb presidential power by shifting checks and balances directly into the President's official family, but chief executives, feeling cornered, might respond by returning to and mobilizing *their* popular, national constituency in a display of independent presidential popularity and power. A curbed imperial presidency, in short, might give way to a dangerously personalistic and plebiscitary one.

These proposals, innovative and daring though they may seem, cannot *by themselves* break the power deadlock in Washington and the country. They do not outwit the Framers' cunning. They do not resolve the separation of powers and checks and balances. They do not overcome Madison's strategy of dividing government not only by separating officials but by pitting them against one another through pinning them to competing constituencies. They do not establish a collective leadership with power and accountability arrayed against a collective opposition offering a responsible alternative credo, set of goals, and program.

There is a missing ingredient in these proposals. It is called party. By developing structured support within the mass electorate, parties provide common political foundations for legislative and executive officials. By shaping a platform—a set of ways and means—parties provide common guidelines to partisans in White House and Congress. By providing a relatively steady flow of political support, parties enable leaders to anticipate problems and plan ahead, knowing that power resources will be available for future needs. By organizing conflict on the basis of partisan rivalry rather than institutional checks and balances, parties provide meaningful and exciting alternatives to the electorate even as they channel and shape public opinion.

The team ticket, in particular, could succeed in unifying government only in a context of strong parties. Members of Congress would continue to act independently of Presidents unless party organizations and leaders served as unifying mechanisms, denying party nomination or renomination to representatives who deserted the party platform, compelling Presidents to work with congressmen on the basis of that platform. The same holds true with the Reuss scheme for a joint presidential-congressional Cabinet. The present political fragmentation would simply be replicated in that Cabinet unless a powerful unifying force could operate among the electorate, in the form of a national party that provided political support for politicians willing to take national positions. Only the unifying "second" constitution of party can overcome the "first" constitution of power separation and division.

CONCEIVING THE INCONCEIVABLE

Some critics of our constitutional system disdain as "half measures" such reforms as the four-year congressional term and the executive-legislative Cabinet. Only a counterstrategy of fundamental constitutional change can overcome the strategy of Madison and the other Founding Fathers, they assert. If the American people are to be advised to consider such drastic action as changing the Constitution, it is urged, they should not waste their efforts on palliatives. Rather they should attack the whole structure of government. If the Constitution reigns as our king, we should remember the old admonition—when you strike at a monarch, strike at the jugular.

Bluntly put, their modest proposal is to substitute the parliamentary system of "unified leadership and collective responsibility" for the American system of "counterbalanced power, fragmented representation, and individual leadership." To the objection that such a change would be inconceivable at this point in the nation's history, they answer that after two hundred years no time for change is better, and that it is equally inconceivable that our present constitutional system can last another hundred years, given the harsh demands and

acute crises that lie ahead. To those who say that the moderate constitutional changes proposed by the process changers is enough, critics respond that the problem is far outrunning step-by-step reform.
Let us call these bold critics structure changers, or structuralists.

The structuralists have their models, living models in the parliamentary and Cabinet arrangements of scores of democratic polities
around the world. For years the British system, with its unification of
party-parliament-Cabinet-prime minister, and with its potent and responsible "H.M. loyal opposition," has served as the leading model
for Americans disenchanted by their checks and balances. More recently, as the British have experienced their own difficulties in governing (at least before Thatcher), structuralists have turned more to
the present French model. Under the Fifth Republic, the president of
France has not only continued as chief of state and as "France's
guide," as Charles de Gaulle put it, but has become the chief executive, politician-in-chief, and to a considerable extent chief legislator.
Popularly elected, and thus possessing their own constituencies, French
presidents can dissolve Parliament and call for a new election, without
themselves having to run (though they may be forced out sooner or
later by the outcome of the new parliamentary elections).

Thus the French have grafted a presidential system onto a parliamentary one, and it works far better than many had expected. Mit-
terrand's difficulties have been more political and policy than institutional. A modified checks-and-balance system remains. "Under the
terms of the present constitution," according to Kay Lawson, "the
president must govern through a prime minister, and the prime minister must have the confidence of parliament. Any legislature with a
firm majority against the president can successfully wrest power back
from the president by consistently voting against the bills presented
by the government." The elevation of the Socialist opposition party to
power in 1981 and the recent tendency toward a relatively strong two-
party system provide the French with the foundations of a stable and
effective government. Miraculously the French have—largely under
the guidance of a transforming leader, General de Gaulle—changed
their constitutional and political structure without major violence.

The American constitutionalists of 1787, willing to reappraise
and reconstitute the existing system under the Articles of Confederation, were the supreme structure changers of American history. The
major transformation they wrought was, of course, the strengthening
of the national government in relation to the states. Of almost equal
importance was their restructuring of the central government—and

especially in setting up a far stronger executive than had existed under the Articles. For some of the Framers, however, creating a powerful presidency was something like creating what, in a later age, would be called a Frankenstein's monster. But, having seen state assemblies succumb to "leveling" movements and even mob rule, they also feared excessive legislative power.

Gouverneur Morris had summed up the dilemma: "Make the Executive too weak: The Legislature will usurp his powers. Make him too strong: He will usurp on the Legislature." How link the two in a fashion to control both?

Back and forth the delegates teetered on this issue. No less than five times they voted in favor of selection of the new chief executive by the legislature. If this plan had stuck, the Framers would have given us the essence of a parliamentary system of government—the first on the globe. To balance executive-legislative power they might have gone on at the convention to add—or later structuralists might have added—a provision allowing the President to dissolve the House of Representatives, or perhaps the whole Congress, and call for new elections. Finally, however, the delegates teetered away from the parliamentary system for good, and instead bequeathed us our present system of legislative-executive separation of powers.

For almost a century the presidential-congressional system was hardly challenged in an intellectually serious way. Rather, American constitutionalists argued over the division of power between the national and state governments—and indeed, ended up fighting a war over it. With this issue partially settled by the northern victory, scholars, lawyers, and politicians could focus on the workings of the national government. *The Nation,* under its redoubtable editor Godkin, published editorials and articles critical of Congress and strongly partial to a more "responsible" government. In 1879, as a Princeton senior still in his early twenties, Woodrow Wilson submitted a paper, "Cabinet Government in the United States," to *The International Review,* edited by another young man named Henry Cabot Lodge. Appearing the same year, the essay took *The Nation* line in its attack on "irresponsible committee government" in Congress and its plea for a national leadership accountable to the people. Six years later Wilson published *Congressional Government,* a powerful attack on the fragmentation and irresponsibility and petty leadership of Congress. Wilson had still not set eyes on the place.

Criticism of the constitutional system and its checks and balances waned around the turn of the century, in part because stronger

Presidents like Grover Cleveland, William McKinley, and Theodore Roosevelt were providing the kind of national leadership that men like Wilson were demanding, and autocratic Speakers like "Czar" Thomas Reed were unifying party ranks in the House. Wilson's own change of attitude was reflected in his *Constitutional Government* (1908). "Greatly as the practice . . . of Presidents has varied," he now wrote, "there can be no mistaking the fact that we have grown more and more inclined from generation to generation to look to the President as the unifying force in our complex system, the leader both of his party and of the nation." The work indeed became an eloquent paean—very quotable and later much quoted—to presidential leadership.

During the first three or four decades of this century there were relatively few searching and critical examinations of the constitutional system. If Presidents like Wilson and the two Roosevelts could provide crisis government at times of great national need, why bother to change the Constitution, or even the machinery? *Crisis Government* indeed was the title of a volume published by Lindsay Rogers in 1934, in which the Columbia professor roundly attacked the weaknesses of Congress and other parliaments, called for more centralized authority in democracies, and predicted that "a Presidential dictatorship like that in Washington may have to be resorted to more and more frequently even in more normal times." Rogers approvingly quoted Wilson's words in *Constitutional Government:* "The President is at liberty, both in law and conscience, to be as big a man as he can."

During the 1930s and 1940s, and especially during the Cold War, journalists, and scholars like E. S. Corwin of Princeton, became increasingly worried about the expansion of presidential power, even while they remained equally concerned by the intermittent stalemate between President and Congress. Americans had not found a means of giving the President his necessary powers without impairing the control of Congress, or of giving Congress control without depriving the President of needed power. Iconoclasts were speaking up, willing to challenge the Constitution's infallibility.

Do we need *"A New Constitution Now"?* asked Henry Hazlitt in 1942. His answer was emphatically yes, and his proposals were almost revolutionary. Congress would choose the President, and the President would have the power to dissolve the legislature. The powers of the Senate would be reduced to make the houses more equal. A Cabinet system would be established. Hazlitt would also abolish the vice-presidency; give representatives staggered four-year terms, with

one-quarter of the House elected each year; shift Supreme Court appointment power from the President to state governors and legislators;
and give the President the item veto over appropriations. And to help
enact such controversial amendments, he would amend the amending
clause itself, substituting a national referendum for the present laby-
rinthine process.

Other bold proposals followed. In 1945 Thomas Finletter advocated the dissolution power for the President; upon dissolution there
would be new elections for the President and for members of Congress, all of whom—senators and representatives alike—would have
six-year terms concurrent with the President's nonrenewable six-year
term. Leland Baldwin proposed presidential power to dissolve a re-
constituted unicameral Congress, two hundred members of which
would be elected for five-year terms. Baldwin added some intriguing
gimmicks: the President could select enough at-large congressmen to
give his party a 55 percent majority in Congress; he could also pick
fifty at-large senators with congressional consent. Baldwin too would
abolish the vice-presidency (no one seems to like this institution) and
the Electoral College.

Perhaps the most thoughtful of proposals for fundamental change
came from Charles M. Hardin, a political scientist long concerned
about divided government and the need to create a unified government and a vigorous opposition. Hardin proposed in 1974 that Presidents, senators, and congressmen be elected for concurrent four-year
terms; that 150 members be added to the present size of the House,
these members to be elected at-large and so divided between the parties that the party winning the presidency would have a clear majority
in the House; that presidential candidates be nominated by party committees composed of all House members and all House candidates of
the party. To curb excessive executive power, the President's veto
could be overridden by an adverse majority vote in the House. Hardin
would deal frontally with the old "upper-chamber problem." The Senate would lose its power to approve treaties and presidential nominations. If the Senate rejected a measure that had been passed by the
House twice in the same form in not less than a sixty-day interval, the
bill would go to the President. The opposition leader would be provided with a seat in the House, privileged membership on committees
and access to the floor, an official residence, and funds for staff and
travel.

Both the strength and weaknesses of these, and many other, proposals were reflected in the wide range and variety of the persons who

made them. Hazlitt was a very conservative columnist, Finletter a former secretary of the air force and moderate Democrat, Hardin a longtime student of agricultural policy and a liberal Democrat. Rexford G. Tugwell, who in 1974 came out with even more sweeping proposals for constitutional revision, including even a transformation of the system of federalism, was on the left wing of the New Deal. Other reformers also stretched across the political spectrum, indicating that the proposals might have wide appeal but also that they reflected a thin consensus among widely different ideological positions.

It would be easy to dismiss out of hand these sweeping, almost breathtaking proposals on the ground that it would be absolutely inconceivable for the American people, or even for the Senate or House, to accept changes that would go to the very foundation of their existence. But we are venturing here to conceive the inconceivable. These ideas must be subjected to analysis, not dismissal on the easy ground of "impracticality." The question is, what would be the results, in terms of our criteria of government, if such proposals *were* put into effect?

In most of these proposals the cardinal constitutional changes, designed to link and strengthen and stabilize presidential and congressional power, are threefold: to unify the two branches through selection of the President by Congress; through coordinating the terms of office of President, senator, and congressman; or through the power of dissolution in order to seek and act on a mandate from the electorate. Few critics favor congressional selection of the President, for memories of the Third Republic and other weak parliamentary regimes that hire and fire Cabinets almost monthly, warn us of the hairtrigger regimes, exploding under the slightest pressure, that would result. Coordination of terms of office alone, on the other hand, is seen as inadequate to pull the government together because centrifugal forces would still dominate the election process.

The big issue is the third of these proposals, dissolution. If the President, faced with congressional obstruction or deadlock, could send the senators and congressmen home to face an election campaign, it is urged, and if the President ran for re-election at the same time, the two branches would be brought into unity at the grass roots. The mere threat of dissolution by the President, indeed, would tend to discourage deadlock, because neither President nor legislators would relish the thought of the effort, expense, and possible defeat involved in an election campaign. Hence White House and Hill would "go to the people" only if irrevocably divided over the most fundamental of issues—and in that event they *should* go.

Would Presidents in fact employ their power of dissolution? It might be a useful weapon under certain circumstances, but typically chief executives would have to face the hard facts of American pluralism. If they dissolved Congress and ordered an election, many senators and congressmen would return to their own constituencies denouncing "presidential tyranny" and appealing to the single-interest, ethnic, and parochial forces that helped them get elected in the first place. Presidents would have to fear the possibility that a Congress still hostile to them, or even more hostile, might be returned to Washington, in which case the chief executives would seem to have been repudiated and the White House would be more frustrated than ever.

If under this dissolution system *Presidents* also ran for re-election, they might lose the election, thus presumably enabling their congressional adversaries to choose a new chief executive. Why should Presidents risk venturing into such a political thicket? Typically, it would seem far more prudent for them either to let the existing deadlock continue, or to follow a "consensus" game, trimming sails whichever way the popular and congressional winds blew, veering always toward the safe and innocuous "middle way" in order to hold the support of various blocs and single-interest groups. All this would hardly encourage leadership on either end of Pennsylvania Avenue.

On occasion a President might win re-election at the same time that a dissolved Congress won renewal of its own mandate in the same election; that is, the election results might simply restore the status quo ante. In that event stasis would doubtless persist, as both Congress and White House continued to claim that it truly spoke for the people. Conceivably the President and the dominant party in House and Senate (assuming they were of the same party) would be brought more closely together in the somewhat unified campaign effort, and if successful, the chief executive and the congressional party majorities might enjoy a honeymoon like the one usually accorded to Presidents after their inauguration, but this honeymoon might be the briefest of all.

The chances of success for a parliamentary system in the United States, like those of the less sweeping constitutional changes discussed earlier, would turn on the influence—the numbers, unity, organization, agreed-on credo, leadership—of national political parties in the states and localities. If local parties could order their ranks sufficiently to adopt candidates and policies in accord with other state and local parties, and above all in accord with the national party and its President or presidential candidate, then the party leadership at all levels could re-elect Presidents after dissolution, if they should be defeated, or at least give them the kind of support that would establish and maintain them as the head of a strong and responsible opposition. But Americans do not possess such a party system; our weak, decentralized parties under present conditions would far more likely make a shambles of a parliamentary system. We would probably end up with a multiparty system like that of the Third Republic in France, as regional and ideological interests tried to maximize their influence on the presidential election and later in a re-elected Congress.

Some champions of the parliamentary alternative grant that strong and unified parties are the necessary means of bracing our political system and that such parties are presently lacking. But that alternative, they contend, is precisely what we need in order to build a party system that in turn could make parliamentary government work in America. In particular, they contend, the President's power of dissolution would provide powerful leverage to national party leadership over state and local parties. The stakes would be so high—the stakes of winning or gaining the presidency, House and Senate in an election in which *all* national elected offices were up for grabs—that the whole party organization would need to be pulled together and tuned high in order to make a serious effort to win, and to be able to do this any time during the year, not merely in November.

There might have been a time—back in the days of Federalists and Democrats and Whigs, or in the days of strong party control of Senate and House and in big cities—when a system of parliamentary dissolution would indeed have strengthened national parties. But it is probably too late now; we may have passed the point of no return. To graft parliamentary arrangements on the present parties would expose their weaknesses rather than overcome them. If, for example, the President and other national party leaders tried to discipline or even unseat congressional rebels in the party by appealing to local voters, they could hardly be more successful than Franklin D. Roosevelt in his attempt to "purge" southern senators in 1938. Local economic interests, ethnic groups, "cause" movements, and party organizations here and there would hold the trump cards.

The secret of the parliamentary system does not lie in the power of dissolution. *It lies in the party system that makes dissolution an effective weapon.* In Britain, indeed, the process of dissolution is rarely exercised, though the *power* to use it is a disciplining factor. What has been crucial in Britain has been the existence of centralized national parties with relatively unified ideology and relatively homogeneous memberships that included rank-and-file activists—third cadres—that could link national leaders and programs with parties' grass-roots efforts. Dissolution is a technique for applying party discipline, not the primary cause of that discipline.

Thus party change becomes pivotal in any constitutional change; party is the essence of structure. It is for this reason that the proposals of Charles Hardin become so significant.

By granting the party winning the presidency enough representatives-at-large to guarantee control of the House to that party, by vesting the national party leadership with control over the choosing and rejecting of candidates for nomination as representative-at-large, by placing party control of presidential nominations in the hands of House party members and candidates, by giving the House of Representatives dominant status and reducing the Senate to "second-chamber" rank, and by allowing members of Congress to serve in the executive branch—and by combining all these changes in one package—Hardin would provide the kind of party centrality and vigor crucial to a parliamentary system for the United States. By setting up a party opposition with a collective leadership arrayed against the party in power, he would strengthen and regularize the battle between "ins" and "outs" so crucial to a democracy. To be sure, some of his proposals might seem retrogressive, such as re-creating a "caucus" system in the House for nominating Presidents that would much resemble the exclusive congressional system for choosing Presidents that the Jacksonians threw out as undemocratic. But in this case Hardin's congressional nominating process could be made part of a broader presidential nominating convention that also included delegates locally chosen under party loyalty provisions.

But even as one considers these proposals and views them as both reasonable and urgent, one questions the prospects of Americans, however reform-minded, putting them into effect. The proposals of Hardin and other reformers would work only if instituted as a package, and both the American temper and the American amending process would militate against that approach. The parliamentary system could not be established without sharply reducing the powers of the Senate, and some believe that the Senate's powers, because of the implied protection for small states in Article Five of the Constitution, are beyond the reach of even constitutional amendment. But above all, the parliamentary system would assume strong parties, nationally organized, firmly structured, participatory of grass roots. The United States has never had such parties and they do not exist now.

In short, if the Framers designed a *constitutional* system that fragmented governmental authority by diffusing it among cross-checking institutions (President, Senate, etc.), can we re-create a *party* system powerful enough to bind those institutions together? Would party renewal do the job alone, or do we need both party *and* constitutional reformation?

NINE

The Realignment of Power

$\mathbf{M}$AN an' boy," Mr. Dooley said to Mr. Hennessy, "I've seen th' dimmycratic party hangin' to th' ropes a score iv times. . . . I've gone to sleep nights wondhrin' where I'd throw away me vote afther this an' whin I woke up there was that crazy-headed ol' loon iv a party with its hair sthreamin' in its eyes, an' an axe in its hand, chasin' raypublicans into th' tall grass. . . ." Many another bartender-philosopher since Mr. Dooley's day could make the same observation—most notably when Harry Truman chased Republicans from whistle-stop to whistle-stop in 1948.

But in 1980 we witnessed quite a different spectacle. Now it was the GOP elephant, its ears flapping and its trunk raised high, chasing Jimmy Carter and other Democrats into the high grass. It was indeed a wondrous sight, especially after all the predictions that the Republican Party was dying. But Ronald Reagan, defeated in 1976 in his bid to lead the Republican Party, had gathered his followers together again, captured the Republican nomination, revitalized the Grand Old Party, and—in a feat the country had not seen in fifty years—ousted an elected White House incumbent. Now, in office, he was building a presidential team, establishing close ties with Senate and House Republican leaders, pushing big budget and tax programs through Congress, and—most remarkable of all—sharing campaign money and other political resources with the party that had put him into the White House.

Ronald Reagan, in short, was giving us a textbook demonstration of how a leader both mobilizes and engages with his followers, wins office, and works closely with party leadership in governing the nation. How long he could continue this virtuoso performance was not clear at the end of his third year in the White House, especially in the wake of Republican loss of House seats in 1982. But for the time being, at least, he was refuting those who had predicted, in the backwash of Watergate, that the Republican Party was doomed. Even more, he was demonstrating that collective executive-legislative-bureaucratic leadership was possible, at least for a year or two, in a pluralistic society when a President took a strong doctrinal position in response to powerful sentiments in his party, provided clear policy guidance on fiscal issues, and nurtured the political party that served as the foundation of his power and authority.

He was reminding us of something else too—that a party leadership did not have to cling to the center to win high office, that a party that knew its own mind could draw a huge new constituency to the polls, and that "extremists" might govern more effectively than "moderates." Observing his first days in office, Meg Greenfield was moved to confess that moderation was not necessarily a virtue, that moderates simply stood in the center of a spectrum defined not by themselves but by the "extremists." Maybe Barry Goldwater, who had been editorially thwacked right and left for crying out that moderation in the pursuit of justice was no virtue, had had a point after all!

Reagan was demonstrating something even more important— that political polarization was not necessarily bad for the American people and might even be good for it. This was bracing news for a people too long lulled by bland and comforting paeans to compromises, centrism, consensus, bipartisanship, "national unity." Leaders of opinion had forgotten that the great forward movements of American democracy had emerged not out of consensus but fiery conflict— out of the struggles between Federalists and Jeffersonians, Whigs and Jacksonians, Free Soil Republicans and slaveholding Democrats, Bryanites and McKinleyites, Roosevelt Progressives and Old Guard Republicans, FDR Democrats and Hoover and Taft Republicans. These conflicts produced a reinvigoration of American democracy and new and more positive directions for the American people.

To be sure, the conflict of 1980 was a truncated one, for the Democrats had not responded in kind. Jimmy Carter had moved so far toward the center during his last two years in office that the Democracy could mount only a feeble defense against Reagan's onslaughts. But the sting of defeat might be making the Democrats of 1981–1984 more willing to respond to Nicholas von Hoffman's exhortation: "Politicize, polarize, ignite the rancors of politics, disunite, crack open the one-party state; no change, no democracy is possible without friction." The question as always was not *"whether* conflict"—it would inevitably appear in some form, malign or benign—but how we organized it.

Ronald Reagan in effect was conducting an experiment for us all—an experiment in party government. He was depending less on the reorganization of *machinery* to enact and implement his policies than on the organization of *power* rising out of militant conservative Republicanism and flowing into the federal government. He might not conduct this experiment well; he might even fail; but he was forcing the American people to re-examine a century-and-a-half-old formula—party government—as a foundation for successful presidential leadership and a strategy for effective government.

REPAIRING THE MAINSPRING

Political parties can serve as the mainspring of democracy, as the vital link between voters and rulers. They organize and focus public opinion. They aggregate "special" interests. They provide meaningful cues to voters, present them with alternatives at election time, propose programs, develop among party followers and party leaders in office support for such programs. They unify legislators and executives among themselves and with one another. They help hold government officials accountable to voters. They mobilize popular support for candidates and officeholders and hence are indispensable to democratic leadership.

No wonder Schattschneider could state that "political parties created democracy," that modern democracy was "unthinkable save in terms of parties," that parties were not merely "appendages of modern government" but were "the center of it and play determinative and creative roles in it."

Despite the confusion inside and outside of parties as to their proper role in the American democracy, and despite their organizational disarray, party watchers see heartening signs. One of these has been the increased interest in the role and potential of political parties on the part of the media. When David Broder made the case for strong political parties in *The Party's Over,* published in 1971, he stood virtually alone as a newsperson eager for the revitalization of parties. Although media coverage as a whole still focuses disproportionately on individual candidates rather than on the party structure that still undergirds electoral politics, one finds in both the print and electronic media a deeper understanding of the party system, its current defects and potential strength. Members of the fourth estate have been willing to re-evaluate the role of the press itself in the political process. In the last decade, Broder has been joined by Richard L. Strout of *The Christian Science Monitor,* Morton M. Kondracke of *The New Republic,* Ken Bode of NBC, Robert Shogan of the Los Angeles *Times,* Robert M. Kaus of *Harper's,* and other journalists whose coverage contributes to, as well as reports on, progress in the cause of party renewal and constitutional change.

The chief sign that some party resurgence may be under way comes from the parties themselves. Both national party committees have so developed modernized structures and promulgated specific issue positions as to suggest that they may have the capacity to become more relevant actors in the political process. In the last decade, the Democratic Party has led the way in party reorganization, the Republicans in grass-roots campaigning. A national bipartisan Committee for Party Renewal, numbering several hundred practitioners and scholars, actively promotes thinking on this matter.

One of the few positive outcomes of the turbulent 1968 Democratic National Convention was the establishment of a Rules Commission that not only dealt with convention procedures but assumed a much broader responsibility. Under the leadership of then Congressman James O'Hara and working with its sister Commission on Party Structure and Delegate Selection chaired by then Congressman Donald Fraser, the commissions jointly recommended to the 1972 Democratic National Convention a major restructuring of the national party, calling in particular for the convening of national party conferences in nonpresidential election years. Most of the recommendations were referred to a subsequent commission, chaired by former Governor Terry Sanford of North Carolina. The Sanford Charter Commission reported to the 1974 Democratic Midterm Conference—the first to be held by any major political party—which adopted a comprehensive national party charter, another first in party history. The 1974 conference defined the organizational structure of the party, codified its rules, and with the adoption of an economic agenda embraced by both the party's rank and file and elected leadership, set the stage for more policy-oriented conferences in the future.

In 1978, unhappily, the potential for a full-fledged issues discussion at the 1978 Democratic Midterm Conference was severely curtailed by an incumbent President in control of the party apparatus. Like most Presidents, Jimmy Carter feared rather than welcomed internal debate over his Administration's programs. Even in the absence of an incumbent President, the Democratic leadership's plans for the 1982 midterm conference demonstrated a distrust of the "grass-roots" component of the party by the adoption of a tightly controlled delegate selection process. But despite this "two-steps-forward-and-one-step-backwards" approach, some progress has been made. On a national level, the question is now at least framed in terms of *what type* of midterm conference will be held, rather than *whether* such a conference will occur at all.

The concept of party accountability has also won greater support and legal standing within the Democratic Party. During the civil rights battles of the sixties, some Democratic National Committee members unsuccessfully advocated that the committee publicly urge the Democratic Congressional Caucus to deny committee chairmanships and seniority privileges to Democratic members who condoned segregationist policies. Although the Democratic Caucus has yet to discipline its members on policy grounds, the national committee itself has taken a firmer stance, acting upon the mandate of its most recent national convention.

In a very specific resolution, the 1980 Democratic National Convention adopted a rule prohibiting national party support of candidates who opposed the ratification of the Equal Rights Amendment. Although criticized as an example of "special-interest" politics, this requirement enforcing a long-standing party commitment to securing the rights of a majority of our population can hardly be construed as a "single-issue" concern. Even those of us who are wary of "litmus tests" can view the Democratic Party's ERA stand as a healthy move toward the idea of formulating a basic statement of party principles to which party candidates will be held accountable. The relationship between a party and its elected officials is always a thorny one, and in American politics, where the organized party has little or no control over the designation of its nominees, applying party accountability standards is an especially challenging task. But the Democratic Party has at least begun the process of exploring avenues for closer ties between the party in office, the organized party, and the party-in-the-electorate by the establishment of a Commission on Party Accountability.

While Democrats were fighting over issues of organization and accountability, the Republican Party was developing informal mechanisms for shaping party policy positions, apart from the traditional adoption of a platform at its national nominating conventions. The

Tidewater Conferences of Republican officeholders, initiated by Senator Robert Packwood of Oregon, received considerable press attention. Although no binding commitments are made nor formal party positions taken at these conferences, they at least provide a forum for an exchange of policy views among one component of the Republican Party, its elected officials.

The real forte of the Republican National Committee has been the nuts-and-bolts aspects of electoral politics, fueled by ample funds. The great innovating leader in this effort was Ray Bliss, an unsung hero of American party development. The GOP has carried on the Bliss tradition in recent years by expanding its professional staff, actively recruiting and grooming candidates, and, most of all, exploiting the latest technological advances in such fields as computerization, direct-mail fund raising, and Madison Avenue advertising techniques. The Republican success in the 1980 elections was the grand climax of more than a decade's efforts. With a presidential candidate able to capitalize effectively on his opponent's record ("Are you better off today than you were four years ago?"), backed by a well-planned and coordinated media and direct-mail campaign ("Vote Republican—For a Change"), the party enjoyed substantial, if ephemeral, victories at every electoral level.

In the ideal world of a strong two-party system, each party would have pursued the various avenues of revitalization simultaneously and hence maximized their combined potential for issue orientation, party accountability, party restructuring, and electoral politics. But parties least of all live in an ideal world. Although they are pursuing a path that can ultimately lead to their renewal, it is a crooked path, often looping back on itself. More hopeful signs can be found on the state level.

State parties such as Minnesota's and Iowa's have long served as models of party organization, but they have stood almost alone. There are signs of party renewal in other states, however. In Massachusetts, long the epitome of individualistic, anti-party politics, the Democratic Party has become revitalized through its Charter movement. Spurred by the model of the 1974 Democratic National Midterm Conference, the state committee held a series of meetings throughout the Commonwealth in 1976 to solicit the opinions of rank-and-file Democrats of the role the party should play in Massachusetts politics. The result was a twelve-point "action plan" that called for strengthened party organization and for an issues convention to be held in June 1977. That convention in turn established a state Charter Commission whose most

controversial responsibility was to decide the question of whether to
hold preprimary party endorsing conventions. The commission, nearly
unanimous in its decision, voted in favor of an endorsing convention
for statewide offices. Based on the Connecticut challenge primary
model, the Massachusetts Democratic Party Charter requires that candidates win a majority of the convention vote to gain the endorsement,
while permitting nonendorsed candidates who receive at least 15 percent of the convention vote to contest the endorsed candidate in a
primary. The Charter also provides for nonelection-year statewide issues conventions where resolutions adopted by local caucuses form the
policy agenda for the convention itself.

The Massachusetts Charter movement can stand as a model for
other state parties bent on self-renewal. That movement engaged the
interest, energy, and ideas of hundreds of Democrats throughout the
state, both the "party activists" and the "party regulars." The network
thus formed provides a stronger grass-roots organizational base for the
party. The movement restructured the party organization, giving more
responsibility to local party committees, thus making those party positions more politically meaningful. The institutionalization of the issues convention provides an effective structure, starting with caucuses
(open to all registered party members) at the town and ward level,
for formulating a programmatic agenda every two years. Most significantly, the party regained some measure of control over its nominating
process by its call for endorsing conventions. Candidates seeking statewide office will now have to prove themselves to the organizational
party before having the opportunity to make a broader appeal to the
general electorate.

Of all the improvements adopted by the Massachusetts Democracy, by far the most important was the local caucus system. This device was by no means new; indeed, the caucus is one of the oldest
institutions in American politics and lies at the foundation of the Democratic parties of Minnesota, Iowa, and a few other states. But the local
caucus had not spread widely before its adoption by Massachusetts.
The genius of the caucus is that it exemplifies both *reform* and *renewal. Reform,* because the caucus must allow all rank-and-file Democrats to take part, is required to make a special effort to gather in
women, young persons, the elderly, and members of minority groups,
and gives everyone—whether a college sophomore or the biggest
Democrat in town—an equal voice and vote. To the degree that the
caucus actually attracts women and other groups ordinarily under-
represented in party organization, it can help meet affirmative-action

requirements. *Renewal,* because hundreds of local, participatory, active caucuses debating issues, recruiting members, choosing party officials, and discussing candidates are bound to have a supportive and indeed rejuvenating impact on the whole party structure above. And if the caucuses can come to have the central role in *nominating* candidates, displacing nominating primaries, the parties will have returned to their historic role in recruiting American political leadership.

But that is a big if, as a look at the presidential nominating process makes clear.

PRESIDENTS AND—OR VERSUS?—PARTIES

One fact towers over all others in the relation of party renewal to presidents and other political incumbents: The average officeholder hates a strong party, unless she or he happens to control it. That hate is somewhat logical. Most politicians in America gain high office not through party organizations, as we have seen, but through their personal organizations. They win nominations not by working through the party structure but by winning a primary election. Of course vote seekers are greedy and will accept all the party support they can get. But their heart belongs to the men and women who have worked for them, over the years, through thick and thin, sometimes across party lines.

All this is triply the case with the President. He does not win his actual nomination through the party convention, but long before the convention, in the state presidential primaries. The national party is of use to him to the degree it can help win the election; after the election its importance to him dwindles. It was not always thus. Great Presidents and other national leaders—John Adams and Alexander Hamilton, Thomas Jefferson and James Madison, Andrew Jackson and Martin Van Buren, Abraham Lincoln and William McKinley and Woodrow Wilson—were to varying degrees party builders, or at least party sustainers, and dependent on party once in office. But that was in the day when parties dominated the nomination system through their caucuses and conventions.

From the point of view of *party* leadership, the most important decision a political party makes is of course the choice of the persons who will carry the party's banner in the general elections as its presidential nominees. These candidates assume the role of chief spokespersons for the party platform as well as their own, later bearing public responsibility for the legislative enactment of the party's program. Yet most chief executives, wrapping themselves in the cloak of "President of All the People" on reaching the White House, sooner or later distance themselves from the national party. They tend to view it either as a vehicle to be used merely for the purpose of their own renomination and re-election or as irrelevant to their success. In 1980 Jimmy Carter called the Democratic Party an albatross around his neck. Thus national committees are either turned into a personalized campaign apparatus for the President or are left to wither on the vine.

To a large extent, the weakness of the party system itself permits and encourages casual disregard of the party on the part of other officeholders as well as the President. The gap between candidates and parties will not be bridged until the party regains control of its own nominating process. For as Schattschneider warned years ago, "Unless the party makes authoritative and effective nominations, it cannot stay in business. The nature of the nomination procedure determines the nature of the party; he who can make nominations is the owner of the party." Or as Boss Tweed put it more succinctly: "I don't care who does the electin' as long as I do the nominatin'."

The failure of parties to control their own destiny is most obvious and ominous at the presidential nominating level, and has long been painfully apparent to the parties themselves. Yet the steps the parties have taken in the name of "reform" have not always been toward renewal, and much of the debate has served to cloud rather than clarify the fundamental issues involved.

The Democratic Party took the initiative in subjecting its nominating process to critical examination after its divisive and chaotic national convention of 1968. Torn over the question of the Vietnam War, Democrats on both sides of the issue found themselves frustrated by a complex set of state regulations and party rules governing the nominating process, laws that seemed to thwart their attempts to have their views reflected at the national convention. Faced with "blind" delegate election in primaries where no presidential preferences appeared on the ballot, unable to find out the time, place, and procedures for local caucuses, angered by discovering that some delegates had been chosen well before the presidential election year, and outraged at such procedural abuses as proxy manipulation, a number of Democrats joined together to form an Ad Hoc Commission on the Democratic Selection of Presidential Nominees. Chaired by then Iowa Governor Harold Hughes, the commission took its case to the Rules Committee and ultimately to the floor of the 1968 convention itself to gain adoption of a resolution establishing a commission to ensure that all Democrats in the future would have a "full, meaningful, and timely" opportunity to participate in the presidential nominating process.

Thus was born the first in a series of commissions to examine party rules, the McGovern-Fraser Commission. Each Democratic National Convention has authorized a successor commission, popularly known by the name of its chairperson: the Mikulski Commission after 1972, the Winograd Commission after 1976, and the Hunt Commission after 1980.

In the continuing debate, it is easy to overlook one very real achievement of the original McGovern-Fraser Guidelines. Adopted in 1969, they did succeed in introducing and enforcing in the presidential nominating process fundamental standards of fairness that have prevailed to this day. They banned racial and sexual discrimination; required state parties to publish and make available adequate party rules describing the "when," "where," and "how" of participation; prohibited the imposition of fees that served as barriers to participation; required that public notice be given of party meetings; and put party apportionment on a "one Democrat, one vote" basis. These were true reforms and ought to be applauded. Yet the McGovern-Fraser and subsequent commissions failed adequately to address and resolve certain of the most fundamental questions for those of us who are *primarily* interested not in party reform but in party renewal.

The reformers did not understand that the most imperative task facing all those who would "come to the aid of their party" was less to rectify or redeem it than to repair and regenerate it. Trying to purge the Democracy of its sins in the 1960s was like trying to rid a terminal-cancer patient of his drinking habit. The invalid needed succor more than sermons. Carried along by the anti-Establishment spirit of the late 1960s and early 1970s, the reformers tried to cleanse the presidential primary system of its exclusive and elitist elements rather than containing it. Still influenced by old reformist and progressive fears of boss-controlled caucuses and back-room deals, they did not seize the opportunity to regenerate the one alternative to media-oriented, money-dominated presidential primaries—an alternative that was not new but had had a vital part in the expansion of American democratic politics.

That alternative was the national convention. I do not refer, of course, to our present national convention, often a sorry affair of media hype, political bombast, and artificial suspense that slavishly endorses the presidential candidate who won the most delegates in the earlier state primary "beauty contests." I refer to a deliberative, decision-making convention composed of *"thinking* delegates" (as Terry Sanford likes to term them), selected democratically in open, participatory local and state caucuses, accountable to the party rank and file back home but not slavishly bound to them; a convention that would typically open its proceedings with several candidates in the running, because no aspirant would have been able to "sweep" thousands of caucuses in several hundred congressional districts, and hence a convention that would be exciting and important because it truly would render a collective decision; a convention of a thousand or so third-cadre activists who not only could recruit presidential leaders but could help mobilize party support for a leader once nominated and congressional support for that leader if elected.

To restore the national convention to its commanding role in the presidential nomination process, to restore state and local conventions and caucuses to a central role in nominations of candidates for all major offices, we must rethink many aspects of our present selection process. We must ask first, whom have we allowed into the nominating process by opening it up to anyone who wants to come to the polls on presidential-primary day? Largely, to any persons who care to call themselves Democrats or Republicans on one specific day every two or four years. But parties cannot function well if they lack an identifiable membership base, composed of persons who have a demonstrable and long-term commitment to the party. Allowing voters to declare their party affiliation at the primary-election polls (and de-affiliating shortly thereafter if they wish) undermines the foundation on which responsible parties must be built. The first step, then, is the introduction of a mandatory party registration or enrollment requirement necessitating that those persons participating in party processes must be members of that party.

Already, I can hear cries of "elitism!" but I challenge any critic to name a major organization that permits nonmembers to vote for the officers that represent that organization in public life. Why should our political parties operate under different standards when the stakes —for all of us—are so much higher? Such a requirement need not be elitist, exclusionary, nor burdensome—which is why participation reforms are so necessary. It would be the responsibility of the party and election officials overseeing the system to provide notice of enrollment and registration deadlines, actively recruit new members, and develop simple, well-publicized procedures for registration and enrollment.

Secondly, the presidential-primary tide must be reversed, even while we try to salvage the better features of the present nomination method. Presidential primaries do expose candidates to public scrutiny, allow them to demonstrate their popularity and electability in November, and provide a forum for discussing issues, however superficially. The problem is that primary outcomes turn on media appeal rather than party support. Let's recognize primaries for what they really are: popularity contests, political "beauty contests." A few states in diverse areas of the country should be permitted to hold advisory presidential primaries so that candidates could demonstrate their political and popular support, *but no national convention delegates would be awarded to candidates on the basis of primary results.* Delegates would be chosen through a party caucus and convention process and allocated proportionately on the basis of the presidential preferences expressed by those participating in this process, not by the voters in the primary. The "beauty contest" results would be merely one of many factors that a party member might take into account in deciding which presidential candidate to support.

My reasons for opposing primaries are not limited to the drawbacks I see in the primary system itself, but also reflect a more positive belief that a caucus-convention system is a superior method for choosing our nominees and has important fringe benefits for our political system. Caucuses offer the party an opportunity for its members who are primarily enthusiastic about a particular candidate to widen their participation by supporting candidates for other offices and taking part in a variety of party activities. Ideally, participants in a caucus not only would come to register their presidential preferences, but would be enlisted as party committee members, assigned to a working subcommittee with a specific function, such as fund raising, membership recruitment, publicity, issue development, or the like, thus reinforcing and expanding the active organizational base of the party.

In a caucus system, members have the opportunity to meet face-to-face with those who share their own commitment to the party and can engage in discussion over the merits of specific candidates, the policies they support, and their electoral prospects. This kind of exchange challenges members to articulate and defend their reasons for supporting a particular candidate, makes for a better-informed decision, and develops the political skills of the participants. And it's a lot more fun than merely entering a beauty-contest primary, casting a lonely ballot, and returning home.

The proposal to prohibit binding primaries and institute the caucus-convention system is not only desirable; it now seems wholly legal. Recent court decisions like *Wigoda* and *La Follette* have upheld a party's right to impose reasonable rules and restrictions on state party procedures. I believe that legally the national committees could adopt and impose national rules banning the binding primary. That they have the will to do so is less certain.

The national committees' authority to limit the number, timing, and location of *advisory* presidential primaries—the beauty contests— is a different question. Because such primaries would not be an integral part of the nominating process, the national parties would be hard put to find a legal basis for challenging states who adopted such preferential primaries outside the framework of national party rules. This obstacle could be overcome, however, by adopting sanctions against presidential candidates who entered primaries not permitted by the party. Requiring one's candidates to abide by the rules of the party whose nomination they seek introduces a measure of accountability and rationality to the process, not dissimilar from the DNC's current position on candidate support for the ERA.

What sanctions or disincentives, then, could the party impose? If matching funds were now funneled through the party rather than directly to candidates, the solution would be at once obvious and effective: No money would be distributed to candidates who violated the rules. In the absence of such a provision—which I would strongly support—the parties must find other mechanisms. Parties could sponsor televised issue forums, picking up the media "tab," in order to stimulate debate between and among its candidates and prohibit from participation any candidate violating its rules. Party-sponsored televised debates of this nature would serve two purposes: providing an appropriate and meaningful sanction, and lifting the level of issue discussion in the campaign.

Finally, the presidential nominating process must try to foster a better relationship among the party's candidates, officeholders, party officials, and party cadres at all levels. The thorniest issue here is the extent to which officeholders should claim favored, even automatic, membership in party nominating conventions—especially, of course, the presidential. The debate on this issue has been clouded by myths, simplistic solutions, and a lack of understanding of the primary reason why the participation of public and party leaders is crucial to the party.

One myth that has long made the rounds is that party leaders and elected officials have been *excluded* from the nominating process. Let's examine that myth. What the McGovern-Fraser Commission Guidelines and subsequent rules actually did was require that party leaders and elected officials compete under the same rules applicable to all other Democrats: no Democrat was made "more equal" than another; each had to run as a candidate for delegate, declare a presidential preference, support a presidential candidate who had sufficient popular strength to be entitled to delegates, and win her or his election as delegate. Some of those purporting to speak on behalf of these officials suggest that such equality is an indignity not to be visited upon our public officeholders, that it is politically undesirable to place elected officials in the position of having to "choose sides" and thus alienate a portion of their constituency by declaring for a presidential candidate, and that said officials are embarrassed to be forced into a competition that they might lose.

One might indeed weep for such officials, unless one remembered that they must declare a presidential preference only if they wish to serve as delegate; otherwise they could stay uncommitted as long as they wished. I submit that officeholders still remain "more equal" than others in terms of their ability to win election as a delegate: they have higher name recognition, an ongoing political organization upon which they can rely for support, access to the media, and other advantages generally denied to a third-cadre activist seeking a delegate position.

Further, those same persons who rail against requiring elected officials to endorse a presidential candidate speak just as vociferously on behalf of the "peer review" function these officials are supposed to perform. Elected officials—particularly senators, representatives, and governors who are more likely to have had the opportunity to work personally with those seeking a presidential nomination—should be encouraged to exercise their influence in choosing the presidential nominee, the argument goes. Agreed, but the issue is *when* and *how* that judgment should be exercised. Officeholders bear a special leadership responsibility in choosing the highest leader in the land. They should make their judgment early, when it most counts, be willing to "go public" with it, and use every resource at their command to influence the nominating outcome.

This leadership function is most appropriately performed early in the process, when endorsements for candidates have higher public visibility, provide more meaningful cues for voters, and can be used to rally support for the chosen candidate. Designating a specific category of public officials as automatic, uncommitted delegates too easily permits them to slip out from under their leadership obligations, offers no guarantee that they will actually participate in the convention, does not force them to become involved in the consensus-building process, nor does it guarantee their support of the eventual nominee or their own further involvement in party affairs. It is a simplistic solution. Provision for categorical ex-officio delegates may have real or anticipated benefits for a particular presidential candidate, but it has no redeeming political value as a proposal that would strengthen the party system.

Apart from the reasons why such a rule would not produce positive benefits, it could have a negative impact on existing party policy, the length of the nominating process, and the concept of party accountability.

Women and ethnic minorities have engaged in a long but victorious struggle to win their battle for inclusion in party affairs. The automatic granting of voting-delegate status to categories of office-holders—the vast majority of whom are white males—will undercut the party's actual and philosophical commitment toward equal rights and equal opportunity for participation, regardless of race or sex. Even if the "numbers" remained the same—an outcome that is problematic at best—a special class of delegates would be created: an uncommitted bloc numerically significant enough to have disproportionate influence at the convention. Once again, and more significantly so, one group of Democrats would be "more equal" than all others.

Then too, the categorical granting of delegate status precludes the imposition of any standard of party accountability. In the present situation where the party cannot deny its label to any candidate who wins a primary, regardless of the policy positions that candidate takes, nor is able to enforce discipline in an elected candidate's actual votes, why should the party automatically bestow voting privileges upon a group of persons, many of whom have no deep allegiance to the national party? What party purpose is served by having Phil Gramm and other "Boll Weevils" on the floor of the Democratic National Convention, participating in the choice of the party's next presidential nominee? As one Hunt Commission member remarked, "Why should we Democrats guarantee Phil Gramm national television coverage for organizing Democrats for Reagan on the floor of our convention by giving him an automatic delegate seat?" I have yet to hear a good answer to that question, especially since Gramm turned Republican.

Categorical delegate blocs aside, there is a legitimate role for party leaders and elected officials to play in the convention. Those incentives must be tied to the question of party accountability. The key word here—as throughout this chapter and most of the book—is *party*. Let the *party* leadership choose a specific proportion of the delegates, unfettered by present constraints. Although National Democratic Party rules for 1980 empowered *state committees* to select up to 25 percent of their state's delegation, their range of choices was severely limited. First of all, national-convention delegates elected at the congressional-district level were usually the ones authorized to choose the 10 percent "add on" portion of the delegation set aside for party leaders and elected officials. The delegates selected by the state committee were primarily for the purpose of "balancing" the overall delegation, stood committed to presidential candidates, and were subject to the approval of those presidential candidates. In many of our largest states, the candidates actually handpicked the delegates, thus leaving no choice to the state committees.

State party committees should particularly have the right and responsibility for selecting the at-large delegates, especially those in the party leader/elected official category. Control over the selection of these delegates would give the party a means of rewarding its friends and punishing its enemies: only supporters of the party need apply. The appropriate percentage range is probably in the 20 to 25 percent range: significant enough to be meaningful, but not so large as to negate the obvious outcome at the grass-roots level. Chosen delegates should still be required to state their presidential preference to those selecting them, or be prepared to defend their uncommitted status. Some leeway should be given in the proportional allocation of delegates to presidential candidates at this level, but safeguards should also be provided to ensure that no widespread manipulation of the process occurs on behalf of a specific candidate.

Such party changes may seem technical and humdrum, but they go to the heart of the problem of linking party to government. They could also help solve other pressing problems in presidential and lesser nominations. They could shorten the present interminable nomination process by requiring delegates to be chosen in the final weeks before the convention. They could diminish excessive media influence by enhancing the parties' deliberative processes. They could elevate the role of the individual delegates in a Burkean sense by making them true representatives of the party electorate.

These are the kinds of party *reform* that immensely strengthen party *renewal*. Hence my emphasis on the three major steps I have proposed: formalizing party membership, drastically reducing the number of binding presidential primaries, and enlarging the role of all *party* cadres and leaders in presidential conventions. Other rules may influence the nature of the game and may influence candidate strategies for participating in it, but none will have as significant an impact as any of those three in terms of the long-range growth and true renewal of our parties.

REALIGNMENT: WAITING FOR LEFTY

We have been discussing party organization, structure, mechanisms, procedures, but a party is much more than this. It is also a popular movement with a set of principles, goals, and policies. Critics say that American parties speak only in platitudes, but this is not true of the national Republican and Democratic parties today. Their platforms are explicit, specific, comprehensive. The failure lies not in doctrine but in parties' inability to carry out the promises they make. Nevertheless, party politicians fight hard over the quadrennial platforms—and now the Democrats' midterm declaration—because they define roughly where the party stands, whom it may favor for leadership, what it *proposes* to do if given power and the opportunity to act. The failure of parties to perform in office stems from the parties' internal weaknesses—hence the vital importance of party *renewal* to the party's capacity to convert promise into policy.

Every few decades, moreover, responding to rising moral imperatives, one or both parties transcend their routine transactions and obfuscations, take highly controversial positions on the most burning issues, and reshape the structure of American politics. The replacement of the Federalists by Jeffersonian Republicans in the period before mass parties, the forging of a new Democratic Party under Jackson and Van Buren, the rise of the Republican Party in the 1850s during the crisis over slavery and its transformation into the dominating Grand Old Party, the realigned Democratic-Republican party competition following the labor and agrarian tumult of the 1890s, the renewed struggle between the two major parties in the upheaval following the Great Depression—all these forced politics out of its normal channels and headed the nation in new directions.

These eras varied markedly from one another in many respects, of course, but they showed some significant uniformities. The "realigning" elections and periods were precipitated by explosive ideas, such as anti-slavery or anti-capitalism, that aroused people to a new consciousness and evoked a mighty popular response overflowing the normal channels of politics. The existing party leadership usually resisted the intrusion of new conflicts, but within one or both parties— more typically the party out of power—ideological groups polarized around new and divisive ideas. When both major parties persisted in their resistance to new doctrines and forces, third parties gained strength, but usually one or both major parties came around because of the threatened third-party competition and because of protest leaders within their own ranks. In any case the resulting "realignment reaches its climax in one or more critical elections that center on the realigning issue and resolve it, but the realigning process may extend over a considerable period before and after the critical election."

Critical realignments, as defined by Walter Dean Burnham, were "relatively short, sharp, and dramatic movements of many voters" from one party to another; arose as a result of "severe, cumulative, but uneven stress" in the social system; were triggered by some powerful "detonating" event such as the Kansas-Nebraska Act; saw sharp conflict over national policy; settled down into a new "stable phase" in the electoral cycle; and were "followed by significant alterations in national public policies and by changes in the relative effective political power of our separate national policy institutions."

Perhaps the most fascinating aspect of these critical elections was their apparent regularity, going back even to the early years of party politics. Realigning eras seemed to escalate to a "flash point" every thirty to forty years. This was not to say that things returned to normal after the critical election. Both parties tended to "modernize" their programs and rhetoric following the realignment. The critical election era of 1890–1916, moreover, brought not only party and electoral change, but also institutional alterations, unlike the other such elections (the changes in federalism after the Civil War were seen as results of northern military victory rather than Republican Party election victory). But the thirty-to-forty-year electoral revolution seemed to have a natural, regular rhythm.

Hence by the late 1960s and early 1970s it was only natural that some political analysts would be looking for another historic realignment of electoral pattern and party control. Not only had the proper thirty-five years or so elapsed since the critical election era of the New Deal, but the basic political situation seemed to have reached another flash point. Many of the conditions that appeared to have precipitated earlier realignments seemed present. Public opinion was in a state of political disarray. Richard Dawson noted that changing patterns of opinion did not relate effectively to the means of political expression; opinions did not relate to one another in an orderly and coherent manner; issue groupings did not have a natural congruence. Race, crime, and foreign policy—especially Vietnam—cut across normal socioeconomic alignments. The parties too seemed in disarray, as the presidential Democrats and Republicans allied with one another against coalitions of congressional Democrats and Republicans, while the largest third-party movement in years—George Wallace's American Independent Party of 1968—gained ten million votes. Even the voters seemed in disarray, as they shifted between the two major parties, between third parties and major parties, and in and out of the electoral arena. Above all, social and political conflict was intensifying, as the nation's values seemed in disarray under the impact of the youth culture, evangelical politics, Vietnam, Watergate, and an explosion of conservative, liberal, and radical causes.

But the expected realignment did not come. Why were things different in this political era?

The most obvious explanation was that the major parties had become so weak and disintegrated that little remained to realign. Party decomposition and disaggregation, to use Burnham's terms, had left the parties so fragmented that the pieces were hardly worth reshuffling, and were too devitalized to realign on their own. This was clearly not a complete explanation, however, because a partial realignment did take place—on the part of the Republican half of the realignment potential.

Because the political pundits had been anticipating that party realignment would begin on the Democratic side, as conservative and radical Democrats finally broke with each other, the early signs of Republican realignment were less noticed. Party experts did not grasp the importance of Barry Goldwater's nomination in 1964, the 1968 and 1972 choice of Richard Nixon as a man of mixed but mainly conservative tendencies, of Reagan's near-seizure of the Republican nomination in 1976 over a Republican President, culminating in the final engorgement of the Eisenhower-Lodge-Rockefeller-Javits Republicans by the Taft-Goldwater-Thurmond party. By 1981, as Reagan men took over the Republican National Committee and most state GOP committees, the Republican realignment was complete.

What about the Democrats during Republican presidencies? How could there be a real party realignment if the opposition party remained "unrealigned"? In fact, most of the critical alignments in history had been produced by one party, leaving the other fundamentally divided. Federalists did not basically change after their rout by Republicans; they lingered, divided between doctrinaire and "practical" Federalists, and then expired. The resurgent Democrats left the Whigs still a conservative party; the realigning Civil War Republicans left the Democracy so divided that it nominated Horace Greeley for President one year and then a string of conservatives culminating in Grover Cleveland; the realigning Republicans of the turn of the century left a Democratic Party that could nominate William Jennings Bryan three times and a conservative judge, Alton B. Parker, in between. The Republican Party moved a bit to the left after its smashing defeats by FDR and Truman, but for some years it was a frustrated party, deeply divided between left and right.

This historical record suggests, in short, that one realigning party does not necessarily produce realigning tendencies in the other. Even when leaders "cross the aisle" to join the opposition, the policy direction of neither the deserted nor the joined party may change. Over the years prominent Republicans have occasionally turned Democratic: Wayne Morse, John Lindsay, Ogden Reid. For years noted Democrats have been turning Republican: John Connally of Texas, Mills Godwin of Virginia, Strom Thurmond of South Carolina, Phil Gramm of Texas. Voting with their feet, these leaders started a rebellion in neither party. Rather they reinforced the main ideological thrust of the party they joined.

The issue of party realignment seems to lie not with politicians who cross party lines but with leaders who stay in their party and half persuade, half drive it into a more principled or ideological direction. This had been the case with Jefferson in the Republican Party, Jackson in the Democratic, Lincoln in the reborn Republican Party, and the two Roosevelts in their parties. FDR had encountered such obstruction in his party on the part of conservative southern Democrats that he tried to purge the party of them. Although he toyed with the idea of a new party of liberal Democrats and Republicans, he never got to the point of leaving the Democracy. Rather he reshaped its doctrine. So with Reagan. Originally a Democrat, he turned Republican in the 1960s despite repeated rebuffs and frustrations, until he could bend the GOP to his own will.

Thus the conservative Republicans by 1980 found Mr. Right and married him. The liberal Democrats were still waiting for Lefty. But was Lefty dead?

Would it matter? Would it not be better to have one ideological party, like the GOP, and one consensual, "pragmatic" party, like the Democracy today—or even two moderate, middle-of-the-road parties?

The answer to this question turns on one's preferred form of government. A case can be made for consensual leadership, moderate parties, subdued conflict, step-by-step policy making, gradual reform, incremental change. Such a strategy of government may be needed some of the time, perhaps most of the time. But there arise occasions in a nation's history when government must take a strong lead and direction, gather its forces together, act decisively, move comprehensively and authoritatively on many fronts, and bring about concerted and energetic social change. And for most of a democracy's history, it may have to pursue steady and vigorous efforts for social justice and equality. In either event we would need strong, united parties, unified and collective leadership, credible and coordinated national government.

The question of party realignment turns ultimately on one's philosophy of representative and responsible leadership. I believe in majority rule as the foundation of this kind of leadership, because it requires popular consent, not consensus; because it permits leaders to act only after they gain the consent of the wide variety of interests represented in the majority coalition without requiring leadership to weaken its program and policies by gaining more than a majority; because it focuses responsibility in the majority party and leadership. I believe in majority rule because, in the American tradition, it also means the rights of the minority not only to exist, to assemble, speak, propagandize, but to prod the government, offer alternatives to the voters, and be prepared to govern. Together, the concept of majority rule and minority rights is one of the most powerful in the democratic arsenal. Fundamentally, majority rule is a leadership system, allowing leaders to act even while it pins responsibility on them.

The strongest case against such a system is that it sharpens conflict and fosters violence. In my view, it does the former but not the latter. By organizing conflict between two parties, by rejecting the Constitution's strategy of distributing friction throughout the twisting coils of government, a realigned party system dramatizes conflict between two great programs of government, channels that conflict into elections, poses grand alternatives, and enables a majority of the people to settle the matter. There is no blood in the streets. On the contrary, by granting the majority party leadership the right to govern, and the opposition party leadership the duty to oppose, majority rule and minority rights under a two-party system make both the holding and transfer of power more orderly, legitimate, and tolerable.

Today the responsibility lies clearly on the Democratic Party leadership to build a unified and responsible opposition, establish clear alternatives to Reagan Republicanism, and to be prepared to take power after the next swing of the party and electoral pendulum. When and how will all this happen? Not automatically with the passage of time, in my view. The forces of resistance to Democratic Party realignment are quite powerful. Those forces persist in thousands of communities, especially in the South and the Sun Belt, where many conservative rural, business, and suburban folk are still voting Democratic because their forebears did for generations. Their Democratic leaders will fear to turn Republican on the national level as long as these voters persist in their ancient Democratic voting habits. These conservative Democratic officeholders—the "Boll Weevils" and the rest—do not stay with the national Democracy mainly out of any lofty sentiment or sense of loyalty, but out of careful calculation about what best favors their own re-election prospects.

Rather Democratic Party realignment will come about, we can expect, through a combination of transformational leadership and a detonating incident. The latter will have to be an intense one in order to jar people out of their normal thinking and voting habits in the face of a moral crisis like that of slavery, or an economic crisis like that of the Great Depression. Given the dire condition of the end-of-century world, this incident might be a stupendous international or foreign-policy crisis, though in the past the detonating event has almost always been a domestic one.

The transformation of the Democratic Party into a committed liberal-labor-left vehicle requires resolute leadership on the part of national chieftains of the Democracy. Even more it will require vigorous action by grass-roots leadership inside and—presently—outside the party. It will be the nature of the interaction of these two levels of leadership that will spell success or failure for a liberal-left strategy for the Democrats. Huge cadres of grass-roots leaders lie waiting to be mobilized by national party leadership, waiting also to strengthen the national leadership politically and stiffen its resolve. Women, blacks, Hispanics, peace activists, are recognizing that they must play both protest *and* electoral politics, both movement *and* party politics, to reach their goals. The cutting edge will be registration of voters and mobilization of them at the polls, and as Cloward and Piven have suggested, a rousing and intensive grass-roots registration effort, especially if it provokes conservative resistance, can serve as a crucial mobilizing force. The result would be the true engagement of local and national cadres of leadership. The "relationship between disruptive mass movements and electoral institutions is interactive," as Cloward and Piven point out; "voter influence is not likely to be realized without the instigating force of protest, and protest movements in turn depend upon the relative size of the electoral constituencies that polarize in their support" or in opposition to the demands of the protesters.

The crucial unknown factor in the next political realignment will be, above all, leadership. What Democrat will match the bold realigners on the right? It will be a leader who can move beyond the usual transactional skills of piecing together a liberal-radical coalition out of existing electoral fragments. It will be a transformational leader who can expand the electoral base of the Democratic liberal-left and mobilize and politicize the tens of millions of Americans who have become politically alienated, apathetic, or anomic, but whose wants and needs can be converted into hopes and expectations, and ultimately into demands on government. Even more, this leader must be committed, once in office, to transforming our present anti-leadership system into one that can convert hopes and aspirations and demands into *outcomes;* he or she must, in other words, show the same political and constitutional creativity in seeking to shape a structure of leadership as the Framers of 1787 did in creating a structure of leadership fragmentation.

The supreme leader of such an undertaking may not even be on the political horizon at this time. But thousands of third-cadre activists and other potential foot troops are already in place, and ready to march. And ready to run as well. For as Mr. Dooley also said, "That's wan good thing about th' dimmycratic party, it always has plenty iv candydates." He said something else too, as a perpetual reminder to the Democratic liberal-left. The Democratic Party "is niver so good as whin 't is broke, whin rayspictable people speak iv it in whispers."

NEEDED: TRANSFORMING LEADERSHIP

What is the prospect, then, of achieving a constitutional system that fosters majority rule, firm governmental authority, consistent policy, collective leadership, vigorous and principled opposition, open and responsible government? Our only chance, I believe, lies in beginning with modest efforts to strengthen both the constitutional and party structures in the hope that gradual renewals and reforms simultaneously in both the party and constitutional spheres would set up a symbiotic relationship out of which might come major changes. This is a strategy for gradual structuralists.

I would start with the force that serves as the indispensable cutting edge in social or structural change—ideas. In this case the ideas would be policy proposals embodied in party platforms, candidates' promises, and official utterances by leaders in office and in opposition. No basic change is possible, and no change if adopted would work, unless each set of party leaders stands united behind a coherent and balanced set of foreign and domestic policies. A few years ago even this small idea would have seemed quixotic. But now the Republicans have provided a case study in the capacity of the Grand Old Party to find itself ideologically, to renew itself organizationally, to win office on the basis of a relatively clear program, to support its leadership, and—to a considerable extent—to enact its program.

Now the shoe is on the Democratic foot. No real structural change is possible in the long run unless the Democratic Party, in the short run, carries through the current process of party realignment and formulates and fights for a clear, comprehensive, and radical alternative to Reagan rule.

Once both parties have made up their mind, efforts to strengthen the linkage between grass-roots cadres and national leadership could be stepped up. Increasingly, party nominating caucuses could be substituted for "party" primaries; local recruitment, organization, and leadership could be strengthened; county, state, and national conventions could gain stronger financing and organization as well as powers; the politics of House and Senate could be grounded more firmly in national party politics; campaign funding could increasingly be channeled to candidates through responsible party organizations; and the national party committees and leadership could be immensely improved. Here again the Republicans have led the way and the Democrats, if only for competitive reasons, must follow suit.

Once renewal was well on its way in both parties, modest efforts to amend the Constitution could be initiated. If the parties had managed sharply to reduce the number of state presidential primaries in which delegates were chosen, it would be safe to amend the Electoral College to make it more equitable, dependable, and more clearly representative of popular majorities. The presidential impeachment process might be strengthened to allow Congress to encourage or effect a resignation or removal of a President who had as clearly lost the confidence of the country for personal or political reasons as Richard Nixon had for moral dereliction. We might adopt the Reuss plan allowing the President to choose for high executive posts members of Congress who would retain their seats, from which they could seek to unify the executive and legislative efforts at collective governing. The "team ticket" might be established, at least covering presidential and House candidates.

Effective party renewal combined with a set of moderate constitutional "process" changes would bring about some modest improvement, at least, in our governance; and each would fortify the other. The question is whether it would be necessary, or even possible, to proceed to *structural* change. This is hard to predict. If the initial moves toward party renewal and moderate constitutional change worked well, the pressure for major constitutional restructuring, such as adoption of a parliamentary system, might be lessened. Indeed, these party and constitutional changes might be enough to make the system work tolerably well. If they did not, some leaders would want to return to the old system of divided powers and individualistic leadership.

Others might press for major constitutional restructuring. I doubt that Americans under normal conditions could agree on the package of radical and "alien" constitutional changes that would be required. They would do so, I think, only during and following a stupendous national crisis and political failure. By then any reform might be too late, but if not, at least we should have done our homework. And we can watch the unfolding constitutional experiments abroad. If we should ever make fundamental changes, the remarkable French combination of presidential and parliamentary government may be especially relevant to the American situation. I doubt that we would ever import the pure, classic form of parliamentarianism, as in Britain.

One thing is clear in all this murk. Major changes in process and structure will not be brought about by spontaneous action on the part of the mass public. People as a whole are not interested in the complexities of party organization and constitutional structure; they are interested in practical results. Changes will be brought about by leadership, as in the drafting and adoption of the Constitution of 1787. But today such changes will not be allowed to remain in the hands of a small set of elites, like the fifty-five men who drew up the Constitution. The second and third cadres of American leadership must be fully involved. The most heartening precedent for constitutional change today goes back to the thousands of grass-roots activists who took part in the state constitutional ratifying conventions of 1787–1788.

Do we have a third-cadre leadership of similar intellectual power and creativity today? The answer can be found in the civic and religious groups, in the local Leagues of Women Voters and local bar associations, in the unions and Chambers of Commerce, in the professional organizations, in the schools and colleges and universities of America.

Drawing on my arguments in Part Three of this volume, I would propose:

1. Strengthening party and collective leadership in House and Senate and between Congress and the President through reorganizing and integrating committees, agencies, and liaison offices.

2. Converting impeachment into a means of removing Presidents not only when they have committed high crimes and misdemeanors but when they have dramatically and irremediably lost the confidence of the nation.

3. Make the major parties more organized, disciplined, programmatic, and principled so that they might offer meaningful alternatives to the voters, sustain their leadership in office, and pull the government together behind the winning platform.

4. Through constitutional amendment create the "team ticket" by which the voter could cast a single party ballot for President, senator, and congressman (as voters do now for President and Vice-President), thus creating electoral support for congressional-presidential linkage.

5. Through constitutional amendment adopt the Reuss proposal, enabling the President to choose senators or representatives for Cabinet membership without requiring these legislators to give up their seats in Congress.

Crucial to this whole effort is the development of a leadership and a followership in the Democratic Party that will move the party to the liberal-left, draw to the polls a huge army of the presently nonvoting, strengthen the grass-roots foundation of the party, and make clear to the American people not only *what* it proposes to do but *how* it proposes to do it. Inevitably, this would compel the Democratic Party leadership to confront the structural weaknesses discussed in this volume.

There is a grand precedent for such a grand strategy—the leadership that Jefferson and Madison and their fellow Republicans demonstrated in the 1790s in organizing a new "party of the people," leading it to victory, converting the opposition party into the governing party, creating party instruments in the executive and legislative branches, and generating new sets of leaders in nation, state, and community. Where are the Jeffersons and Madisons today?

Epilogue:
Catch '87 –Thinking Our Way Out

PHILADELPHIA, *September 17, 1987. A great throng stands before Independence Hall. The long military parade is over, the floats filled with "Founding Fathers" have rumbled off into the distance, the bands have stopped. Waiting to speak, dignitaries crowd the long platform in front, their backs against the old statehouse. The President of the United States pays lavish tribute to the Constitution of the United States, completed on this spot two hundred years before. The Chief Justice of the United States lauds the genius of the Founders. The president pro tem of the Senate speaks for the upper chamber, the Speaker of the House for the lower. Then the governor of Pennsylvania, the mayor of Philadelphia, the French ambassador . . .*

What would we do in these years if we were really to honor the Founders—honor them not with the usual pieties but with an effort to take the same kind of intellectual and political leadership today that they did during that long Philadelphia summer two centuries ago?

We would acclaim the Framers for the greatest collective feat of intellectual leadership in the history of the nation—for their creative vision in recognizing the changing needs of their fellow Americans, for their sunburst of institutional innovation, for the lasting charter they produced, which still mocks those who say that humans can advance only by tiny, faltering steps and piecemeal, "practical" changes.

But we would do more than pay tribute. We would try to match their example of standing back from the existing political system and coldly assessing its capacity to meet rising human expectations and demands and heightened international challenges. We would not fear to take an intellectual and theoretical approach to the 1980s system, just as they did in confronting their 1780s system. Hence we would put our contemporary problems in historical perspective, exploit accumulated theory and data, study the experience of other political systems, think analytically as well as creatively.

In analyzing governmental institutions and proposing changes, we would seek to put them in their proper context of political power. We would be content neither with mechanical tinkering that hardly touched the structure of power, nor with grandiose changes that ignored the interplay of perceptions, motivations, and ambitions bolstering existing political systems.

We would not shrink from moral leadership. The Framers wished to nurture republican virtue and civility and to protect men's liberties against government. Today we wish to protect people's liberties in all their Bill of Rights dimensions and to expand freedom, equality, and justice in every dimension of human life.

We would innovate boldly but always with an eye to what was possible, assuming we could demonstrate some of the leadership that the Framers did in the 1780s. Thus like them, we would obey the ancient injunction, "Think as men of action, act as men of thought."

To undertake all this we would have to recognize a fact that will hardly be mentioned that September 1987 day in Philadelphia—the fact that the Framers bequeathed us a structure of power that today not only fragments creative and collective leadership but frustrates any major effort of leaders to rid it of its anti-leadership qualities. We cannot make political (mainly party) changes unless we make structural (mainly constitutional) changes first, but we cannot do the reverse either. It's like trying to start a stalled car on a highway—we can't start the engine because the battery is dead, but we can't charge the battery because the engine won't run. This is Catch '87.

So today, we cannot create leadership teamwork in government unless we provide unified political backing for executives and legislators in office, and for the minority; and we cannot do that without strengthening both the "in" party and the "out" party. We cannot do this unless we establish the "team ticket" of jointly elected President, senator, and representative, but this is impossible without a constitutional amendment establishing such a ticket. Yet a party effort would be necessary in order to gain such an amendment. The proposed joint executive-legislative Cabinet raises the same dilemma—such a Cabinet would strengthen the role of party and collective leadership in government, but a unified party effort would be necessary to bring about the constitutional amendment that would be required to establish the joint Cabinet, and only a strong party could make it work. That too is Catch '87.

Is there a way out of Catch '87? Yes, and a difficult one. This would be the conversion of the Democratic Party into a far more principled, programmatic, and committed party than it is today. This would call not so much for liberalizing its platform—the Democratic platform is already radical in rhetoric—as for encouraging and requiring the Democracy to live up to its existing principles. This in turn would call for the choosing of Democratic Party leadership that would break away from the present centrist and incremental tactics of the national Democracy and to mobilize the support of the tens of millions of Americans presently antagonized or bored by both parties. But that new leadership would be committed not only to winning but to *governing*.

Thus the sequence of action would have to go something like this: the winning of the Democratic Party nomination by such committed leadership; that leadership's anticipation, or early discovery, that enactment and execution of the full program will be utterly impossible without a party team in government and that in the long run such a team is impossible without structural changes; the willingness of that leadership to make constitutional reframing and party renewal a central part of a new appeal to the people, along with the substantive or policy goals that such changes would help realize; and battling it out along this line over an extended period of time.

We can learn something from the Framers about time. Writing the new Constitution of 1787 was only one phase of a generation-long era of transforming change. Even before 1787, the Founders spent years experimenting with state and national governments, taking small steps, reflecting deeply on their experiences. The new charter had to be ratified, which meant that many hundreds of delegates rode horseback and carriages, canal and river boats, to meet in convention centers like Richmond and Boston and Poughkeepsie, where they debated for weeks. Once authorized, the new government had to be established, which meant that elections had to be held, George Washington had to journey to Manhattan from Mount Vernon to become the first President, and legislators, judges, and bureaucrats had to assume their offices. A Bill of Rights had to be adopted. Then an Administration party had to be created to sustain the Federalist leadership during the 1790s, and an opposition party had to be created to challenge it. That opposition party—the first Republicans—had to be allowed peacefully to take over the government after the new party won the presidential and congressional elections of 1800.

The lesson for us today is that no major changes in our system will take place overnight or in one long summer or even in a year or two. The Founders drafted and established the new Constitution by operating outside the existing government (the Articles of Confederation) through conventions, and then using their new system to make further changes in it. Today we would have to work largely through existing institutions, which would make the process slower and riskier. Basic structural change would probably take a decade or two, if possible at all.

Why place the burden of such change on the Democrats? Why not on the Republicans? Because the Grand Old Party has already done its part. Under Ronald Reagan's leadership it has become the principled conservative party of this nation. It has shown that a committed party can become a government party, and is all the more effective because of this commitment. But it is not the job of conservatives to be innovators, institution changers, reframers. That is the job of liberals, leftists, and radicals. And in any event, Reagan Republicanism has become far too narrow, negative, and reactionary a doctrine to include thoughts about changing the system; on the contrary, a system that thwarts governmental effectiveness is basically acceptable to Reagan conservatism.

For the Democrats the question is one of moral leadership. To call for a principled party of the left to match the present doctrinal party of the right is not merely for the sake of achieving two meaningful, competitive, programmatic parties, or of re-enlisting the people's interest in American politics so that at least they show up at the polls, or both empowering and constraining leaders in office, important though all these are. It is to recognize that tens of millions of poor and lower-income Americans are not represented in the present party system, that some American liberals have so concentrated on the defense of Bill of Rights liberties that they have neglected the aspirations of millions of their fellow citizens for equality and justice, that tens of millions of present, nominal, and potential Democrats are unrepresented by a party that somehow cannot struggle persistently, consistently, and militantly for peace and détente.

Can we imagine men or women in this decade or the next who would dare to exercise the kind of transforming leadership necessary to duplicate the Framers' feats of institution building in meeting modern social and economic needs? We can, if we imagine such leaders not as heroes riding to our rescue on white chargers but as committed persons responding to needs and hopes welling out of grass-roots activism. We know that among the general public, distrust in government and lack of confidence in leadership have escalated in the last quarter century, and not only since Watergate and Vietnam; hence there is a mass potential for change. We know that new leaders are coming to the fore in the Democratic Party, as they did in the Republican, eager for a politics of issues, program, and governmental responsiveness and action.

Still, can we depend on the voters to respond? Yes, if the need for transforming change is expressed not in terms of arid institutions but in the satisfaction of human wants and needs. Yes, if would-be transforming leaders are bold enough. But, more than political courage, it will take intellectual audacity and inventiveness. Powerful vested interests grow thickly around ideas as well as institutions. Foes of change will arouse fears rather than provoke thought. In particular they will evoke the old American fear of popular rule, even though we are used to majority decisions in town meetings, corporation boards, professional organizations. They will provoke fear of polarization, even though militant but peaceful polarization is vital in stimulating political and institutional change.

It is hard to believe that we cannot find, among a nation of 235 million embracing a rich profusion of talents, the kind of transforming leadership, at the grass roots and in Washington, that will rival the Jeffersons and Van Burens, the Roosevelts in both parties, the Adamses and Lincoln and Wilson, Jane Addams and Eugene Debs, Carrie Chapman Catt and Martin Luther King, Jr., Brandeis, Warren—and even the men of Philadelphia 1787.

Notes

PROLOGUE: THE DESERTION OF THE SYSTEM

Nonvoting: Raymond E. Wolfinger and Steven J. Rosenstone, *Who Votes?* (New Haven: Yale University Press, 1980); Everett Carll Ladd, *Where Have All the Voters Gone?*, 2nd ed. (New York: W. W. Norton, 1982).

Decline in confidence in government and leadership: Seymour Martin Lipset and William Schneider, *The Confidence Gap* (New York: The Free Press, 1983); Lipset and Schneider, "Confidence in Confidence Measures," *Public Opinion*, August/September 1983, pp. 42–44. See also *New York Times*, July 15, 1983, pp. 1, B6.

Rating of officeholders on honesty and ethical standards: Gallup Poll, August 1983.

Lessened faith in democratic institutions: Lester W. Milbrath, "Can Anyone Successfully Govern Modern Democratic Society?," paper, World Congress of the International Society of Political Psychology, August 1982; *ISR Newsletter* (Autumn 1979), "Deepening Distrust of Political Leaders Is Jarring Public's Faith in Institutions," Institute for Social Research, University of Michigan, quoted in Milbrath, p. 3.

Reverse representation: Robert E. Goodin, "Voting Through the Looking Glass," *American Political Science Review*, Vol. 77, No. 2 (June 1983), pp. 420–434.

Concern about the system on the part of both scholars and practitioners: "Political Economy and Constitutional Reform," *Hearings* before the Joint Economic Committee, Congress of the United States, 79th Cong., 2nd Sess., November and December 1982, Vols. 1 and 2 (Appendix) (Washington: U.S. Government Printing Office, 1983), chaired by Rep. Henry Reuss (hereafter referred to as Reuss, *Hearings*).

Public perception of no difference between the major parties on key policies: *Public Opinion*, August/September 1982, p. 32.

David S. Broder on failure of Democratic Party opposition: North Adams (Mass.) *Transcript,* June 25, 1982, p. 4.

Nonendorsement of either party's economic approach: *Public Opinion,* December/January 1983, p. 5.

Janowitz on leadership failure: Morris Janowitz, *The Last Half-Century: Societal Change and Politics in America* (Chicago: University of Chicago Press, 1978), as reviewed and summarized by Jonathan Rieder, *American Journal of Sociology,* Vol. 88, No. 1, pp. 173–180.

One: CARTER: THE VERDICT OF NOVEMBER

Kennedy Library dedication: Hank Klibanoff, "And once again, there was Camelot," Boston *Globe,* October 21, 1979, p. 37; Martin F. Nolan, "A day of poetry, politics and wit," Boston *Globe,* October 21, 1979, pp. 1, 33–34; Eleanor Roberts, "The beautiful join best and brightest," Boston *Herald-American,* October 21, 1979, pp. A1, A3; Peggy Simpson, "Camelot at Columbia Point," Boston *Herald-American,* October 21, 1979, pp. A1, A9.

"what a bunch of turkeys!": Earl Marchand, "A day of glittering celebs, a herd of pols, press . . . ," Boston *Herald-American,* October 21, 1979, p. A2.

"greatest concentration of America's political elite": Sidney Blumenthal, *The Permanent Campaign: Inside the World of Elite Political Operatives* (Boston: Beacon Press, 1980), p. 245.

Jacqueline Kennedy's reaction to Carter: "Jimmy in Camelot," *Newsweek,* October 29, 1979, p. 32.

Spender poem: "A poem 'to capture the spirit of our father,' " Boston *Globe,* October 21, 1979, p. 29.

Joe Kennedy's speech: "Joe's fiery remarks," Boston *Globe,* October 21, 1979, p. 31; Chris Black, "Joe II gives tough talk and surprises listeners," Boston *Globe,* October 21, 1979, p. 29; Peter Lucas, "Young Joe Kennedy . . . He came out slugging," Boston *Herald-American,* October 21, 1979, pp. A1–A2.

Carter's speech: "Carter's remarks," Boston *Globe,* October 21, 1979, p. 2; Curtis Wilkie, "For Carter, the jest was 'appropriate,' " Boston *Globe,* October 21, 1979, p. 2.

Kennedy's speech: "Text of Sen. Kennedy's address," Boston *Globe,* October 21, 1979, p. 2.

Columbia Point reaction: Joe Heaney, "While across the tracks . . . ," Boston *Herald-American,* October 21, 1979, pp. A1, A3.

The Hopes of January

Carter's personality and political style: See Jimmy Carter, *Why Not the Best?* (Nashville: Broadman Press, 1977); Betty Glad, *Jimmy Carter: In Search of the Great White House* (New York: W. W. Norton, 1980); William E. Miller, *Yankee from Georgia: The Emergence of Jimmy Carter* (New York: Time Books, 1978); Clark Mollenhoff, *The President Who Failed: Carter Out of Control* (New York: Macmillan, 1980).

Carter's "first hundred days": Robert Shogan, *Promises to Keep: Carter's First Hundred Days* (New York: Crowell, 1977).

Carter as an insider: Glad, *op. cit.,* p. 160.

Carter "a good, but not extraordinary, governor": *Ibid.,* pp. 186–187.

Carter switching friendships: *Ibid.,* p. 203.

Carter as restless and aggressive: Shogan, *op. cit.,* p. 204.

Jack Germond on Carter's self-confidence: Quoted in Glad, *op. cit.,* p. 229.

Carter's own aspirations for his presidency: *Ibid.,* p. 353.

Carter grading his presidency on *60 Minutes:* Martin Schram, "Carter: Toll of a Clockwork Presidency," Washington *Post,* October 27, 1980, pp. A1, A4, Carter quoted at p. A4.

Califano on Carter's evaluation of his presidency: Joseph A. Califano, Jr., "Getting fired by Jimmy Carter," Washington *Post,* May 24, 1981, pp. C1, C5, Carter quoted at p. C5. See also Joseph A. Califano, Jr., *Governing America: An Insider's Report from the White House and the Cabinet* (New York: Simon and Schuster, 1981).

Carter at Princeton: "Could have been more effective, Carter admits," Washington *Post,* March 19, 1981, p. A17.

Carter's broken promises: John Steuart and Steve Lietman, "Carter's unkept '76 promises—a time bomb?" *New York Times,* September 7, 1980, p. E19.

The Loneliness of the Long-Distance Jogger

Strauss on Carter: Interview with Robert S. Strauss, Washington, D.C., January 12, 1981.

Carter's political aptitude: Meg Greenfield, "The Cult of the Amateur," *Newsweek,* June 16, 1980, p. 100.

Carter's relationship with the Democratic Party: Interview with Richard C. Moe, Washington, D.C., January 13, 1981.

Carter's comments on his party leadership in retrospect: Interview with Jimmy Carter, Atlanta, April 21, 1982, by the author and Michael Beschloss; notes transcribed by Michael Beschloss.

Carter's lack of an identifiable program: Meg Greenfield, "The Passionless President," *Newsweek,* August 11, 1980, p. 84.

Carter's reversals on policy: Howard J. Silver, "Presidential Power and the Post-Watergate Presidency," *Presidential Studies Quarterly,* Vol. 8, No. 2 (Spring 1978), p. 207. See also Michael Krasner, "Why Great Presidents Will Become More Rare," *Presidential Studies Quarterly,* Vol. 9, No. 4 (Fall 1979), pp. 367–375; and Ben W. Heineman, Jr., and Curtis A. Hessler, *Memorandum for the President: A Strategic Approach to Domestic Affairs in the 1980s* (New York: Random House, 1980), especially pp. 251–302.

Califano on Carter's vacillation: Joseph A. Califano, Jr., "Carter's cabinet lacked cohesion from first year," Washington *Post,* May 23, 1981, pp. A1, A10, quoted at p. A10.

Anne Wexler's role: "Reflecting on feminism, politics, and the Democratic Party," Washington *Post,* December 9, 1980, p. A19; interview with Anne Wexler, the White House, January 15, 1981.

So—Why Not the Best?

Hamilton Jordan on the Carter presidency: Dom Bonafede, "A Sense of Relief," *National Journal,* December 20, 1980, p. 2183. See also "Hamilton Jordan: looking back," Washington *Post,* December 2, 1980, p. A19.

The "impossible situation" theory: Erwin C. Hargrove in a review of Betty Glad, *Jimmy Carter: In Search of the Great White House, American Political Science Review,* Vol. 75, No. 2 (June 1981), pp. 493–494.

Carter's staffing of the presidency: Edward D. Feigenbaum, "Staffing, Organization and Decision-making in the Ford and Carter White Houses," *Presidential Studies Quarterly,* Vol. 10, No. 3 (Summer 1980), especially pp. 370–377; and R. Gordon Hoxie, "Staffing the Ford and Carter Presidencies," *Presidential Studies Quarterly,* Vol. 10, No. 3 (Summer 1980), especially pp. 384–401.

New ideological groupings and political factions: Richard M. Scammon and Ben J. Wattenberg, "Is It the End of an Era?" *Public Opinion,* October/November 1980, pp. 6–7.

Horney's description of the introverted personality: Quoted in Glad, *op. cit.,* p. 495.

Kellerman's observations on the introvert as President: Barbara Kellerman, "Introversion in the Oval Office," Institute for Leadership Studies, Fairleigh Dickinson University, June 1981, p. 33.

1980 Iowa debate: Richard Harwood, ed., *The Pursuit of the Presidency* (New York: Berkley Books, 1980), p. 108.

Carter's 1980 TV ads: *Ibid.,* p. 105.

Vance on the primary system: Cyrus Vance, "Reforming the Electoral Reforms," *New York Times Magazine,* February 22, 1981, pp. 16–17, 62–69, quoted at p. 62.

Two: REAGAN AND THE NEW REPUBLICAN PARTY

Expectations for the Reagan presidency: "A Remodeled Conservative," *Newsweek,* November 3, 1980, pp. 35–36; James David Barber, "Reagan's sheer personal likability faces its sternest test," Washington *Post,* January 20, 1981, p. 78; Lou Cannon, "The man: an optimism for future rooted in past," Washington *Post,* January 20, 1981, pp. A1, A9; Lou Cannon, "The two Reagans: conflicting images," Washington *Post,* October 11, 1980, pp. A1, A9; Richard J. Cattani, "What kind of President would Reagan make?" *Christian Science Monitor,* July 15, 1980, pp. 1, 14; Robert Lindsey, "What the Record Says About Reagan," *New York Times Magazine,* June 29, 1980, pp. 12–20, 32–34; "Meet the Real Ronald Reagan," *Time,* October 20, 1980, pp. 18–22, 27; T. R. Reid, "Reagan: a life built on performing," Washington *Post,* October 22, 1980, pp. A1, A10; Richard J. Whalen, "Reagan's agenda: innovations for a new era," Washington *Post,* November 9, 1980, pp. D1, D5.

The Two Republican Parties: Conservative Roots

The Reagan conservative ideology: A. James Reichley, *Conservatives in an Age of Change: The Nixon and Ford Administrations* (Washington, D.C.: The Brookings Institution, 1981), p. 3.

The development of conservative thought: M. Stanton Evans, *The Future of Conservatism: From Taft to Reagan and Beyond* (New York: Holt, Rinehart and Winston, 1968); Allen Guttmann, *The Conservative Tradition in America* (New York: Oxford University Press, 1967); Robert McCloskey, *American Conservatism in the Age of Enterprise* (Cambridge: Harvard University Press, 1951); George H. Nash, *The Conservative Intellectual Movement in America since 1945* (New York: Basic Books, 1976); Clinton Rossiter, *Conservatism in America: The Thankless Persuasion* (New York: Alfred A. Knopf, 1962).

Individualism: Herbert Hoover, *American Individualism* (Garden City, N.Y.: Doubleday, Page, 1922), p. 9. See also Horace M. Allen, *Individualism: An American Way of Life* (New York: Liveright, 1933); J. R. Pole, *American*

Individualism and the Promise of Progress (New York: Oxford University Press, 1980).

Whigs: Daniel Walker Howe, *The Political Culture of the American Whigs* (Chicago: University of Chicago Press, 1979); E. Malcolm Carroll, *Origins of the Whig Party* (Durham, N.C.: Duke University Press, 1925).

"the hero of Horatio Alger": Louis Hartz, *The Liberal Tradition in America* (New York: Harcourt, Brace, 1955).

Trustbusting: Richard C. Hofstadter, *The Age of Reform. From Bryan to FDR* (New York; Knopf, 1955), especially Chap. 6; Richard C. Hofstadter, ed., *The Progressive Movement 1900–1915* (Englewood Cliffs, N.J.: Prentice-Hall, 1963), especially Part Four.

Goldwater: John H. Kessel, *The Goldwater Coalition: Republican Strategies in 1964* (Indianapolis: Bobbs-Merrill, 1968); Stephen C. Shadegg, *What Happened to Goldwater?* (New York: Holt, Rinehart and Winston, 1965).

Presidential versus congressional Republicans: James MacGregor Burns, *The Deadlock of Democracy: Four-Party Politics in America* (Englewood Cliffs, N.J.: Prentice-Hall, 1963).

"I am now a Keynesian": quoted in Rowland Evans, Jr., and Robert D. Novak, *Nixon in the White House: The Frustration of Power* (New York: Random House, 1971), p. 372.

Herbert Stein on Nixon's budget: Quoted in Reichley, *op. cit.,* p. 229.

The New Federalist: William Safire, *Before the Fall: An Inside View of the Pre-Watergate White House* (Garden City, N.Y.: Doubleday, 1975), pp. 219–222.

The Ford presidency: Robert T. Hartmann, *Palace Politics: An Inside Account of the Ford Years* (New York: McGraw-Hill, 1980); Jerald terHorst, *Gerald Ford and the Future of the Presidency* (New York: Third Press, 1974).

Three Right Wings: Reagan's Dilemma

Reagan's political development: William E. Leuchtenburg, "Ronald Reagan's Liberal Past," *The New Republic,* Vol. 188, No. 20 (May 23, 1983), pp. 18–25.

"My speeches underwent a kind of evolution": Ronald Reagan and Richard G. Hubler, *Where's the Rest of Me?* (New York: Duell, Sloan and Pearce, 1965), p. 266.

Goldwater's comments on Reagan's 1964 Republican convention speech: *Newsweek,* July 21, 1980, p. 38. For the text of the Reagan speech, see "Where it began: 'Rendezvous with Destiny,' " Washington *Post*, January 20, 1981, pp. 38–39.

Seeing ourselves in a mirror: Reagan and Hubler, *op. cit.*, p. 78.

The photogenic Reagan: Bill Boyarsky, *Ronald Reagan: His Life and Rise to the Presidency* (New York: Random House, 1981), p. 5.

"I'm hurt but I'm not slain": Remer Tyson, "How Reagan captured the GOP," Miami *Herald*, July 13, 1980, p. E1.

Reagan's philosophical consistency: Lindsey, *op. cit.*, quoted at p. 18.

"less change": Quoted in "Meet the Real Ronald Reagan," *Time*, October 20, 1980, p. 20.

Reagan's view of Carter as "ineffective": Richard Wirthlin, Vincent Breglio, and Richard Beal, "Campaign Chronicle," *Public Opinion*, February/March 1981, pp. 43–49.

"we have the talent": Richard Harwood, ed., *The Pursuit of the Presidency* (New York: Berkley Books, 1980), p. 32.

November 1980 exit polls: "Why They Pulled the Reagan Lever," *National Journal*, November 8, 1980, p. 1877.

Republican Party development in the last decade: John F. Bibby, "Party Renewal in the National Republican Party," in Gerald M. Pomper, ed., *Party Renewal in America: Theory and Practice* (New York: Praeger Publishers, 1980), Chap. 7; Timothy B. Clark, "The RNC Prospers, the DNC Struggles As They Face the 1980 Elections," *National Journal*, September 27, 1980, pp. 1617–1621.

National Review's twenty-fifth birthday party: Nicholas Lemann, "Trying to turn a collective sentiment into a government," Washington *Post*, February 24, 1981, p. A4.

Neo-conservatism: Peter Steinfels, *The Neo-Conservatives: The Men Who Are Changing America's Politics* (New York: Simon and Schuster, 1979). On Will's more recent views, see George F. Will, *Statecraft as Soulcraft* (Simon and Schuster, 1983).

Russell Kirk on conservatism: Russell Kirk, *A Program for Conservatives* (Chicago: Henry Regnery, 1962), p. 207.

Conservative Political Action Conference: Reagan quoted in Dom Bonafede, "New Right Preaches a New Religion and Ronald Reagan Is Its Prophet," *National Journal*, May 2, 1981, p. 779.

The "Moral Majority": Seymour Martin Lipset and Earl Raab, "The Election and the Evangelicals," *Commentary*, March 1981, pp. 25–31.

The Moralistic Right: Bonafede, *op. cit.*, p. 780.

Conflicts between the three rights: Alan Crawford, *Thunder on the Right* (New York: Pantheon Books, 1980), Chap. 6.

The "Good Right Fight": William Safire, "The Good Right Fight," *New York Times*, November 17, 1980, p. A23. See in general F. Clifton White and William J. Gill, *Why Reagan Won: The Conservative Movement 1964–1981* (Chicago: Regnery Gateway, 1981).

Foreign Policy—Strategy or Stance?

Ronald Reagan's pre-presidential views on Communism: Betty Glad, "Black and White Thinking: Ronald Reagan's Approach to Foreign Policy," paper prepared for presentation at the 50th Anniversary Program for the Institute for Psychoanalysis, n.d. (quoted with permission), pp. 17–20. See also pre-presidential radio transcripts, Ronnie Dugger, *On Reagan: The Man and the President* (New York: McGraw-Hill, 1983), Appendix.

Reagan's 1981–1983 views: Robert Dallek, *Ronald Reagan and the Politics of Symbolism* (manuscript, 1983), pp. 5–37.

Hedrick Smith on the ideological shift in Reagan: *New York Times*, May 20, 1982, p. A28.

Glad on lack of change in Reagan: Glad, *op. cit.*, p. 54.

Reagan's liberal Democratic, pro-labor phase: Leuchtenburg, *op. cit.*, pp. 18–25.

Glad on Reagan's displacement of anger: Glad, *op. cit.*, p. 50.

Men around Reagan reinforcing his ideology: Ronald Brownstein and Nina Easton, *Reagan's Ruling Class* (New York: Pantheon Books, 1983), Chap. 7, "The White House."

Dugger on Reagan making anti-Communism part of his liberalism: Dugger, *op. cit.*, p. 10.

Stanley Hoffmann on Reagan finding remedies in old verities: Quoted in Dallek, *op. cit.*, Chap. 4, p. 1.

Reaganism Without Reagan

Warning to Ronald Reagan as to the governmental problems he would face as President: Arnold J. Meltsner, "Memorandum to Ronald Reagan," in Meltsner, ed., *Politics and the Oval Office: Towards Presidential Government* (San Francisco: Institute for Contemporary Studies, 1981), pp. 3–9, quoted at p. 9.

Reagan on his unchanging intentions: Interview with Marvin Stone, *U.S. News & World Report,* October 25, 1982, p. 98.

Phillips on Reagan's coalition: Kevin P. Phillips, *Post-Conservative America* (New York: Random House, 1982).

Reagan on coming back for more: Interview with Marvin Stone, *loc. cit.*

Reagan as a hedgehog: Isaiah Berlin, *The Hedgehog and the Fox* (New York: Simon and Schuster, 1970), quoted at pp. 1–2.

Three: KENNEDY: GOVERNING WITHOUT CAMELOT

Kennedy announcement speech: "Kennedy declares his candidacy, vowing new leadership for nation," *New York Times,* November 8, 1979, pp. A1, A17; "Teddy Makes It Official," *Newsweek,* November 5, 1979, p. 51; "The Kennedy Challenge," *Time,* November 5, 1979, pp. 14–26; "Teddy Kennedy launches from Faneuil Hall," North Adams (Mass.) *Transcript,* November 6, 1979, p. 2; personal report on the proceedings by Michael Beschloss, an observer.

Kennedy's definition of leadership: Quoted in Elizabeth Drew, *Portrait of an Election* (New York: Simon and Schuster, 1981), pp. 34–35.

Public opinion polls on leadership: Thomas E. Cronin, "Looking for Leadership 1980," *Public Opinion,* February/March 1980, pp. 14–16.

JFK: Memories of the Future?
    The subtitle of this section is taken from the name of a *pulqueria* I saw on the outskirts of Mexico City in 1933.

John F. Kennedy's political background: Theodore Sorensen, *Kennedy* (New York: Harper & Row, 1965); David E. Koskoff, *Joseph P. Kennedy* (Englewood Cliffs, N.J.: Prentice-Hall, 1974); Richard J. Whalen, *The Founding Father: The Story of Joseph P. Kennedy* (New York: New American Library, 1964); James MacGregor Burns, *John Kennedy: A Political Profile* (New York: Harper & Row, 1960); Kenneth P. O'Donnell and David F. Powers with Joe McCarthy, *"Johnny, We Hardly Knew Ye"* (Boston: Little, Brown, 1970).

Kennedy's 1960 campaign: Theodore White, *The Making of the President 1960* (New York: Atheneum, 1961); Sorensen, *op. cit.,* Part Two; Lawrence O'Brien, *No Final Victories* (Garden City, N.Y.: Doubleday, 1974), Chaps. 4–5; Pierre Salinger, *With Kennedy* (Garden City, N.Y.: Doubleday, 1966).

John Kennedy's role and performance: Arthur Schlesinger, Jr., *A Thousand Days* (Boston: Houghton Mifflin, 1965); Henry Fairlie, *The Kennedy Promise* (Garden City, N.Y.: Doubleday, 1973); John F. Kennedy, "As Kennedy Foresaw the Presidency," *U.S. News & World Report*, November 28, 1960, pp. 76–78; Lewis J. Paper, *The Promise and the Performance: The Leadership of John F. Kennedy* (New York: Crown Publishers, 1975); James MacGregor Burns, "New Size-Up of the President," *U.S. News & World Report*, December 4, 1961, pp. 44–49; Helen Fuller, *Year of Trial: Kennedy's Crucial Decisions* (New York: Harcourt, Brace & World, 1962); James L. Sundquist, *Politics and Policy* (Washington, D.C.: The Brookings Institution, 1968); Garry Wills, *The Kennedy Imprisonment* (Boston: Little, Brown, 1982).

Kennedy's presidential character and personality: Biographical works cited above; Evelyn Lincoln, *My Twelve Years with John F. Kennedy* (New York: David McKay, 1965); Benjamin C. Bradlee, *Conversations with Kennedy* (New York: W. W. Norton, 1975); William Manchester, *Portrait of a President* (Boston: Little, Brown, 1962); Nancy Gager Clinch, *The Kennedy Neurosis* (New York: Grosset & Dunlap, 1973); Tom Wicker, *Kennedy Without Tears* (New York: William Morrow, 1964).

Structure of power behind the congressional committee system: James MacGregor Burns, *The Deadlock of Democracy* (Englewood Cliffs, N.J.: Prentice-Hall, 1963).

Schlesinger on nature of Kennedy's mind: Schlesinger, *op. cit.,* p. 104.

Kennedy's practicality and "pragmatism": Bruce Miroff, *Pragmatic Illusions* (New York: David McKay, 1976); Fairlie, *op. cit.,* quoted at pp. 256, 233; Schlesinger, *op. cit., passim.*

Kennedy's foreign policy: See especially Roger Hilsman, *To Move a Nation* (Garden City, N.Y.: Doubleday, 1967); Richard J. Walton, *Cold War and Counter-Revolution* (New York: Viking, 1972); and relevant works cited above.

Kennedy's civil rights policy: Carl M. Brauer, *John F. Kennedy and the Second Reconstruction* (New York: Columbia University Press, 1977); and relevant works cited above. I quote Brauer on the "turning point" at p. 265.

On major aspects of Kennedy's presidency see the authoritative Herbert S. Parmet, *JFK: The Presidency of John F. Kennedy* (New York: Dial Press, 1983), and sources cited therein; for a comprehensive and informative bibliography, see James Tracy Crown, *The Kennedy Literature* (New York: New York University Press, 1968). I quote Parmet at pp. 336, 259, 271; and Sorensen is quoted in Parmet at p. 336.

1980: The Death of Camelot

Threat of assassination: James MacGregor Burns, "Advice to Kennedy, other candidates: avoid political macho," *New York Times,* September 14, 1979, p. A25.

Press coverage of the Kennedy campaign: Elizabeth Drew, "A Reporter at Large: 1980: Kennedy," *New Yorker*, February 4, 1980, pp. 42–95; Stephen V. Roberts, "Ted Kennedy: Haunted by the Past," *New York Times Magazine*, February 3, 1980, pp. 54–58, 64; Tom Shales, "Petty for Teddy: the anti-Kennedy bias in TV news reporting," Washington *Post*, January 30, 1980, pp. B1, B11; "Teddy's Ragged Start," *Newsweek*, December 10, 1979, pp. 56–57; B. Drummond Ayres, Jr., "Reporter's notebook: style eludes Kennedy on stump," *New York Times*, December 7, 1979, p. A28. Interviews with Edward M. Kennedy, April 27, 1981; Ken Bode, January 15, 1981; Robert Shrum, April 29, 1981.

Shah statement: Kennedy quoted in B. Drummond Ayres, Jr., "Kennedy, after denouncing Shah, assures support of Carter's efforts," *New York Times*, December 4, 1979, p. A1; Strauss quoted in Terence Smith, "Kennedy chided by the leaders of both parties," *New York Times*, December 4, 1979, p. B18.

Impact of Iran crisis: Adam Clymer, "Crisis in Iran alters '80 race," *New York Times*, December 13, 1979, p. A22; Richard Harwood, *The Pursuit of the Presidency* (New York: Berkley Books, 1980), pp. 43–44, 106–108.

Reader's Digest: John Barron, "Chappaquiddick: The Still Unanswered Questions," *Reader's Digest*, February 1980, pp. 65–72, 219–242.

Impact of Iowa caucuses: Interview with Edward M. Kennedy, Washington, D.C., April 27, 1981.

Georgetown speech: Interview with Arthur M. Schlesinger, Jr., New York City, January 17, 1981; "Transcript of Kennedy's speech at Georgetown University," *New York Times*, January 29, 1980, p. A12; Robert Healy, "Kennedy regroups, plans major address," Boston *Globe*, January 26, 1980, pp. 1, 15; "Ted Tries, Tries Again," *Newsweek*, February 11, 1980, pp. 29–31.

Kennedy floundering: Interview with Arthur M. Schlesinger, Jr., New York City, January 17, 1981.

"the personalization of our politics": Ronnie Dugger, "Ganging up on the prince of Camelot," Boston *Globe*, June 29, 1980, p. A4.

Kennedy's resiliency: Interview with Arthur Schlesinger, Jr., New York City, January 17, 1981.

Divided Democrats: Two Lefts and a Right

Liberalism in American politics: Louis Hartz, *The Liberal Tradition in America* (New York: Harcourt, Brace, 1955), *passim;* Otis L. Graham, Jr., "A Historical Perspective on the Future of Liberalism," *The Center Magazine*, March/April 1981, pp. 58–63.

The four-party system: Burns, *The Deadlock of Democracy, op. cit., passim.*

Acceptance of the New Deal approach: Everett Carll Ladd, Jr., "The Democrats Have Their Own Two-party System," *Fortune,* October 1977, p. 213 and *passim.*

Lowi's description of contemporary liberal government: Theodore J. Lowi, *The End of Liberalism: The Second Republic of the United States* (New York: W. W. Norton, 1979), p. x.

"Democrats must face the music": Ben Wattenberg, "What do the Democrats stand for?" Washington *Post,* April 16, 1981, p. A19.

"shameless caricature of liberalism": Described by Arthur Schlesinger, Jr., in "Is Liberalism Dead?" *New York Times Magazine,* March 30, 1980, p. 42.

The future of liberalism: Marcus G. Raskin, "Progressive Liberalism for the '80s," *The Nation,* May 17, 1980, pp. 577, 587–591; Gary Hart, "Democrats: a new path to old goals," Washington *Post,* September 23, 1980, p. A15; Senator Tsongas and Stuart Eizenstat quoted in Tom Wicker, "Democrats in Search of Ideas," *New York Times Magazine,* January 28, 1981, pp. 30–42.

Neo-liberal proposals: Frederic S. Nathan, Jr., "The Pioneering of a New Liberalism," typescript, Williams College, 1983.

Four: THE ROOTS OF LEADERSHIP FAILURE

Harris poll on public confidence: Jim Luther, "Garbagemen rated over White House," Washington *Post, op. cit.*

I will contend that the system does not work: I have treated some aspects of these systemic problems in earlier works, especially in *Congress on Trial* (New York: Harper & Row, 1949); *The Deadlock of Democracy* (Englewood Cliffs, N.J.: Prentice-Hall, 1963); and *Presidential Government* (Boston: Houghton Mifflin, 1965). In all of these I have emphasized the problem of a dangerously powerful or personalized presidency existing within a system of balanced and static powers.

Transforming the System

Transforming leadership: James MacGregor Burns, *Leadership* (New York: Harper & Row, 1978). See also Glenn D. Paige, *The Scientific Study of Political Leadership* (New York: The Free Press, 1977).

Transforming leadership in the Revolutionary period: Bernard Bailyn, *The Ideological Origins of the American Revolution* (Cambridge: Belknap Press, 1967); Gordon S. Wood, *The Creation of the American Republic: 1776–1787* (Chapel Hill: University of North Carolina Press, 1969).

Hofstadter's definition of leadership: Richard Hofstadter, *Anti-Intellectualism in American Life* (New York: Alfred A. Knopf, 1963), p. 25.

Founding Fathers' attitudes toward liberty and tyranny: James MacGregor Burns, *The Vineyard of Liberty* (New York: Alfred A. Knopf, 1982), Chaps. 1–3; George W. Carey, "Separation of Powers and the Madisonian Model: A Reply to the Critics," *American Political Science Review*, Vol. 72 (March 1978), pp. 151–164; Robert A. Dahl, *A Preface to Democratic Theory* (Chicago: University of Chicago Press, 1956); Paul Eidelberg, *The Philosophy of the American Constitution* (New York: The Free Press, 1968); Richard Hofstadter, *The American Political Tradition* (New York: Alfred A. Knopf, 1948); Garry Wills, *Explaining America: The Federalist* (Garden City, N.Y.: Doubleday, 1981); John H. Scharr, "Anti-Federalists Arise!", *The Nation*, January 22, 1983, pp. 84–87.

George Washington on Shays's Rebellion: Quoted in Burns, *Vineyard, op. cit.*, pp. 15–16.

Rule by popular majorities through elected representatives: Henry Steele Commager, *Majority Rule and Minority Rights* (New York: Oxford University Press, 1943); Jean Yarbrough, "Thoughts on the *Federalist*'s View of Representation," *Polity*, Vol. 12 (Fall 1979), pp. 65–82.

Madison's fifty-first Federalist paper: Jacob E. Cooke, ed., *The Federalist* (Middletown, Conn.: Wesleyan University Press, 1961), p. 349.

"parchment barriers": Quoted in Gene W. Boyett, "Developing the Concept of the Republican Presidency, 1787–1788," *Presidential Studies Quarterly*, Vol. 7, No. 4 (Fall 1977), p. 201. For a different point of view see Wills, *op. cit.*

Pitting Ambition Against Ambition

Framers' attitudes toward the presidency: Charles N. Thach, Jr., *The Creation of the Presidency, 1775–1789* (Baltimore: Johns Hopkins University Press, 1922); Donald L. Robinson, "Inventors of the Presidency," *Presidential Studies Quarterly*, Vol. 12, No. 1 (Winter 1982), pp. 8–25.

Convention at sea: Calvin Jillson, "The Executive in Republican Government: The Case of the American Founding," *Presidential Studies Quarterly*, Vol. 9, No. 4 (Fall 1979), p. 395.

Experience of the delegates: Clinton Rossiter, *1787, The Grand Convention* (New York: Macmillan, 1966), p. 146.

Morris on the election of the President: Quoted in Richard M. Pious, *The American Presidency* (New York: Basic Books, 1979), p. 28.

Direct election of the President: Discussed in Boyett, *op. cit.*, p. 205.

"bad edition of a Polish king": *Ibid.*, p. 204.

The Tamed Jungle and the Rogue Presidency

Framers' views on the judiciary: Joseph M. Bessett and Jeffrey Tulis, *The Presidency in the Constitutional Order* (Baton Rouge: Louisiana State University Press, 1981); Richard E. Ellis, *The Jeffersonian Crisis: Courts and Politics in the Young Republic* (New York: Oxford University Press, 1971); Benjamin Wright, *The Growth of American Constitutional Law* (Boston: Houghton Mifflin, 1942); Charles Warren, *The Supreme Court in United States History* (Boston: Little, Brown, 1932).

Conflict over the Alien and Sedition Acts: Burns, *Vineyard, op. cit.,* pp. 125–133; 183–193.

Powers of the presidency: Raoul Berger, *Impeachment: The Constitutional Problems* (Cambridge: Harvard University Press, 1973); Irving Brant, *James Madison: Father of the Constitution, 1787–1800,* Vol. 3 (Indianapolis: Bobbs-Merrill, 1950); Louis Fisher, *President and Congress, Power and Policy* (New York: The Free Press, 1972).

Schlesinger on the Constitution: Arthur M. Schlesinger, Jr., *The Imperial Presidency* (Boston: Houghton Mifflin, 1973), p. 7.

Corwin on the Constitution: Quoted in Schlesinger, *ibid.*

Response to Macaulay's taunt: Louis Henkin, *Foreign Affairs and the Constitution* (Mineola, N.Y.: The Foundation Press, 1972), p. 271.

Limitations on congressional power: James L. Sundquist, *The Decline and Resurgence of Congress* (Washington, D.C.: The Brookings Institution, 1981); Louis J. Fisher, *The Politics of Shared Power: Congress and the Executive* (Washington, D.C.: Congressional Quarterly Press, 1981).

The Path Not Taken

European parliamentary systems: Carl J. Friedrich, *Constitutional Government and Democracy: Theory and Practice in Europe and America* (Waltham, Mass.: Blaisdell, 1950); Peter H. Merkl, *Modern Comparative Politics* (New York: Holt, Rinehart and Winston, 1970); E. N. Williams, ed., *The Eighteenth Century Constitution: 1688–1815, Documents and Commentary* (Cambridge, Eng.: Cambridge University Press, 1960); J. H. Plumb, *England in the Eighteenth Century* (London: Penguin Books, 1953); Walter Bagehot, *The English Constitution* (London: Oxford University Press, 1955).

Friedrich on nonadoption of the American system: Carl J. Friedrich, *The Impact of American Constitutionalism Abroad* (Boston: Boston University Press, 1967).

Five: THE RISE AND FALL OF PARTY LEADERSHIP

James Madison on factions: Edward Mead Earle, ed., *The Federalist* (New York: Modern Library, 1937), pp. 53–62.

Fission or Fusion?

Founders' attitudes toward parties: William Nisbet Chambers, *Political Parties in a New Nation: The American Experience* (New York: Oxford University Press, 1963); Joseph Charles, *The Origins of the American Party System* (New York: Harper & Row, 1961); Noble E. Cunningham, *The Making of the American Party System, 1789–1809* (Englewood Cliffs, N.J.: Prentice-Hall, 1965); Seymour Martin Lipset, *The First New Nation* (New York: Basic Books, 1963); Charles H. McCall, "Political Parties and Popular Government," in George G. Graham, Jr., and Scarlett G. Graham, eds., *Founding Principles of American Government: Two Hundred Years of Democracy on Trial* (Bloomington: Indiana University Press, 1978), pp. 280–304; Austin Ranney, *Curing the Mischiefs of Faction* (Berkeley: University of California Press, 1975).

Plumb on violence: Quoted in Richard Hofstadter, *The Idea of a Party System: The Rise of Legitimate Opposition in the United States* (Berkeley: University of California Press, 1969), p. 12.

Hume on parties: Quoted in *ibid.*, p. 25.

Bolingbroke on parties: Quoted in *ibid.*, p. 10.

John Adams on parties: Quoted in *ibid.*, p. 28.

Hofstadter on Burke: *Ibid.*, p. 33.

Origins of political parties in Congress: Rudolph M. Bell, *Party and Faction in American Politics: The House of Representatives 1789–1801* (Westport, Conn.: Greenwood Press, 1973); John F. Hoadley, "The Emergence of Political Parties in Congress, 1789–1803," *American Political Science Review,* Vol. 74, No. 3 (September 1980), pp. 757–779.

Grass-roots political parties: Eugene P. Link, *Democratic-Republican Societies, 1790–1800* (New York: Columbia University Press, 1942).

Manning on political parties: William Manning, *The Key of Libberty* (Billerica, Mass.: The Manning Association, 1922).

Washington on political parties: "Farewell Address," September 19, 1796, in John C. Fitzpatrick, ed., *The Writings of George Washington* (Washington,

D.C.: Government Printing Office, 1931–1944), Vol. 35, pp. 214–238, quoted at pp. 226, 225.

The election of 1800: James MacGregor Burns, *The Vineyard of Liberty* (New York: Alfred A. Knopf, 1982), pp. 144–155.

Jefferson on parties: Quoted in Hofstadter, *op. cit.*, p. 115.

Harper on parties: Quoted in *ibid.*, p. 116.

Party Leadership—the Vital Balance
Jefferson's inaugural address: Paul Leicester Ford, ed., *The Writings of Thomas Jefferson* (New York: G. P. Putnam's Sons, 1892–1899), Vol. 8, pp. 1–6. See also Burns, *op. cit.*, p. 160; Hofstadter, *op. cit.*, p. 167.

Jefferson as a party leader: Burns, *op. cit.*, Chap. 5; Robert M. Johnstone, Jr., *Jefferson and the Presidency* (Ithaca: Cornell University Press, 1978).

Jefferson on "appointments and disappointments": Ford, *op. cit.*, Vol. 8, p. 31.

The decline of the Federalist Party: Linda K. Kerber, *Federalists in Dissent: Imagery and Ideology in Jeffersonian America* (Ithaca: Cornell University Press, 1970); Shaw Livermore, Jr., *The Twilight of Federalism: The Disintegration of the Federalist Party, 1815–1830* (Princeton, N.J.: Princeton University Press, 1962).

America "swarms with lesser controversies": Alexis de Tocqueville, *Democracy in America* (New York: Alfred A. Knopf, 1945), Vol. 1, p. 177.

The "people's" constitution: Burns, *op. cit.*, Chap. 10.

The Albany Regency: *Ibid.*, pp. 371–373; Robert V. Remini, "The Albany Regency," *New York History*, Vol. 39, No. 4 (October 1958).

Whigs: See Chapter Two, pp. 50–51; William R. Brock, *Parties and Political Conscience: American Dilemmas, 1840–1850* (Millwood, N.Y.: KTO Press, 1979); Lynn L. Marshall, "The Strange Stillbirth of the Whig Party," *American Historical Review*, Vol. 72, No. 2 (January 1967), pp. 445–468.

Origins of the Republican Party: Hans L. Trefousse, "The Republican Party, 1854–1864," in Arthur M. Schlesinger, Jr., ed., *History of U.S. Political Parties* (New York: Chelsea House Publishers, 1973), Vol. 2, pp. 1141–1172.

Voter coalitions: Richard Jensen, "Party Coalitions and the Search for Modern Values," Chap. 2, in Seymour Martin Lipset, ed., *Emerging Coalitions in American Politics* (San Francisco: Institute for Contemporary Studies, 1978), p. 22.

Political machines: Denis W. Brogan, *Politics in America* (New York: Harper & Brothers, 1954), p. 125.

Plunkitt: Quoted in William L. Riordan, *Plunkitt of Tammany Hall* (New York: E. P. Dutton, 1963), p. 25.

How to Dismember a Party

The election of 1896: James L. Sundquist, *Dynamics of the Party System: Alignment and Realignment of Political Parties in the United States* (Washington, D.C.: The Brookings Institution, 1973); Walter Dean Burnham, *Critical Elections and the Mainsprings of American Politics* (New York: W. W. Norton, 1970).

TR on Bryan: Quoted in James MacGregor Burns, *The Deadlock of Democracy* (Englewood Cliffs, N.J.: Prentice-Hall, 1963), p. 79.

Kleppner's assessment of political parties in the 1890s: Paul Kleppner, "From Ethnoreligious Conflict to Social Harmony," Chap. 3 in Lipset, *Emerging Coalitions, op. cit.,* p. 43.

The Progressive movement: Herbert Croly, *Progressive Democracy* (New York: Macmillan, 1914); see also his *The Promise of American Life* (New York: Macmillan, 1914); Benjamin Parke DeWitt, *The Progressive Movement* (Seattle: University of Washington Press, 1968).

A more responsible party system: Committee on Political Parties, American Political Science Association, *Toward a More Responsible Two-Party System* (New York: Rinehart, 1950). See also John Kenneth White, *The Fractured Electorate* (Amherst, Mass.: University Press of New England, 1983).

Schattschneider on parties: E. E. Schattschneider, *Party Government* (New York: Farrar & Rinehart, 1942), p. 1.

1964 Democratic National Convention: Carol F. Casey, "The National Democratic Party," in Gerald M. Pomper, ed., *Party Renewal in America: Theory and Practice* (New York: Praeger Publishers, 1980), p. 88.

Hughes Commission: Commission on the Democratic Selection of Presidential Nominees, "The Democratic Choice," *Congressional Record,* Vol. 114, Part 25 (90th Cong., 2nd Sess.), October 15, 1968, p. E1972.

GOP's positive action: Austin Ranney, "The Political Parties: Reform and Decline," in Anthony King, ed., *The New American Political System* (Washington, D.C.: American Enterprise Institute for Public Policy Research, 1978), pp. 213–214.

The "DO" committee: Austin Ranney, "Changing the Rules of the Nominating Game," in James David Barber, ed., *Choosing the President* (Englewood Cliffs,

N.J.: Prentice-Hall, 1974). See also Austin Ranney, "Recent Changes in the Nominating Process," *The Key Reporter,* Vol. 48, No. 4 (Summer 1983), pp. 3–5.

Rethinking Party

Inadequacy of the party system: Committee on Political Parties, *Toward a More Responsible Two-Party System, op. cit.,* pp. 13–14.

Party renewal versus party reform: Pomper, *op. cit.;* Robert A. Goldwin, ed., *Political Parties in the Eighties* (Washington, D.C.: American Enterprise Institute for Public Policy Research, 1980); Ranney in King, *op. cit.,* pp. 215–247; Jeane Kirkpatrick, *Dismantling the Parties: Reflections on Party Reform and Party Decomposition* (Washington, D.C.: American Enterprise Institute for Public Policy Research, 1978).

"Be bold": Letter from the author to the members of the Democratic National Committee's Commission on Presidential Nomination, August 17, 1981.

Six: THE NEW LEADER: KING OF THE ROCK

My own race for Congress: James MacGregor Burns, *The Deadlock of Democracy* (Englewood Cliffs, N.J.: Prentice-Hall, 1963), pp. 229–233.

The Media: Pack Leadership

FDR's Good Neighbor League: James MacGregor Burns, *Roosevelt: The Lion and the Fox* (New York: Harcourt, Brace, 1956), p. 270.

The politics of the media: David Halberstam, *The Powers That Be* (New York: Dell Publishing, 1979).

1840 campaign of William Henry Harrison: James MacGregor Burns, *The Vineyard of Liberty* (New York: Alfred A. Knopf, 1982), pp. 419–422.

An "exhibition of abuse": Richard B. Morris, ed., *Encyclopedia of American History* (New York: Harper & Row, 1976), pp. 218–219.

Partisanship of the American media: Robert D. McClure, "Mass Media Activities and Influence in the Politics of 1980," in Paul David and David Everson, eds., *The Presidential Election of 1980 in State and Nation* (Springfield, Ill.: Sangamon University Press, 1982), pp. 9–10; Richard Jensen, "Armies, Admen and Crusaders: Strategies to Win Elections," *Public Opinion,* October/ November 1980, p. 46; Richard Jensen, *Grass Roots Politics* (Westport, Conn.: Greenwood Press, 1981).

Senator Kennedy's Georgetown speech: See Chapter Three, pp. 87–88;

Thomas E. Patterson, *The Mass Media Example* (New York: Praeger Publishers, 1982), p. 7.

Broder on the Washington press corps: David S. Broder, "The press corps gap," Washington *Post,* March 25, 1981, p. A19.

Hess on the Washington press corps: Stephen Hess, *The Washington Reporters* (Washington, D.C.: The Brookings Institution, 1981), Chap. 4.

"pack journalism": Timothy Crouse, *The Boys on the Bus* (New York: Random House, 1973).

Galbraith on Washington journalism: Quoted in Ben H. Bagdikian, "All that glitters is not news," Washington *Post,* April 12, 1981, p. 7.

Transactional leadership: James MacGregor Burns, *Leadership* (New York: Harper & Row, 1978), Chaps. 10–14. See also Charles E. Lindblom, *The Intelligence of Democracy* (New York: The Free Press, 1965); Andrew S. McFarland, *Power and Leadership in Pluralist Systems* (Stanford, Cal.: Stanford University Press, 1969).

Personalismo: The Rose Garden Presidency

Proliferation of primaries: Rhodes Cook, "Presidential Primaries Reach Record Level," *Congressional Quarterly,* August 4, 1979, pp. 1609–1616; Kenneth A. Bode and Carol F. Casey, "Party Reform: Revisionism Revised" in Robert A. Goldwin, ed., *Political Parties in the Eighties* (Washington, D.C.: American Enterprise Institute for Public Policy Research, 1980), pp. 16–18.

Campaign costs: Herbert E. Alexander, *Financing Politics: Money, Elections and Political Reform* (Washington, D.C.: Congressional Quarterly Press, 1980); Gary C. Jacobson, *Money in Congressional Elections* (New Haven: Yale University Press, 1980).

"horserace" phenomenon: McClure in David and Everson, *op. cit.,* p. 14.

Connally's use of TV: William J. Lanouette, "You Can't Be Elected with TV Alone, but You Can't Win Without It Either," *National Journal,* March 1, 1980, pp. 344–348.

Michael Robinson on TV news: Michael J. Robinson, "Television and American Politics: 1956–1976," *The Public Interest,* Vol. 48 (Summer 1977), p. 23.

Media coverage of national conventions: David L. Paletz and Martha Elson, "Television Coverage of Presidential Conventions: Now You See It, Now You Don't," *Political Science Quarterly,* Spring 1976, pp. 109–121.

The job of the President: Reo M. Christenson, "Presidential Leadership of Congress: Ten Commandments Point the Way," *Presidential Studies Quarterly,*

Vol. 8, No. 3 (Summer 1978), pp. 257–268; Stephen Hess, *The Presidential Campaign: An Essay* (Washington, D.C.: The Brookings Institution, 1978).

Kassebaum on the presidency: Nancy Landon Kassebaum, "The Essence of Leadership," *Presidential Studies Quarterly,* Vol. 9, No. 3 (Summer 1979), p. 240.

Plebiscitary presidency: Aaron Wildavsky, "The Plebiscitary Presidency: Direct Election as Class Legislation," *Commonsense,* Winter 1979, pp. 1–10.

President as chief of state: Harold M. Berger, "The Prominence of the Chief of State Role in the American Presidency," *Presidential Studies Quarterly,* Vol. 8, No. 2 (Spring 1978), pp. 127–139.

Voters Adrift: The Decline of Followership

Truman on "the powers of selfishness and greed": Robert H. Ferrell, ed., *Off the Record: The Private Papers of Harry S. Truman* (New York: Harper & Row, 1980), p. 102.

"reservoir of perennial nonparticipants": Warren E. Miller, "Disinterest, Disaffection, and Participation in Presidential Politics," *Political Behavior,* Vol. 2, No. 1 (1980), p. 11.

Nonvoting generally: Martin Plissner and Warren Mitofsky, "What If They Held an Election and Nobody Came?" *Public Opinion,* February/March 1981, pp. 50–51.

Unrepresentative and inegalitarian effects of nonvoting: Miller, *op. cit.;* Howard L. Reiter, "Why Is Turnout Down?" *Public Opinion Quarterly,* Vol. 43 (Fall 1979), pp. 297–311.

Split-ticket voting: Norman H. Nie, Sidney Verba, and John R. Petrocik, *The Changing American Voter* (Cambridge: Harvard University Press, 1979), p. 1.

Decomposition of the American electorate: Walter Dean Burnham, "Politics in the 1970's—Beyond Party?" in Jeff Fishel, ed., *Parties and Elections in an Anti-Party Age: American Politics and the Crisis of Confidence* (Bloomington, Ind.: Indiana University Press, 1978), pp. 333–341.

Increasing number of independents: Nie, Verba, and Petrocik, *op. cit.;* Hugh L. Leblanc and Mary Beth Merrin, "Independents, Issue Partisanship, and the Decline of the Party," *American Politics Quarterly,* Vol. 7, No. 2 (April 1979), pp. 240–256; David C. Valentine and John R. Van Wingen, "Partisanship, Independence, and the Partisan Identification Question," *American Politics Quarterly,* Vol. 8, No. 2 (April 1980), pp. 165–185; William Schneider, "1980–a Watershed Year?" *Politics Today,* January/February 1980, pp. 26–32.

Sundquist on independents' searching for candidates' qualities: Personal communication to author, July 1983.

Art of followership as well as leadership: Burns, *Leadership, op. cit., passim.*

Seven: REORGANIZATION: THE POLITICS OF TINKERING

Reston on the crisis of government: *New York Times, op. cit.*

Teamwork: My ideas on this subject are set forth more fully in *Congress on Trial* (New York: Harper & Row, 1949) and *Uncommon Sense* (New York: Harper & Row, 1972).

Congress: Mess or Mesh?

Background on Congress generally: James L. Sundquist, *The Decline and Resurgence of Congress* (Washington, D.C.: The Brookings Institution, 1981); Roger H. Davidson and Walter J. Oleszek, *Congress Against Itself* (Bloomington, Ind.: University of Indiana Press, 1977); Samuel C. Patterson, "The Semi-Sovereign Congress," in Anthony King, ed., *The New American Political System* (Washington, D.C.: American Enterprise Institute for Public Policy Research, 1978), pp. 125–177.

Woodrow Wilson on Congress: Woodrow Wilson, *Congressional Government* (Boston: Houghton Mifflin, 1885), p. 9 and *passim.*

Congressional reorganization: Godfrey Hodgson, *All Things to All Men: The False Promise of the Modern American Presidency* (New York: Simon and Schuster, 1980), pp. 119–160.

Proliferation of congressional subcommittees: President's Commission for a National Agenda for the Eighties, *The Electoral and Democratic Process in the Eighties* (Washington, D.C.: U.S. Government Printing Office, 1980), pp. 43–47; "American Renewal," *Time,* February 23, 1981, p. 42.

Rodino on the committee system: Quoted in Trent Lott, "Blueprint for a House that works," Washington *Post,* April 14, 1981, p. A21.

"there has to be a way": President's Commission, *op. cit.,* p. 43.

Nixon and impoundment: Sundquist, *op. cit.,* p. 203.

Congressional Budget and Impoundment Control Act of 1974: Norman C. Thomas, "Presidential Accountability Since Watergate," *Presidential Studies Quarterly,* Vol. 8, No. 4 (Fall 1978), pp. 423–424; Allen Schick, "The Battle of the Budget," in Harvey C. Mansfield, Sr., ed., *Congress Against the President*

(New York: Praeger Publishers, 1975); Louis Fisher, "Congressional Budget Reform: The First Two Years," *Harvard Journal on Legislation,* Vol. 14 (April 1977), pp. 413–458.

Congress and foreign policy: James L. Sundquist, "The Crisis of Competence in Government," in Joseph A. Pechman, ed., *Setting National Priorities: Agenda for the 1980s* (Washington, D.C.: The Brookings Institution, 1980), p. 533.

Congressional staffing: Steven K. Bailey, "Improving Federal Governance," *Public Administration Review,* Vol. 40, No. 6 (November/December 1980), pp. 548–552, quoted at p. 551; Sundquist, *Decline, op. cit.,* pp. 409–411; Donald L. Robinson, "If the Senate Does Want Leadership," paper for Committee on Operation of United States Senate (1974).

Policy reorganization of committees: President's Commission, *op. cit.,* p. 50.

Congressional leadership: Quoted in Sundquist, *Decline, op. cit.,* pp. 398–399.

The Presidency: What Price Teamwork?

Hamilton's call for a "vigorous Executive": Federalist Paper #70, *New York Packet,* March 18, 1788, in Edward Mead Earle, ed., *The Federalist* (New York: Modern Library, 1937), pp. 454–455.

Brownlow Committee: Report of the President's Committee on Administrative Management, "Administrative Management in the Government of the United States," January 1937; 1980 Commission: "A presidency for the 1980s: a report on presidential management by a panel of the National Academy of Public Administration," November 10, 1980, p. 10.

Indictment of presidential disorganization: President's Commission, *op. cit.,* p. 72; John E. Harr, "The Planning Function in the Executive Office," paper prepared for the presidential management review panel of the National Academy of Public Administration, Washington, D.C., 1980.

Vice-President as chief of staff: "American Renewal," *Time,* February 23, 1981, p. 41.

Role of the Cabinet: *Ibid.;* President's Commission, *op. cit.,* pp. 82–85; Thomas E. Cronin, *The State of the Presidency,* 2nd ed. (Boston: Little, Brown, 1980); Walter Mondale, *The Accountability of Power: Toward a Responsible Presidency* (New York: David McKay, 1975); Ben W. Heineman, Jr., and Curtis A. Hessler, *Memorandum for the President: A Strategic Approach to Domestic Affairs in the 1980s* (New York: Random House, 1980), p. 127; George Reedy, *Twilight of the Presidency* (New York: Mentor Books, 1970), p. 77.

The bureaucracy: Robert Wood quoted in Hodgson, *op. cit.,* p. 115.

Civil service reform: President's Commission, *op. cit.,* pp. 76–77.

Limit White House assistants: Harry A. Bailey, Jr., "An Administrative Approach to Constraining the American Presidency," *Presidential Studies Quarterly,* Vol. 8, No. 3 (Summer 1978), pp. 268–275.

Public ombudsman: Arthur S. Miller, "Separation of Powers: An Ancient Doctrine under Modern Challenge," *Administrative Law Review,* Summer 1976, p. 32.

Historical proposals for a six-year term: Paul B. Davis, "The Future of Presidential Tenure," *Presidential Studies Quarterly,* Vol. 10, No. 3 (Summer 1980), pp. 469–475.

Valenti on a six-year term: Quoted in James J. Kilpatrick, "Four years better than six," North Adams (Mass.) *Transcript,* November 28, 1979, p. 18.

Vance on a six-year term: Cyrus Vance, "Reforming the Electoral Reforms," *New York Times Magazine,* February 22, 1981, pp. 16–17, 62–69, quoted at p. 69.

Reedy's opposition to a six-year term: Reedy, *op. cit.,* pp. 135–136. See also Thomas E. Cronin, "Against a Single 6-Year Presidential Term," *Newsday,* January 4, 1983.

Neustadt's opposition to a six-year term: Richard Neustadt, *Presidential Power: The Politics of Leadership from FDR to Carter* (New York: John Wiley and Sons, 1980), p. 232.

Repeal of the 22nd Amendment: Attitudes of the Presidents cited in Paul B. Davis, "The Results and Implications of the Enactment of the Twenty-Second Amendment," *Presidential Studies Quarterly,* Vol. 9, No. 3 (Summer 1979), pp. 289–303. See also John Charles Daly, "How Long Should They Serve? Limiting Terms For the President and Congress" (Washington, D.C.: American Enterprise Institute for Public Policy Research, 1980).

Congress and President: Wedlock or Deadlock?

Madison's strictures: Federalist Paper #51, in Earle, *op. cit.,* pp. 335–341.

Legislative oversight: Sundquist, *Decline,* Chap. 11; Morris S. Ogul, "Congressional Oversight: Structures and Incentives," in Lawrence C. Dodd and Bruce I. Oppenheimer, eds., *Congress Reconsidered* (New York: Praeger Publishers, 1977), pp. 207–221.

Legislative veto: Peter Schauffler, "The Legislative Veto Revisited," *Public Policy* (Harvard University, Graduate School of Public Administration, 1958), pp. 296–327; Thomas, "Presidential Accountability," *op. cit.,* pp. 424–426; James Abourezk, "The Congressional Veto: A Contemporary Response to Executive Encroachment on Legislative Prerogatives," *Indiana Law Review,*

Vol. 52 (Winter 1977); James L. Sundquist, "Without the Legislative Veto," Washington *Post,* June 26, 1983, p. D8.

War Powers Resolution: Comments of the Presidents cited in Sundquist, *Decline, op. cit.,* pp. 263, 290–291, and 309. See also Thomas, "Presidential Accountability," *op. cit.,* pp. 420–421; W. Stuart Darling and D. Craig Mense, "Rethinking the War Powers Act," *Presidential Studies Quarterly,* Vol. 7 (Spring/Summer 1977), pp. 126–136; Graham T. Allison, "Making War: The President and Congress," in Thomas E. Cronin and Rexford G. Tugwell, eds., *The Presidency Reappraised,* 2nd ed. (New York: Praeger Publishers, 1977), pp. 228–247.

Eight: TAKING THE "PATH NOT TAKEN"

Woodrow Wilson's comments: Woodrow Wilson, *Congressional Government* (Boston: Houghton Mifflin, 1885), p. 318.

A call for leadership: I have developed these ideas more fully in *Leadership* (New York: Harper & Row, 1978).

Confronting a Sacred Cow

Question period for Cabinet members: Walter Mondale, *The Accountability of Power: Toward a Responsible Presidency* (New York: David McKay, 1975), pp. 148–151.

Executive-legislative Cabinet: Godfrey Hodgson, *All Things to All Men: The False Promise of the Modern American Presidency* (New York: Simon and Schuster, 1980), pp. 256–257.

Six-year term: See Chapter Seven, pp. 180–182.

"Problems are *national* or *planetary*": Arthur S. Miller, "Constitutional Law: Crisis Government Becomes the Norm," *Ohio State Law Journal,* Vol. 39, No. 4 (1978), p. 741.

"totem and fetish": Max Lerner quoted in Larry R. Baas, "The Constitution as Symbol," *American Politics Quarterly,* Vol. 8, No. 2 (April 1980), p. 238.

Public attitudes toward the Constitution: *Ibid.,* pp. 237–256.

"black hole in space": Senator Charles McC. Mathias quoted in George F. Will, "Four years better than six," North Adams (Mass.) *Transcript,* November 28, 1979, p. 18.

Knitting the Government Together

Comments on the Reuss proposal: James L. Sundquist, "The Case for an Easier Method to Remove Presidents," *George Washington Law Review,* Vol. 43, No. 2 (January 1975), pp. 472–484.

Four-year term for Congress: Charles O. Jones, *Every Second Year* (Washington, D.C.: The Brookings Institution, 1967).

"team ticket": Lloyd N. Cutler, "To Form a Government," *Foreign Affairs*, Vol. 59, No. 1 (Fall 1980), reprinted in Reuss *Hearings* (see full citation, Prologue Notes), Vol. 1, pp. 15–40, esp. pp. 28–29; James L. Sundquist, prepared statement submitted to Reuss Committee, Reuss *Hearings*, esp. p. 299.

Reuss proposal for a joint legislative-executive Cabinet: Text of proposed amendment, Reuss *Hearings*, Vol. 2, p. 679.

Conceiving the Inconceivable

Kay Lawson on the French system: Kay Lawson, "The Impact of Party Reforms on Party Systems: The Case of the R.P.R. in France," *Comparative Politics*, July 1981, p. 416.

Woodrow Wilson on Cabinet government: Thomas W. Wilson, "Cabinet Government in the United States," *The International Review*, August 1879, pp. 146–163; reprinted in Reuss *Hearings*, Vol. 2, pp. 680–697.

Wilson's changing attitude: Woodrow Wilson, *Constitutional Government* (New York: Columbia University Press, 1908), p. 60.

Rogers on weaknesses of Congress: Lindsay Rogers, *Crisis Government* (New York: W. W. Norton, 1934).

Corwin comments: Edward S. Corwin, *The President: Office and Powers* (New York: New York University Press, 1957) and *Total War and the Constitution* (New York: Alfred A. Knopf, 1947).

Hazlitt's proposals: Henry Hazlitt, *A New Constitution Now* (New Rochelle, N.Y.: Arlington House, 1974; expanded version of 1942 original).

Other bold proposals: Thomas Finletter, *Can Representative Government Do the Job?* (New York: Reynal and Hitchcock, 1945); Leland D. Baldwin, *Reframing the Constitution: An Imperative for Modern America* (Santa Barbara, Cal.: Clio Press, 1972); Charles M. Hardin, *Presidential Power and Accountability: Toward a New Constitution* (Chicago: University of Chicago Press, 1974).

Tugwell proposals: Rexford G. Tugwell, *The Emerging Constitution* (New York: Harper's Magazine Press, 1974).

The British example: William S. Livingston, "Britain and America: The Institutionalization of Accountability," *Journal of Politics*, Vol. 38, No. 4 (November 1976), pp. 879–894; Howard A. Scarrow, "Parliamentary and Presidential Government Compared," *Current History*, pp. 264–272, reprinted in Reuss *Hearings*, Vol. 2, pp. 987–991.

Other foreign experience: Ferdinand A. Hermens, "Foreign Experience and American Constitutional Reform," Reuss *Hearings,* pp. 992–1052, a comprehensive treatment.

Nine: THE REALIGNMENT OF POWER

"I non iv a party": Finley Peter Dunne, "Discusses Party Politics," in Dunne, *Mr. Dooley's Opinions* (New York: R. H. Russell, 1901), p. 97.

Moderates versus extremists: Meg Greenfield in *Newsweek,* February 11, 1981, p. 104.

"Politicize, polarize, ignite": Nicholas von Hoffman, *Make Believe Presidents* (New York: Pantheon Books, 1978).

Repairing the Mainspring

"political parties created democracy": E. E. Schattschneider, *Party Government* (New York: Farrar & Rinehart, 1942), p. 1. For further readings on "more responsible" political parties, see Chapter Five. See also Evron M. Kirkpatrick, "Toward a More Responsible Two-Party System: Political Science, Policy Science, or Pseudo-Science?" *The American Political Science Review,* December 1971, pp. 965–990.

The media on political parties: David S. Broder, *The Party's Over* (New York: Harper & Row, 1971); Kenneth A. Bode and Carol F. Casey, "Party Reform: Revisionism Revised," in Robert A. Goldwin, ed., *Political Parties in the Eighties* (Washington, D.C.: American Enterprise Institute for Public Policy Research, 1980), pp. 3–19.

Committee for Party Renewal: Jerome M. Mileur (University of Massachusetts), "The Committee for Party Renewal," paper prepared for delivery at the 1983 Annual Meeting of the American Political Science Association, Chicago, September 1983.

The National Democratic Party in the last decade: William J. Crotty, *Decision for the Democrats: Reforming the Party Structure* (Baltimore: Johns Hopkins University Press, 1978); Commission on Party Structure and Delegate Selection (McGovern-Fraser Commission), *Mandate for Reform* (Washington, D.C.: Democratic National Committee, 1970); Commission on Delegate Selection and Party Structure (Mikulski Commission), *Democrats All* (Washington, D.C.: Democratic National Committee, 1974); Commission on Presidential Nominations and Party Structure (Winograd Commission), *Openness, Participation and Party Building: Reforms for a Stronger Democratic Party* (Washington, D.C.: Democratic National Committee, 1978); Lanny J. Davis, "Reforming the Reforms," *The New Republic,* February 17, 1982, pp. 8–13.

The national Republican Party in the last decade: John F. Bibby, "Party Renewal in the National Republican Party," in Gerald M. Pomper, ed., *Party Renewal in America: Theory and Practice* (New York: Praeger Publishers, 1980), pp. 102–115.

Massachusetts Charter convention: Jerome M. Mileur, "Massachusetts: The Democratic Party Charter Movement," in Pomper, *op. cit.,* pp. 159–175.

Presidents and—or versus?—Parties

Schattschneider on presidential nominations: Schattschneider, *op. cit.,* p. 64.

Hughes Commission: Commission on the Democratic Selection of Presidential Nominees, "The Democratic Choice," *Congressional Record,* Vol. 114, Part 25 (90th Cong., 2nd Sess.), October 15, 1968. For an ingenious alternative to the present presidential nominating system, see Thomas Cronin and Robert Loevy, "The Case for a National Pre-primary Plan," *Public Opinion,* December/January 1983, pp. 50–53.

"thinking delegates": Terry Sanford, *A Danger of Democracy: The Presidential Nominating Process* (Boulder, Colo.: Westview Press, 1981), Chap. 14. See also Lloyd N. Cutler, "Getting Rid of Incoherent Government," Washington *Post,* March 27, 1983, pp. B1, B4.

Court decisions on political party authority: *Cousins* v. *Wigoda,* 419 U.S. 477 (1975); *Democratic Party of U.S.* v. *La Follette,* 67 L. Ed. 2d 82, 97 (1981).

1980 Democratic National Convention rules: *Delegate Selection Rules for the 1980 Democratic National Convention* (Washington, D.C.: Democratic National Committee, June 9, 1978).

Realignment: Waiting for Lefty

On party realignment generally: See James L. Sundquist, *Dynamics of the Party System: Alignment and Realignment of Political Parties in the U.S.* (Washington, D.C.: The Brookings Institution, 1973); Walter Dean Burnham, *Critical Elections and the Mainsprings of American Politics* (New York: W. W. Norton, 1970); Adam Clymer and Kathleen Frankovic, "The Realities of Realignment," *Public Opinion,* June/July 1981, pp. 42–47; Everett Carll Ladd, Jr., and Charles D. Hadley, *Transformations of the American Party System* (New York: W. W. Norton, 1978); Seymour Martin Lipset, ed., *Emerging Coalitions in American Politics* (San Francisco: Institute for Contemporary Studies, 1978).

"realignment reaches its climax": Sundquist, *op. cit.,* pp. 294–295.

critical realignments: Walter Dean Burnham, "American Politics in the 1970s: Beyond Party?" in Jeff Fishel, ed., *Parties and Elections in an Anti-Party Age* (Bloomington, Ind.: Indiana University Press, 1978), p. 333.

Dawson on changing patterns of public opinion: Richard Dawson,

Views on the 1980 election as a realigning one: Robert Kelley, "America's 6th major vote shift," *New York Times,* November 11, 1980, p. A15; Adam Clymer, "A warning for the G.O.P.," *New York Times,* November 5, 1981, p.

B18; David Broder, "GOP rediscover unity to forge government policy," North Adams (Mass.) *Transcript,* August 4, 1981, p. 4.

Majority rule and minority rights: I have developed these ideas more fully in *Uncommon Sense* (New York: Harper & Row, 1972).

Cloward and Piven on transforming the Democratic Party: Richard A. Cloward and Frances Fox Piven, "Toward a Class-Based Realignment of American Politics: A Movement Strategy," *Social Policy,* Vol. 13, No. 3 (Winter 1983), pp. 3–14, quoted at p. 6. See also John Atlas, Peter Dreier, and John Stephens, "Progressive Politics in 1984," *The Nation,* July 23–30, 1983, pp. 62, 82–84; and the symposium, "Post-ERA Politics," *Ms.,* January 1983, pp. 35*ff.*

Mr. Dooley on the Democratic Party "whin't is broke": Finley Peter Dunne, *op. cit.*

Acknowledgments

I wish to thank Michael B. Beschloss, Thomas E. Cronin, Donald L. Robinson, and James L. Sundquist for their critical readings of the manuscript. I was privileged to receive intellectual benefits from Dr. Sundquist's major work on political parties, Congress, and public policy; Professor Robinson's research and analysis in the areas of the origins of the presidency and other constitutional and political questions; Professor Cronin's broad grasp of presidential politics and of the whole system of checks and balances; and Michael Beschloss's recent research and analysis in 20th century American history and foreign policy.

My heaviest debt is to Carol F. Casey, political scientist and political activist, who worked with me on research and interviews, provided her findings and analyses on major questions of party organization and reform, helped draft sections within her area of expertise in party politics, and made this effort a collaborative and fruitful one.

My wife, Joan Simpson Burns, devoted her fine critical and creative eye to the manuscript, much to its benefit. Professor Patricia Hunt-Perry read portions of the manuscript and made useful suggestions. Milton Djuric helped mightily on manuscript preparation. My associate on another project, Jeffrey P. Trout, found time to help on this one. The reference librarians at Williams College were typically helpful and generous with their time. Lisl Cade gave useful advice from the point of view of a trade audience. Catherine Trout provided vital last-minute manuscript assistance.

I thank my editor, Frederic W. Hills, for helping me broaden the whole concept of the book, and all those at Simon and Schuster who sped the book toward publication, as well as Patricia Miller for her expert copy editing.

J.M.B.

Index